Introduction

The title to this book of homilies, "No to Yes" reflects the age old beckoning to conversion. So, in one way or another, here they are—all 70 of them. Often drawn from everyday headlines and columnists, the reader will notice that they range from the inspirational to the challenging and that there is a distinct bias in theme towards the conflict of culture and faith. That our attractive and almost totally pervasive secularism—think movies, billions of commercials, celebrity worship, nine-hour daily dedication to social media—is hostile to the interior life is a gross understatement and so my urgings—hectorings?—to step back a bit and reflect are frequent.

Then there are the stories, a hallmark of my homilies. The more I preach the more I am convinced of their importance. Decades later people will tell me they remember the stories and the homiletic weight attached to them. Research has shown that stories form our lives for better or worse. Those stories that grapple with the deep questions—God, suffering, loneliness, and death—produce the myths we live by, myths that give us humans living on a decaying star some sense of identity, community, meaning and purpose. That is why we are a storytelling people and stories, unlike the "facts-only" one-dimensional statements our age favors, have their own flexible, shape-shifting meanings that challenge (and often upend) each era. That's why the Bible, rightly read, is not a volume of history but an anthology of stories. It is also why I use stories to interpret where we are now. Occasionally I will use the same story or recycle some stories into different contexts to demonstrate their flexibility, ever mindful that fiction is the lie that tells the truth.

Although the homilies are generally identified according to the liturgical seasons and scripture citation, those in the "Ordinary Time" are also fluid enough to fit a wide range of many situations and the homilist can apply them according to preference. The *O Tempora! O Mores!* section (Cicero's version of "what awful times we're in") contains free floating homilies of contemporary import that need no scriptural citations other than what the homilist might choose.

A study of former Catholics has identified poor preaching as the second single most common complaint of why they stopped attending church. Clearly people want words that reflect where they are, that deal with matters they must face every day, and words that help them name their spiritual longings. As Christianity declines, at least here in the West with the Catholic Church hemorrhaging most severely of all, there is a need for reaching out to those who have left organized religion but who have not necessarily abandoned the quest for spirituality.

Part of that outreach must begin with preaching the word of God whose aim, in the words of a Pope Francis book title, makes "Walking with Jesus" more inviting, more approachable. Hopefully these homilies may help.

Dedication

In gratitude for sixty years of priesthood and for those who encouraged, guided, and forgave me along the way.

Contents

ORDINARY TIME

FUNERAL HOMILIES

O TEMPORA! O MORES!

NOTES AND CREDITS

Advent–Christmas

ADVENT
CYCLES A, B, C

1

Advent, RIP

Advent, like Jacob Marley, is dead.

Advent has been swallowed up by commercial Christmas. No one really celebrates it anymore. Advent is not a byword. We come here to church to remember it, note the purple vestments, and sing the lovely Advent hymns but it evaporates the moment we leave church.

The Christmas flyers have long since arrived. TV is showing Christmas movies before November's turkey is being thought of. Black Friday steadily absorbs Thanksgiving. The stores are already aglitter with Christmas merchandise and Christmas music. My town already has its Christmas decorations up. A good number of houses in town are already decorated with Christmas lights and inflated cartoon icons. Christmas office parties have begun, school plays and festivals are in motion.

In a word commercial Christmas, well before Advent's arrival, has saturated the public square, luring us into secular festivity without the spiritual preparation of Advent. The truth is that, in reality, Advent exists only for the short time we are here in church, and even if we light our wreath at home or scan a daily meditation, we are inevitably pulled into commercial Christmas whether we like it or not. Especially if we have children who must be a part of Christmas or, these days, holiday activities.

So, I repeat: for all practical purposes, Advent is dead. There's no time before the birth of Jesus to look at those people who unknowingly were a part of the first drama, people who could tell us so much about what happened back then or what it meant.

But at least, for our short time here today, we can go back to the era before the catalogs, Black Friday, online shopping, and artificial lights. Back then the only light would eventually be a star. Before that, a lot of darkness, and in that darkness are the stories of four people we will briefly look at. We know them as Mary of Nazareth, Joseph, also of Nazareth, Elizabeth of the far country, and the old widow, Anna of Jerusalem. Each one had a secret burden one way or another.

We begin with Mary. She was a young girl and she is suddenly, mysteriously scared out of her wits by a heavenly vision, a voice beyond a human voice, an unmistakable intrusion she could not fathom but could not deny.

If this voice were from some other place she had every right to be frightened, even if the voice were from God. Mary knew her tradition: to be confronted, called by God, was always scary, always dangerous. You never knew what this God would want. Whatever it was, the one thing Mary knew, it would be challenging. It would cost.

She knew the stories of Abraham who hesitated; Moses who begged off saying, "Call my brother Aaron, he's a better speaker"; Isaiah, who asked the Lord, "Have you noticed? I stutter! Call someone else"; Jonah who said, "No Way!" and then he ran the other way—they all knew of the danger and they each asked to be excused. "No, not me . . . find someone else" was their common plea. Mary knew that.

So, she was scared. The angelic Messenger understood that and so immediately said, "Do not be afraid." Then he gave his message, but she became even more afraid on hearing it. Could she handle this call to be mother of the Messiah? How would it all happen? What about her parents, the neighbors? What about Joseph?

It was a long and lonely pause. Then she said yes to God. "Be it done unto me according to your word," and her life moved in a direction of which she never dreamed.

Mary is the Advent person for the invitationally challenged, for those hesitant to say yes to God's call to a different life, a fuller and deeper life beyond image, beyond looking out for Number 1, or who want the joy of yes but not its cost. Mary encourages us to say yes to the Lord, and to walk with her during Advent.

Then there is cousin Elizabeth, the deprived one as we might call her, the marginalized. Why did God do this to her: close her womb in a society that highly prized children, who gave her status, acceptance, and a common bond and respect with the other women of her village? Instead everyone could clearly see she was cursed by God: no children, no grandchildren for her old age. It's hard to be different, an outsider, out of the loop, folding dishtowels when others were folding diapers. She was different, seemingly passed over by God, surviving on the margins and she had to live with it.

What was wrong with her? Didn't God love her?

Until one latecomer day she felt a stirring in her body, and that same day cousin Mary came to visit and suddenly two women—both sterile, one by choice and the other by nature—celebrated God's breaking into their lives. She knew then that even if everyone else dismissed her, she had been noticed, she was noticed by the One who counts.

Elizabeth tells us shadowed people that no matter what the emptiness or how sidelined and unpopular we are, *we* are noticed by God. She would tell us to keep faith with our tradition. Read the scriptures. Worship in community. Give alms. God will break into our lives. Elizabeth gives us Advent hope.

Joseph. What can we say about him except that he always seems to be left out? His favorite question is, "What's going on around here? I'm the last person to know." He listens, overhears whispers and conversations that are recorded, and he winds up with not one word in the gospel accounts—or anywhere else for that matter. The silent man. The perennially perplexed. The lost soul. The overlooked.

Even later in those fabulous Renaissance paintings, he's always in the background or off center. The lighting, the spotlight, is always on Mary and Jesus. The forgotten man, the man in the dark. But it is in that darkness that he discovers he was to be one of those special quiet people who make a difference, who remain faithful and obeys even when he does not understand. Yes, faithful, loyal Joseph and those like him who are the context in which great things happen even if they have no clue. For some, he's a good sturdy companion for Advent. *Be a context for great things*, Joseph tells us.

Finally, there is Anna, the old woman, who went daily to the Temple in the hope she might see the Messiah before she dies. She is a woman who knows loss. She lost her husband, and some children. Celebrating Passover will be hard this year because her husband's gone. She has a heavy heart. So many memories!

She's old now and her faith and hope have ebbed. She lives in constant doubt. All those promises too long unfulfilled, all that waiting for the Messiah was a waste of time. She's seen too much tragedy, too much innocent suffering, too many unanswered prayers, too much of God's absence.

But her moment came. Despite dryness of heart, she went to the Temple every day and this day, this special day, she got to look into the face of the Messiah. Her lesson is to remain faithful in spite of doubt, in spite of loss. Keep faith with the community. Those of you for whom Christmas will be hard this year because you have lost a loved one, remember Anna as she will remember you.

These are some of the people who can focus our Advent in the midst of entertaining distraction. I suggest that you take one of them home with you. Even though you and I will be assaulted by commercial Christmas as soon as we leave here, in our hearts let us walk with Mary, Elizabeth, Joseph, or Anna as a little reminder of what the season really is all about. To that extent, dead Advent can live again in our lives and in our hearts.

2ND SUNDAY OF ADVENT
CYCLE B
MARK 1:1-8

2

Comfort My People

Today's first reading opens with the prophet Isaiah's majestic words, "'Comfort, give comfort to my people' says your God. Speak tenderly to Jerusalem . . ."

So I thought that today, this second Sunday of Advent, I would indeed speak tenderly to you; that is, share a woman's true story that will convey to us a sense of why we prepare to celebrate Christmas. She speaks:

One minute I was a 31-year-old part-time music teacher. The next moment, I turned into one of my pre-K students, hyperventilating and sobbing uncontrollably, wishing that Mom and Dad would come to rescue me.

That's what claustrophobia will do to you.

My parents were at home on Long Island, though, and here I was trapped in an elevator in a Manhattan high-rise. All alone. This was exactly what I'd been afraid of when my best friend asked me to come see her new apartment. Unless I wanted to climb fifteen flights of stairs, this metal coffin was my only way up. So, I said a prayer and went for it. I was doing okay . . . until the elevator car jerked and then came to a halt—between floors! I tried taking deep breaths. Feeling faint, I sank to the floor and tucked my head between my knees and closed my eyes.

Maybe because the next day was Father's Day, I thought back to how Dad had comforted me when I was a little girl. "Catch the kiss!" he'd say as he puckered up his lips, blew a kiss and then laughed as I ran around the room, grabbing handfuls of air trying to hold onto the invisible. Had I ever told him what those moments meant to me? Now I might never get the chance. Not if I suffocated to death in this elevator, or if the cable snapped and I plummeted to my death.

I opened my eyes. Blinking away my tears, I spied a little door below the button panel. *Emergency phone!* Thank God! I snatched up the receiver, "I'm stuck in here!" I cried in panic. "Get me out, please!"

"We're working on it, Ma'am," a voice responded.

"I know you're upset, but the longer we stay on the phone, the longer it will take to free you." I hung up immediately.

Trying to dry my tears, I rummaged through my purse for a tissue. My hand bumped into something hard. It was the mini tape recorder I used for my classes. "Make this time count", I thought. "If I don't make it, at least tell everyone you love what you've always wanted to tell them." I held the microphone to my lips and pressed *Record*. I started with Dad.

"Dad, I remember you at the playground, how you stood at the end of the giant blue slide waiting to catch me. I'm all grown up now, but I continue to count on you to be there for me when I'm scared. You never let me down. In my mind, you'll always be the giant that met me at the bottom of that slide, and I'll always be your little girl. Happy Father's Day, Dad, I love you."

Suddenly, *clang!* What was that? The cable snapping? A panicked heartbeat later, the elevator doors slid open. An emergency worker was there. I nearly leaped into his arms. He looked me over and led me downstairs to the lobby. I buzzed my friend's apartment. She came down. "I'm sorry," she said. "But, really, what were the odds that this would happen to you, of all people?"

I told my parents about this whole frightful episode when I saw them on Father's Day. Then I handed Dad my gift. He looked confused. "A tape recorder?" he asked. "Just press *Play*," I said. He listened to my elevator message. "This is the best gift you could have given me," he said. Now he was the one blinking away tears. Little did I know at the time that it would be our last Father's Day together. Dad was soon diagnosed with leukemia and succumbed swiftly.

It took a while before I could bring myself to sort through the bag of belongings he'd brought with him to the hospital: some magazines, his father's watch. But at the bottom of the bag I was startled to find the tape recorder I'd given him. I rewound the tape and pressed *Play*.

That time in the elevator had been terrifying. But it had given me the chance to tell Dad how I felt before it was too late. I thought of my words comforting him in his final days the way he had always comforted me. Thank you, Lord, for that.

My old elevator message ended. I was about to turn it off when I heard the sound of someone clearing his throat. It was Dad's voice steady and clear.

"Dear Princess. When you find this recording, I will no longer be here. Know that I love you more that life itself. You are the greatest blessing a father could hope for. When you close your eyes, listen for my voice and know that you are never alone. I am with you always." Just before the recording clicked off, I heard the unmistakable sound of him blowing a kiss. I reached up with both hands and clasped them together in the air, catching something invisible, something that had never felt more real."

It's not too hard to imagine that this woman's story is the Advent story in another guise, which means it is the story of us: a people sometimes in the dark, sometimes stuck between the floors of our life in what she calls a metal coffin—what we call a spiritual, social, emotional coffin—waiting and yearning for salvation and, while waiting, desperately clinging to Isaiah's promised words of comfort.

I suggest that her father's words are those words of comfort.

"Know that I love you . . . You are my greatest blessing. Close your eyes and listen to my voice and know that you are never alone. I am with you always."

These are Advent-like words that are the heart and soul of Christmas. At the beginning of the gospel, they come from the mouth of the angel Gabriel who described the savior-to- come as Emmanuel which, he says, means 'God with us'; they also come at the end of the gospel when Jesus says, "I am with you all days, even to the end of time."

Advent is promise. Christmas is fulfillment. With our story in mind, let's keep on singing with confidence, "O come, O come Emmanuel."

3RD SUNDAY OF ADVENT
CYCLE B
JOHN 1:6-8, 19-28

3

John's Question, Jesus' Answer

John the Baptist.

John the forerunner, the voice crying in the wilderness, the one who prepares the way for some other whose sandal strap, he says, he is not worthy to tie; John the baptizer who calls the people, the soldiers, the Pharisees, to repentance. He is forceful and fascinating, popular and feared. He even catches the attention of superstitious King Herod who was anxious one day to meet him. He is riding high, confident, sure of himself.

But, as happens to us all, especially in midlife, one day, John's fortunes begin to turn. He's caught up in the politics of those who do not want to repent, whose vested interests he has hurt, and eventually finds himself in Herod's dreaded prison fortress of Machaerus that overlooks the city of Jerusalem.

There he has enough time in that rat-infested hole to think, to feel sorry for himself, to wonder if it was all worthwhile. After all his preaching, all his calls to repentance, all his fierce dedication, all his ultimate acknowledgement of Jesus as the Messiah, he begins to have his doubts. The dream begins to fade.

So much so, you recall from hearing or reading in the gospels, that he sends two of his disciples to find Jesus and ask him outright, "Are you the one who is to come or shall we look for another?"

When they finally found Jesus, who had just finished preaching to the crowd and taking some downtime, they told him what John said. After he heard their message, Jesus sighed and bowed his head in sadness and thought for a long, long time.

He sympathized with John. He is right to ask. Look around. After all of John's efforts, after all of his own preaching and healing and working miracles, there's no doubt about it: the bad guys seemed to be winning—and, Jesus probably thought to himself, sooner or later, they'll catch up with me.

After what seemed like an eternity, Jesus raised his head, smiled, and said, "Look, go back and tell John what you have seen and heard: how the blind see, the deaf hear, the poor have the good news, the gospel, preached to them and tell him, *Blessed are those who are not scandalized in me*."

How current! How contemporary! How aching John's question is, a question which is now the question of so many of us: Jesus, *are* you the one who has come to establish your kingdom or shall we look somewhere else? We're getting desperate.

We ask this because, after 2,000 years, the world is still in such a terrible mess, maybe worse than ever. It's aflame with endless war, deceit, and betrayal. Millions upon millions of refugees from Syria—those who haven't been slaughtered—are homeless, living in tent cities if they're lucky. Christians, in the greatest persecution of them in history, continue to be beheaded by Islamic radicals.

Poverty stalks even affluent America. Financial and political meltdowns hobble the middle class. The races clash. The gap between the extremely rich and poor widens. Suffering and alienation have never seemed so widespread. Our national moral life, subverted by a vulgar media and mass overconsumption, seems so empty, so shallow. Keeping up with the Kardashians rather than noble people is sadly our new national aspiration.

The sense that we have lost our way, our soul as a nation, is everywhere. Awash in pagan values and the loud hectoring of the atheists, our moral compass seems off course. Every day in the papers and on our televisions, there's so much bad news. So much electronic connection, yet so little human connection.

Closer to us, there is unemployment and broken families. What further breaks our hearts is that our children and grandchildren, nice and good people, are not here to worship with us. Religion has nothing to say to them, they claim. Their divorces and lifestyles sadden us. We love them, of course, but we grieve.

In short, all over the bad guys seem to be winning and we are all, every one of us John the Baptists, asking, "Jesus, are you the one who was to come or shall we look for another?"

But Jesus' response, "I want to submit to you," is still valid, still compelling, still as true now as it was then, and we should remember and hold on to it. As proof, think of the early Jesus followers: they too were drowning in bad news. Every day they were reviled, ridiculed, persecuted, declared illegal, and sidelined as minorities. They knew loss. Many of their family members and friends died for the faith. Some caved in and apostatized. Life for them meant just trying to survive both politically and morally, as they had to live with the surrounding pagan culture that was the complete opposite of their gospel beliefs.

Yet, for all of this bad news, one found these non-celebrity people century after century quietly telling and retelling the Jesus story, gathering to break the bread and share the cup, doing this behind closed doors and covered windows, in the fields, in the woods, in prisons, in cemeteries. They bravely lived countercultural lives conscious that they might be punished for it, yet also conscious that they had been called by Jesus to make a difference. One thing is sure: living with so much bad news, in their wildest dreams they could never, ever, imagine that within four or five hundred years Christianity would capture the empire and later spread worldwide with whole nations crying out, "Jesus Christ is Lord!"

And this was done not by mighty power and vast bureaucracies but by ordinary weakness: by ordinary people who made the blind see, the deaf hear, the good news lived and proclaimed, who quietly and routinely practiced the spiritual and corporal works of mercy. These people, although out of the spotlight, off the publicity radar, in a one-on-one witness, eventually made the difference. Evil gave way to good and all was made new.

I am here to encourage you. I am here to tell you that

it's still the same today. Just like it happened in those first difficult centuries, so today's unadvertised and uncelebrated goodness will prevail. Why? Because, think about it; the same pieces Jesus cited are all still in place.

Think right now. Before this day is over, out of camera range, billions of people will have gathered to hear the Jesus story again. They will break the bread and share the cup whether in churches like our own or in fields, woods, prisons, cemeteries or other secret hiding places. Think of how many people here and throughout the world today will be carrying the Eucharist to the homebound.

Think of the billions of people today feeding the hungry, clothing the naked, or visiting the sick, the imprisoned, the refugee. Think of the collective worldwide impact of every parish's St. Vincent de Paul Society. Think of the children being taught in schools and in secret meeting places. Think of ordinary people who are caring for the elderly or other family members. Think of your own taken-for-granted care, shelter, food, and clothing for your family. Think of the good marriages rather than the publicized failed ones. Think of all this happening worldwide, every day and off-the-radar, and know that Jesus was right in saying, "Yes. I know about the bad news but go and tell John the good news, how the lame walk, the blind see, the poor have the gospel preached to them. *That's* proof of my holy presence in an unholy world."

So, there we are. Yes, we say, faith is waning. Yes, our children have dropped out. Yes, some have embraced secular values. Yes, the world is a mess. Yes, a steady diet of bad news grinds us down. But, just as those early Christians overcame the bad news by quietly living out and eventually spreading the gospel, so be comforted and do the same. Be faithful. Hold fast. Your being here counts. Your being here is good news. And you are legion.

In a word, know that your unadvertised charity in global unity counts. Your walking to a different drumbeat counts. You may not see it now, you may be in a John the Baptist mode of anxiety, depression and doubt, but someday, in another age, people will find Christ again.

My message is that when, like John the Baptist, weary and frightened and discouraged, we ask Jesus, "Are you the one to come or shall we look for another?" Remember his answer:

"Look around you. Look beyond the everyday advertised bad news to the everyday unadvertised good news. Remember that this very day in countless numbers people will be ministered to, hearts will be mended, bodies will be bandaged, bread will be broken, souls will be soothed, wounds will be healed—and blessed are those who are not scandalized in me."

And then, finally, looking upon us kindly, Jesus adds, "Remember my promise: Behold, I am with you all days until the end of time."

4TH SUNDAY OF ADVENT
CYCLE C
LUKE 1:39-45

4

Crossing Borders

The Advent-Christmas season, as you may have noticed, is full of names we've come to know and cherish: Gabriel, Mary, Joseph, Jesus, Elizabeth, Zachariah, David, John, Anna, Simeon, Herod; full of people: shepherds, soldiers, Pharisees, Elders, innkeeper, Magi; it is full of divisions: Roman occupiers, Palestinians occupied, Pharisees and Sadducees, Jews, and Gentiles.

The shared commonality in the gospel narrative is that these people were all invited to cross borders when it would have been easier to stay with the comfortable and the familiar. Some declined. Most took the chance.

Herod, the Elders, and some Pharisees opted for what they knew, and what they could control. But a frightened teenaged girl named Mary finally closed her eyes, took a breath, and said yes, yes. Yes, let it be done unto me according to your word, and from that point on she crossed the border into the unknown with only her faith to guide her. And she changed history.

Shadowy and perplexed Joseph, the man apparently with no ego at all, thought over a troubling dream and wound up literally crossing the border into Egypt with his now-expectant wife. What would await them there? He had no clue, but it too turned out to change history.

Elizabeth and Zechariah—they're the name of a sterile, childless couple—too advanced in years for adventure, too wedded to the past, but in time they held hands and said we'll cross to parenthood and a promising child. Somehow we'll cope. That promised child, John, said yes and crossed over to begin to his strange mission of making way for the Messiah, whoever he might be, wherever that would lead.

Ancient Anna and Simeon, too old now to have illusions, too near death to expect anything, too disappointed to have hope anymore, nevertheless, weary and unexpectant, crossed the border of the Temple doorway every single day to seek the Messiah—just in case this was the day. They kept faith.

Then Jesus came. If nothing else, he was a person of border-crossings. He crossed the border from divinity to humanity. His border-crossing mercy extended to his ethnic and political enemies: to Samaritans and Romans, Jews and Greeks, a foreign Phoenician woman with a sick child, disgusting lepers, traitorous tax collectors, and possessed madmen. In fact, one of the main criticisms of him was that he crossed borders no decent person would or should cross—right up to his death when he made a promise to a miserable thief and offered forgiveness to some cowardly executioners.

The lessons of these Advent figures—including Jesus—are clear. When God summons us to cross borders. In a way, the spiritual journey *is* about border crossings. Today we remember that there are those who have not yet crossed borders, headline names that spawn slogans like "Black Lives Matter" or "Blue Lives Matter," Congress and the president, Israel and Palestine, Ukrainians and Russian separatists, Isis and Syrians, the very rich and very poor, peacemakers and war makers, atheists and believers. The challenge remains for them: cross the border.

But what about us, we good people? Why don't we cross over more often like Mary and Joseph and the rest? Perhaps the answer is our lifestyles. Closeted only with our electronic partners, we never talk face-to-face with others, never move beyond our ring of interest, our circle of friends. We never meet the world's "others" with whom we might dialogue. A closed circle plus over business and speed are our militant guards against the outside, against those "others," against hearing invitations from God.

Yet, these invitations are out there but we're so busy, so glamorously distracted by a non-stop media and advertising, the hawking and noise are so loud, that we seldom hear the voice gently confronting, the sweet urging to change our ways, the Lover's plea to say yes to God, to deepen our sensitivity to God's holy presence, to discover joy beyond the constant round of mere sensations the world offers us.

Therefore we don't respond to God's gentle invitations to let go as Mary and Joseph did. We don't insist on the requisite downtime to listen to God's invitation to cross over to virtue, or to put aside the shallow lives we're living and go deeper where true love is to be found. In a world of such engaging non-stop distraction crossing borders is hard to do.

Yet, we must try. We must consider that, like our first Advent-ers, we are called to cross borders, called to join Mary and Joseph and the rest. We are prompted by the season to ask ourselves, what borders are we called to cross, to erase, in our lives?

CYCLES A, B, C

5

Christmas: Something Happened—Then and Now

He was a widower and she was a widow. They had known each other for a number of years, being high school classmates and then having attended class reunions in the past without fail. This 60th anniversary of their class, the widower and the widow made a foursome with two other singles. They had a wonderful evening, their spirits high with the widower throwing admiring glances across the table and the widow smiling coyly back at him. Finally, he picked up the courage and blurted out, "Will you marry me?" After about six seconds of careful consideration, she answered, "Yes! Yes, I will!"

The evening ended on a happy note for the widower. But the next morning he was troubled. Did she say yes? Or did she say no? He couldn't remember. Try as he would, he just could not recall. He went over the conversation of the past evening, but his mind was blank. He remembered asking the question but for the life of him he could not recall the response. So with fear and trepidation, he picked up the phone and called her.

First, he explained that he couldn't remember as well as he used to. Then he reviewed the past evening. As he gained a little more courage, he then inquired of her, "When I asked if you would marry me, did you say yes or did you say no?"

"Why, you silly man, I said yes. Yes, I will! And I meant it with all my heart."

The widower was delighted. He felt his heart skip a beat.

Then she continued, "And I am so glad you called because I couldn't remember who asked me!"

Two things: First, it's good to hear laughter in church. Laughter calls us out of our individual selves, our individual needs and sorrows, and for the moment makes us a community—which, when you come right down to it, is what religion is all about.

Second, those who know me know that in those rare times whenever I begin a homily with a joke, it signals that I'm preparing you for something quite serious. And they are quite right, although I have some reservations.

After all, this *is* Christmas. You're here, family and visitors are here and you understandably want to hear from me something engaging, a warm fuzzy for the season, a cheerful story sending you home uplifted. I *will* share the good news but, I admit, not in a way that is necessarily "uplifting" or comfortable—and I apologize for that—but in a way that I hope will lead to deeper reflection. Anyway, so forewarned, let me lead you to a television documentary.

As some of you may already know, television's PBS is airing a five-part series on the holy pilgrimage shrines of all faiths around the earth. The series, just begun, is called "Sacred Journeys with Bruce Feiler." I saw the first in the series and it's that episode in which I want to briefly talk about, although it's not easy to do so. It was devoted to the Catholic shrine of Lourdes—but it had a very special focus. It focuses on some very special pilgrims among the five million who each year make the pilgrimage to Lourdes: severely wounded warriors from Iraq and Afghanistan.

These are soldiers with missing limbs, or who are blind, crippled, deformed and with many demons in their heads, whose lives and families have been upended by the horrors of war. Half of the many soldiers in this particular group are Catholics of one kind or another. Others are not. Some are believers. Others are skeptics pretty much like ourselves in this regard. Interestingly, uniformly, when they are asked why they have come to Lourdes, they all say they would like to be cured but don't expect to be, yet they all want to be healed. Notice the wonderful difference here. Curing refers to the body, healing refers to the soul.

Yes, these soldiers would like to be cured but, more than that, they want to be healed. They want their inner pain to go away. They want those memories of their buddies dying in their arms excised. They want that buzzing in their heads to stop. They want their despair, their depression, their thoughts of suicide, their feeling of being in half-human, half-prosthetic bodies, to disappear.

The film follows a few of these wounded warrior pilgrims. There's the 20-year-old army rifleman, Zach Herrick, who was shot in the face in the mountains of Afghanistan. Once quite handsome, he lost this lower jaw and many teeth. He says he feels uncomfortable with people staring at his deformed face. He has trouble chewing and talking. Then there is James Pierce from North Carolina, who was seriously injured in a suicide bombing. There is Juan Roldan from New Jersey, who suffered a traumatic brain injury and lost both his legs mid-thigh. Others are paralyzed, pushed in wheelchairs by wives and girlfriends.

They each came to Lourdes free. Their expenses have been fully covered by anonymous donations from around the world as part of Lourdes' annual international military pilgrimage, which means each year tens of thousands of soldiers gather at the place where Bernadette Soubirous, just fourteen, said she saw the Blessed Virgin over at the grotto in 1858.

The film shows the soldiers arriving at Lourdes as they are greeted by unstoppable love and care by ordinary people who volunteer their time to assist them in every way. Many of these volunteers are former pilgrims themselves and have come back in gratitude to freely serve others. These wounded soldiers are there an entire week surrounded by the love and service of these volunteers. The soldiers take part in processions, attend Mass, and finally are dipped in the so-called miraculous waters that the Blessed Mother pointed out to St. Bernadette.

A tense moment is when they are plunged into its icy waters. No one is cured. But, strangely, everyone is healed in one way or another. They say they feel different. Darkness of mind is lifted. They come out with a better sense of themselves.

Then later, at the end of their stay, they all meet in the church square where they blow off steam with singing and beer. And the camera shows soldiers, hurt, deformed, laughing, and, most of all—which is some kind of a miracle—embracing other soldiers who were once their enemies, whom they would have killed in the war. Yet here they are, opponents hugging and joking with one another. Quite a moving sight. Some would say, it's a miraculous sight.

What unites them is the common bond of their brokenness and some, for the first time, are able to stand up and speak to the group out loud and let their feelings and struggles be known. They speak of being moved by the kindness and compassion they feel around them at Lourdes.

Most of all, they struggle to speak of "something happening" within them, that some of the demons inside them have subsided, that they no longer feel worthless, no longer feel that they'd be better off dead or that the horrors they've seen, forever etched in their minds, are not the last word. They were each deeply touched by the love, compassion, and attention of the volunteers. They left Lourdes, uncured but not unhealed. They go home knowing "something's happened," and so do their families. A powerful film. The end.

And now I want to process down to our feast, to why we are here this Christmas day. I want to return to that recurrent phrase, "Something happened." I am suggesting that "something happened" is what Christmas is all about.

Something happened over 100 years ago at Lourdes. Whatever it was Bernadette saw over a hundred years ago, "Something happened."

Something happened to make those countless sympathetic, unknown donors pay the fare and the upkeep for soldiers they do not know and will never meet.

Something happened to cause those anonymous volunteers to come and nurse, care for, and love perfect strangers in various stages of woundedness.

Something happened to make them, once pilgrims themselves, to feel the need to return grace for grace.

Something happened to those wounded warriors themselves who, for the first time, found themselves looking beyond their sorrows and injuries.

I suggest, finally, that, whatever the metaphors, the storytelling, the ornamentation, something also happened in Bethlehem 2,000 years ago, something more than meets the eye, something that spiraled 2,000 years later to touch the hearts of these soldiers. That "something" is that Love has come to earth, and has found a home among us. Christmas says that healing has been let loose in Jesus Christ and that's why we celebrate it.

So—you may not leave here with a glow in your hearts, but I hope at least that you leave here with gratitude in your souls; yes, for those soldiers, of course, but especially for the God who came among us and made something happen—and still does.

HOLY FAMILY OF JESUS, MARY AND JOSEPH
CYCLE C
LUKE 2:41-52

6

For a New Year

New Year's is traditionally a time for resolutions: you know—the lose weight, be on time, be nice to my spouse sort of thing. Everybody suggests them. I want to throw my hat in the ring, for I, too, have a suggestion to make. But we need some background. So, I ask you to go back to the time when, on one occasion, Jesus' disciples asked him, "Teach us how to pray." What brought this on is the subject of our reflection.

They had been with Jesus a while and began to see that it was through the medium of prayer that he drew his strength from beyond himself. They notice he prays a lot. Jesus prays when he is joyful and when he is in agony. He prays with others around him and when he is alone at night. He prays high on a mountain and on a level plain.

And this is not lost on his disciples. They see that he is linked at some deep place, to something beyond to the One he calls Father, and they want this for themselves. That's what they mean when they ask Jesus, "Teach us how to pray." They didn't necessarily want words—although he gave them some—they wanted the depth that reaching beyond gave.

They didn't want power to do miracles, the quick intelligence to silence opponents. They wanted the graciousness of soul, the largeness of spirit, the wholeness that Jesus displayed. They wanted his power to love when hated, to forgive when reviled, to be big hearted with small-minded people, to reach beyond his tribe, and to live beyond slogans. They wanted Jesus' ability to see "larger," if you will, and that, obviously, came from beyond.

A little story that makes the same point: a holy monk was once given a most precious Bible by a wealthy man grateful to be freed of his sins and addictions. Though the ancient book was worth a fortune, the monk placed it openly in his small hut as a focus for meditation and prayer.

One day a destitute and sick man wandered by. He was wounded and seemed half alive. The holy monk took him in and for many months cared for him, eventually nurturing him back to health. As he got better, the man, a felon and thief as it turned out, became more and more interested in the Bible that he could see was worth much money. Soon the temptation of greed became too strong. One day while the monk was out ministering to the poor, he snatched the Bible and fled.

As it turned out, he was eventually caught in connection with another crime and put in prison. The police returned the Bible to the monk. Upon receiving it, however, the monk traveled to the village where the man was held. He forgave him, handed him back the book and left. The thief was delighted. It would fetch much money when he was freed. After a year, the thief was released, but during his imprisonment he'd had time to think. It wasn't long before he appeared at the hut of the old monk and handed him back the Bible. "Oh," said the monk. "You can keep it. It will bring you much money." The thief cried out, "I don't want the book, I don't want money! I want—I want whatever it is that made you give it back. I want what's inside of you that makes you able to do this."

That's what the disciples meant when they asked Jesus, "Teach us how to pray. Give us the gift that will help us look beyond, look deeper. What they wanted was Jesus' depth of connection to the Father so that they would not live shallow lives, always determined by peer pressure, the fickle crowds.

We should want the same thing but today, as you know, it's almost impossible to "go beyond," to escape the attractive greed, the incessant distractions, the powerful drive for surface image and acceptance. It's almost impossible to escape the speed of life, the constant activity, to escape the world of sound bites and slogans, to escape the constant call to the "always busy" and "never enough time" syndrome, which is a badge of success in our society even though it's sucking us dry.

You see where all this is leading? It's New Year's, the traditional time for resolutions. We know in our hearts that we need to pull back from the noise, the omnipresent mass media that panders to our greed, confirms our prejudices and homogenizes our morals, a media that will not allow us the time to look beyond.

You know, it would be an interesting experiment to take some paper and write down, say, an account of the past week of our lives and see how much time was spent reading secular magazines, looking online, Facebooking, tweeting, smart phoning, or TV watching—and what you were taking in all this time, day after day. Make a list of the daily diet of *what* you read or watched. Now multiply all that input by months and years.

What we often get is shallowness of soul. What we get is insensitivity and lack of inner peace. What we get from this poor intellectual and moral diet is bad spiritual health that lives by responding to media stimuli and the culture's definition of success and its exultation of speed, being active, always on the move all of which prevent depth so that we can get to the place beyond, the place Jesus tapped.

But for the New Year, I suggest that we imitate Jesus and go apart now and then from the culture. That we imitate Mary of today's gospel of whom it was said, "And Mary kept all these things, reflecting on them in her heart." We need to go apart, reflect, take a break from the TV, from the official secularism of the culture. Like Jesus, we need to tap into the Source. We need to tap something beyond, to tap that spiritual equilibrium that makes us free.

So, finally, we come to the point—my simple recommended New Year's resolution: everyday set aside at least 15 to 20 minutes to do some spiritual reading, whether the gospels or another book. Engage an alternate voice, a different drummer, a deeper vision of life. Tap into the source of life and love.

Socrates famously said that the unexamined life is not worth living. Saints, mystics, and the gospels say he is right. Daily spiritual reading will make not only for a happy New Year but a holy one.

BAPTISM OF JESUS
CYCLES A, B, C

7

Baptism a la Bush

On January 6, 2015 President George H.W. Bush and his wife, Barbara, celebrated their 70th wedding anniversary. President Bush, before leaving the hospital, tweeted his wife the following: "Seventy years ago this very day, Barbara Pierce of Rye, New York, made me the happiest and luckiest man on earth."

In these days when some marriages don't last seven years, or even seven days in the case of some celebrities, when more and more discard marriage or have children without it, his words are beautiful and touching. They remind me of another couple married 67 years. When asked how it survived so long, the wife said, "We were raised in an age when something was broke we didn't throw it away. We fixed it."

Seventy years ago, January 6, 1945 was clearly important for the Bush's. A commitment, a way of life was pledged. It was a significant life-changing moment for them both.

In like manner, think of the day a man or woman, after many years of study and apprenticeship, at last receives his or her medical or legal certification or engineering degree. Think of the day when someone, after a long wait, is accepted by the important powers-that-be into a prestigious country club. Think of any life-changing step and the excitement, joy and even apprehension that go with it. Will I make it? Will I be good at it? Will I advance? Will I succeed in my life's choice? Will I be loyal to its principles? It's all weighty stuff.

Yet, it's so hard, probably impossible for us today, to grasp that, once upon a time, in the early centuries of the Church, baptism was considered precisely like that: a major, life-changing, courageous, thoughtful step undertaken only after years of study and apprenticeship and approval by the powers that be. We shake our heads. No, we say, that can't be. I never heard of that. Baptism today doesn't even provoke a hesitation or a ripple. No one ever thinks of it. More and more, many are not even interested in it. It's a non-item for even the best of Christians.

What a drastic change from the past! That is to say, at one time, baptism into the Christian religion was truly a scary and brave thing with all its dangers of persecution, betrayal, and living radically different from those around you; it meant, say, holding countercultural views that brought distain, job loss, ridicule—like the belief, for example, where two thirds of society were slaves, that every human being is made to the image and likeness of God.

Who would hold such ridiculous things? To love your enemies and pray for those who persecute you was civic nonsense beyond the pale. It was unheard of to hold that exposing unwanted babies to the elements was wrong. Where all this kind of radical, being-out-of-step stuff was part of becoming Christian, not many people were willing to consider it or, if they did, they spent some several years prepping for it. Baptism was serious stuff back then.

But what happened was success. When in the 4th century, Christianity became legal and it became politically correct to become a Christian if you wanted the better jobs; then the standards dropped and at one momentous slippery point in history baptism became casual, one's ticket into society rather than into a faith community, and over the centuries it even became a private thing whereas for centuries it was quite a public, communal event witnessed and encouraged by the entire Christian community.

Further, as believing correctly began to supplant living and acting correctly according to the gospel, then gradually the only question that got to be asked was whether or not you were orthodox, not as previously—to the point of calling in neighbors and witnesses—Are you moral, prayerful and compassionate? Do you intend to live a Christ-like life?

In our time, the ultimate deterioration of this reversal was captured in Francis Ford Coppola's masterpiece *The Godfather*, where in an oft-cited spliced-in scene, simultaneously Michael Corleone is having his son baptized Catholic as his henchmen are machine gunning his enemies. Oh, Michael was orthodox—he didn't deny the Trinity—so he passed muster as a Christian. In former days, he would not make it through the door till he repented of his ways no matter how much money he gave in the collection, or how perfectly he could recite the creed. And so baptism became a social rather than a life-changing, life-challenging event.

So, what's changed with the meaning behind baptism, then vs. now? Let's look.

Gone are the long preparations, the long study. Gone is regular public appearances before the bishop and fellow Christians who questioned you on your lifestyle and practice, your motives and sincerity, and your worthiness.

Gone is the mentoring, the beautiful and exotic ceremony at the end of Lent when you were anointed, when before family and friends—think of that!—in a darkened hall you and the others had to face west, the place of the sinking sun and darkness and shout, "I renounce you, Satan, prince of darkness!" and then turn quickly to the East, the place of the rising sun and shout, "I accept you, Jesus, the light of the world."

Gone are the sponsors, who actually lived the life of Jesus themselves and guided you by their counsel and example. Now people have Aunt Susie as godmother because, even though she is divorced four times and never goes to church, she's family and besides, she asked you to be godparent to her child. Gone is the involvement and support of the whole community as people have their children quietly baptized on a Sunday afternoon with no one there except some close friends.

Gone are those old baptismal pools shaped either like a womb or a tomb, the one emphasizing new life, the other, death to sin and one's former way of life. Perhaps our small basin-like fonts today are emblematic of the diminishing of baptism's meaning.

Gone is any concept—a totally correct one—that being baptized is far more important than being ordained a deacon, priest or bishop, that it is the most important sacrament of all because, like being knighted in medieval times, it is an initiation rite into the whole life-long system of love and service, a very public declaration that, as a Christian, you will seek to live the life of Christ at every moment: at your job, your school, your marriage—even if it costs you.

Gone is the memory of the voice that said to Jesus at his baptism, "You are my beloved, with you I am well pleased." We don't hear it anymore. We don't think of ourselves as forever beloved of God, beholden to God, branded, as it were, with God's seal.

Gone is that sense of calling, of vocation through baptism. The truth is that the secular culture has homogenized us and baptism has fallen into a mere cultural event like having a birthday party with no meaning, and with no promise to try and live the gospel. And it shows.

Anyway, today, on the feast of the Baptism of Jesus, we can at least look back at the ideal to review baptism's history, the way it used to be, was meant to be, to see baptism for a moment for what it really is: a solemn rite of initiation into living as best we can the life and teachings of Jesus Christ.

It's a good time, on this feast of the Baptism of Jesus, to remember that we have been baptized, that we have been christened—"Christ-ened," if you will—that we are identified as Christians—a dangerous label in early centuries and also, as we know, in some parts of the world today. It's a good time to remember what being baptized is all about: a commitment to live as Jesus would have us live.

It's a nice fantasy to think that someday before we die, we too would be able to tweet someone, like George Bush tweeted his wife, Barbara, and say, "So many years ago this very day, Jesus Christ made me the happiest and luckiest person on earth. Through baptism he made me a follower. I hope it has showed."

The Lent–Easter Cycle

8

The Passion of Elvis

Lent once again is upon us and so, naturally, I am going to preach about Elvis Presley.

He would have been 80 at the beginning of this year [2015], but let's go back to when he was much younger. It's June of 1977 and Elvis is preparing for the last movie he ever made as the cameras are readying to film him in concert. He is overweight, looks and feels terrible and within two months, at age 42, he will be dead. His body is filled with painkillers and tranquillizers. He's starting to forget the words to his songs. Larry Geller his hairdresser—and spiritual adviser—yes, his hairdresser is his spiritual guru; remember this is Hollywood—runs over and touches up some gray on his sideburns.

How could the man who had everything be destroyed at the age of 42?

Let's go back. Born in a sharecropper's shack in 1935 in the Deep South of Mississippi, Elvis knew poverty and its effects. Lack of health care cost the life of his twin brother. His parents barely survived economically. His father went to prison for the minor infraction of altering a $4 check to a $14 one, so desperately poor was he. When a teenager, his family moved into one of the projects in Memphis. His family survived the horrendous 1936 tornado. Most people do not know that this tornado that killed hundreds is listed as the second worst natural disaster in U.S. record.

But from the beginning, Elvis knew songs. His mother, carrying him on her back as she picked cotton, would sing sacred songs. He heard gospel music at church, the ultra-conservative Pentecostal church where his father and several of his uncles were deacons. Later he parted from the church when the preacher condemned an Abbot and Costello movie as "Lucifer's work," but he never lost his connection to its music nor to his mother's superstitious and fundamentalist bible reading.

She often told him that since his twin brother had died he needed to have a double strength, two destinies—a belief that was likely passed down from his maternal Cherokee great, great grandmother, Morning White Dove. You can readily see the Cherokee Indian look in Elvis' face.

Eventually Elvis rejected not only his church's fundamentalism but also its racial segregation, and he would often listen to black musicians along Memphis' famous Beale Street. Later, he would appear on stage with them. After his mother's early death in 1958, he found himself drifting, rudderless. Even when praise and wealth came, he always felt empty. He was always searching, forever searching.

At the height of his Hollywood career in 1964 was when he came under the influence of his hairdresser, Larry Geller whom we mentioned before, and through his influence Elvis devoured texts on Hinduism, Judaism, Buddhism, and yoga writings. Elvis kept the King James Bible in his bedside dresser. He wore the Star of David, an Egyptian religious symbol, and his mother's crucifix. He was always the searcher.

"I want to find God," Elvis said more than once. Geller wisely told him that to do this he must first lose his ego. But, like the young man in the gospel story, Elvis couldn't bring himself to do that. Poor too long, he loved his cars and his fame and his wealth. These rescued him from poverty and he couldn't turn back although he always wrestled with them. He kept coming back to his favorite New Testament reading, the saying of Jesus that it was easier for a camel to pass through the eye of a needle than for a rich man to be saved.

Elvis would spend his life skirmishing between his fame and this gospel passage. Hence his legendary deeds of debauchery fought with his equally legendary acts of charity.

Sadly, in the end, neither his spirituality nor his generosity of spirit were enough to save him. In the midst of his 1970s successes and concerts, with the sweat running down his face from the lights and stumbling from stage to stage, he fought to find his center. He had survived his twin brother's death and a tornado, but the whirlwind of his success destroyed him.

You can see this struggle as he continually reached back to the gospel songs throughout his life. "How Great Thou Art" is probably his most celebrated gospel song, but he also often sang others. Those gospel songs were, in reality, his oases, his lifeline, his dying prayers.

A searcher to the end, you should know that Elvis died reading a book on the Shroud of Turin, and perhaps his journey was taking him to Catholicism. He had already dipped into it. Listen to his rendition of "The Miracle of the Rosary" and watch him sing in a Mass folk group in his film about nuns, *Change of Habit*. Elvis, I think, would have been delighted to find out that his name, Elvis, is a Catholic saint's name. Elvis is the Anglicized version of the Irish spelling. St. Elvis, the legend goes, was abandoned by his parents at birth because a king wanted to kill him. He was raised by a wolf and converted the Welsh and the Irish to Christianity. Loving to pray by the sea, St. Elvis would often sing knee-deep in the water. To this day, St. Elvis churches are to be found in England and Ireland. Elvis would have been fascinated.

So, Elvis Presley as a figure for Lent? Why not? Yes, our image of Elvis is the media's version it wants you to see: hip-swirling, scandalous, movie idol, the celluloid "king of rock and roll" who died tragically and left us a legacy of fabulous singing. But you should know that there was another side to him—the passionate seeker, the Rich Young Man, the Prodigal Son—who never quite found what he was looking for, never quite could let go and so he becomes us. Elvis reminds us to take a look at what we can't let go of but should, to search, to seek, to find.

Yes, Elvis' music speaks to our memories and his cultivated celebrity caters to our fantasy needs, but behind it all, it is his search and his sincere flirtation with holiness, that speak to us for Lent. We have forty days to listen carefully.

9

Veronica's Veil

Morris realized that he needed to purchase a hearing aid, but he was unwilling to spend much money.

"How much do they cost?" he asked the salesman.

"That depends," he said. "They run from $2.00 to $2,000."

"Let's see the $2.00 model," said miserly Morris.

The salesman put the device around Morris' neck. "You just stick this button in your ear and run this little string down to your pocket," he instructed.

"For $2.00 how does it work?" asked Morris.

"For $2.00 it doesn't work," said the salesman, "But when people see it on you, they'll talk louder."

That's my lame introduction to the subject of legends. Legends talk loud hidden truths. They turn up the volume of some historical reality and expand and embellish it with colorful language and extraordinary happenings in order to expose a deeper meaning or profound truth.

National legends like Homer, Beowulf, Paul Bunyan, or Johnny Appleseed, for example, give larger than life emphasis to the truths a country embraces as its identity. George Washington chopping down the cherry tree admitting he did it—not factual but true as depicting the great man's integrity. Marie Antoinette saying, "Let them eat cake"—not factual but true enough to portray the callous indifference of the powerful towards the poor. The favorite "Canticle of the Sun" prayer of St. Francis is a prayer that historically he didn't write but which beautifully captures the spirit of the man.

This kind of legendary storytelling isn't meant to be an objective argument, a proof, or a collection of data, but instead a creative and "loud" way of capturing meaning and inspiration. And, remember, legends always have roots in some reality.

Anyway, all this long introduction that you're getting today is not so much a homily but a minor history lesson to expand your general Catholic knowledge. So, class, relax as we go back to our recent Holy Week when the Christian Church rehearsed its drama: spy Wednesday, Holy Thursday, Good Friday, empty Saturday, and glorious Easter Sunday.

I want to single out Good Friday and, further, to single out the devotion that grew out of it, namely the Stations of the Cross—those 14 meditation spots whereby the Christian world paused 14 times to contemplate and pray and wonder. And, in the light of what I have just said, I want to remind you that, while most of those 14 stationary meditation spots are indeed historically recorded, five of them are legendary. These legends, like all legends, are indeed rooted in the facts of the time but have been expanded to make a powerful and memorable point about Jesus and what he was doing.

Three of these legendary embellishments are the three falls of Jesus on the way to Calvary. The falling is not actually in the historical record of the gospels but it is very likely that a weakened and wounded Jesus, carrying a heavy beam, did fall at least once. The one fall, following the rules of storytelling, then easily took on the symbolic number three and moved into a minor legend meant to convey to us the threefold endless determination of Jesus, grounded in love for us, to go all the way for our sakes.

Another legend is where Jesus meets his mother. That, too, is not literally in the gospels, but it is exceedingly likely that Mary was surely among the grieving women of Jerusalem who *are* in the gospel accounts. Naturally, storytellers couldn't let it rest there. The son, Jesus, and the mother, Mary, meeting had to be singled out from the crowd. This poignant meeting then easily morphed into the eternal tableau representing all parents who grieve for their suffering children, suffering physically with sickness, disease, depression, or suffering morally with messed-up lives, drugs, divorces, and unbelief.

The final legendary station, number six, is the one we are going to consider for the rest of the homily, the one we call "Veronica wipes the face of Jesus." We all know the story of how a woman broke through the crowd, wiped spit and sweat from Jesus' face, and later found the imprint of his face on her veil. This legend soon became a part of Catholic legendary lore. Like all legends, this one eventually expanded to say that Veronica later traveled to Rome to present her imaged cloth to the emperor Tiberius and that the veil possessed miraculous properties such as being able to quench thirst, cure blindness and even sometimes raise the dead.

During the 14th century, the legend of Veronica's Veil, so long prominent in the Eastern Church, migrated to the Western Church where it became a firm part of our devotional life and gaining even more details as time went on. Testimony to this is that to this day, on the Via Dolorosa in Jerusalem, there is a small chapel known as the "Chapel of the Holy Face," regarded as the site of the miracle.

But the fact remains that there *was* no specific woman named Veronica, nor her action or imaged veil. It was all a dramatic devotional and fictional story trying to convey a deeper truth. (What that truth is, we'll see in a moment.) So how did the story originate? It's not hard to imagine that it easily sprung from what *was* recorded, namely, what we mentioned already in the case of Mary: those compassionate women who were there to witness the sad event of Jesus' march to Calvary.

Just as it was not unreasonable, as we saw, to assume that Mary was among these women, so it is also not unreasonable to assume that one of these unnamed courageous women in the crowd, ignoring the hostility of the people and the threats of the soldiers, could not restrain her love and compassion; she boldly broke through the mob to show a pitiable and dying man that there were those who still loved and cared for him even as he stumbled to his execution. This likely assumption is the seed that sprouted into the legend of Veronica and her wondrous Veil.

But there's a further intriguing root to this legend. Recall the well-known event recorded by all four evangelists elsewhere of the woman with the hemorrhage who risked the scolding of the apostles and the anger of the crowd. She thought to herself that if she just bolted forward through the crowd to touch the hem of Jesus' cloak as he was on his way to cure Jarius' daughter, then she would be cured. She did and *was* cured.

What if the anonymous woman we just mentioned, the one who broke through the crowd to wipe Jesus' face with her veil, was the same woman who broke through the crowd to touch Jesus to be cured of her hemorrhage? This speculation proved to be so irresistible that, by the fourth century, a full legend had blossomed giving this woman of the hemorrhage a name, Bernice. According to this legend, Bernice went to Rome to cure the emperor of his illness through an image of Jesus that *she herself had painted* on her veil out of gratitude for her healing, and that's the origin of a veil with the image of Jesus.

Later, after Bernice died, the painted cloth was entrusted to the care of the pope. Still later, in medieval times, someone, evidently wanting to symbolically frame the story better and make sure we didn't miss the point, changed the name Bernice to Veronica, Veronica being a combination of the Latin words *vera* meaning true and *icon* meaning image: *vera + icon, true-image*, comes out Veronica. Eventually the whole legend got cemented into the sixth station of the cross as the woman gradually acquired a name, a symbolic one, Veronica.

To this extent the legend of compassionate Bernice, now called Veronica, and Jesus leaving his image on her veil, encapsulated a wonderfully profound truth to live by. This truth is that *those who show compassion to others are imaged to the likeness of Christ*. Those who step out of the crowd to aid faceless humanity, to relieve those relegated to the margins of life, or those exiled by war, revolution, famine and poverty each bear Jesus' image in their hearts. Thus, the legend of Veronica's Veil speaks loudly of a great truth.

So, our lesson for today: "Veronica wipes the face of Jesus" is not just a legend, not just a title of a plaque on our church walls. It is the Christian faith in miniature. It is a piece of Christian devotion about people who did or did not minister to Jesus wherever his bruised face appeared.

It's a reminder that we take on the image of Jesus by doing good deeds; our good and kindly deeds, done in the name of Jesus, speak loudly even as they etch his holy face on our hearts.

I've Got a Little List

In Gilbert and Sullivan's delightful operetta, *The Mikado*, the Lord High Executioner named Ko-Ko, sings a song about a list of people he would happily like to exterminate:

> As someday it may happen that a victim
> must be found
> I've got a little list, I've got a little list
> Of society's offenders who live proudly
> above ground
> And who never would be missed, never
> would be missed . . .

And on he goes ticking off a litany of various fawning bureaucrats, gossipers, bores, people who cut in line or talk loud on their cell phones, and so on.

Lists go way back. We all love them: lists of bestsellers, colleges, songs, cars, movies, weight loss remedies, and so on. As I said, lists go way back. For example, from the start spiritual writers have always been list-minded: follow this and that list of practices and you will be on the way to holiness. In that tradition, let me share a short three-point list to consider for Lent.

First, practice being grateful

A man was suffering from an abdominal ailment and was in pain. One night it was unbearable. He pushed his buzzer and the nurse came into the ward. She washed his face with a cool towel and then administered a painkiller to him. After some minutes, the medication took effect and he relaxed. Just as the nurse turned to leave the room, he said, "I really appreciate you doing this for me." She replied simply, "No need for thanks. I'm only doing my job." But he answered, "Ma'am, it's nobody's job to take care of me. So when you do this for me, I need to say thanks."

To grow spiritually one must feel the urgency, the need to say thanks to many people and often. Give thanks: to God, to family, and to friends. Try to develop an attitude of gratitude. Try practicing it often for Lent. As the great spiritual guide, Meister Eckhart wrote, "If the only prayer you said in your whole life was 'thank you,' that would suffice."

Second, bless more and curse less. In these days, as college kids well know, when Facebook and apps like Whisper, Secret, and Yik Yak can become the ultimate tool for bullies who anonymously post untruthful, character-assassinating, disgusting and vile comments that can drive some vulnerable people to depression and even suicide; when daily and civic language is full of casual invective, lies, insulting, crude, vulgar, and pornographic discourse, this imperative to bless not curse, encourage not destroy, is ever more important to observe for a follower of Jesus.

Un-blessing is destructive. Blessing is generative. A sincere word of praise, affirmation, approval is like sunshine to a flower. Blessing makes people grow. It confirms their goodness and self-worth. As Mark Twain said, "I can live for two months on a good compliment." Use words that make people live. Bless.

A case in point: A week ago, I received a note from a former parishioner. It was part of her Lenten practice, she said, which was to send a note every day for Lent—40 notes in all—to affirm and bless people who have meant something in her life. Maybe we could do that once a week or once a month—a phone call, a note, a word—to let loose a blessing upon the world.

Third, say yes to transform and no to transmit. That is to say, do not give bad things back in kind. Any evil that we transmit but do not transform will simply be recycled and it will go on and on. Jesus, of course, is our model here, Jesus who taught to love your enemies and pray for those who persecute you. As Peter wrote in his first epistle:

Christ suffered for you
And left you an example . . .

When he was insulted
He returned no insult.
When he was made to suffer
He did not counter with threats.

Instead, he delivered himself up
To the One who judges justly

Yes, Jesus took away our sins like a filter purifies water. Just as the filter flushes out toxins and gives back purity so does Jesus.

As one spiritual writer puts it:

> Jesus takes in hatred, holds it, transforms it and gives back love.
> He takes in bitterness, holds it, transforms it and gives back graciousness.
> He takes in curses, holds them, transforms them and gives back blessing.
> He takes in chaos, holds it, transforms it and gives back order.
> He takes in fear, holds it, transforms it and gives back freedom.
> He takes in jealousy, holds it, transforms it and gives back affirmation.
> And he takes in Satan and murder, holds them, transforms them and gives back only God and forgiveness.

Yes, Jesus takes away the sins of the world in the same way a water filter takes impurities out of water, by absorbing and holding all that isn't clean and giving back only what is.

This is hard, but the scripture is clear: do not return evil for evil. I think of that scene in *To Kill a Mockingbird* where the redneck racist, who later tries to kill Atticus Finch's children Jem and Scott, meets Atticus at the home of the black folk whose son he is defending and spits in his face. Atticus, much larger and stronger, could have beaten him to a pulp. Instead, he wiped it off and walked away. He was not going to become like that man.

He was not going to transmit evil.

And Jesus was silent before Pilate.

So, as Ko-Ko sang, "I have a little list," so we have our own little list for Lent—and for life:

Thank.
Bless.
Transform.

2ND SUNDAY OF LENT

CYCLE A

MATT 22: 1-15

11

A Parable Revisited

This is a weird parable, one that has always puzzled us, a parable that, on the surface, sounds so—*unfair*! It's the parable of the king who threw a banquet, sent out servants with invitations, was rejected by those invited and sent out more servants to the byways and alleys of the village to press totally surprised strangers to come.

So they came to the banquet and, when the king comes in, he spies a man not wearing a wedding garment and proceeds to toss him out—this passerby, snatched from the streets and who you think was doing the king a favor by being there in the first place—he throws him out because he was not wearing a wedding garment! We ask: What did the king expect? People don't go around everyday in their wedding garments! Is the Master eccentric, perhaps mad? What can this parable possibly mean?

First, to make sense of the story, we must presume that the king was not mad or sadistic. He was not Gilbert and Sullivan's nutty, whimsical Mikado or Melville's mad Captain Ahab or Anthony Perkins' proprietor of the Bates Motel. In short, he was not demented or unbalanced, but perfectly sane and sensible.

So, with that as a given, then the focus shifts to the man. Somehow—the parable, as so often happens, doesn't fill in the details—somehow, the *man* is at fault. Whether garments were handed out at the time of invitation or at the door, or the fact that "clothing" is often a metaphor for good works and faithful discipleship—as in St. Paul saying that the baptized "have clothed themselves with Christ "—whatever, the man was at fault. The point being made then is that for all the king's graciousness, the man insulted him. For all the king's undeserved generosity, the man spurned it.

And we're doubly sure the man was at fault because, when accosted by the king asking the fateful question—why are you here without your wedding garment?—the man says nothing. *He says nothing because he has nothing to say*. He's speechless because he knows he's in the wrong. As the parable says tersely, "He was silent."

Looking around I suspect that most of you are too young to remember the very funny sitcom, *The Honeymooners*, replayed now and then on television, channel 3. For those of you who missed some great fun, it's the story of overweight, bumbling, loudmouth bus driver, Ralph Kramden, and his long-suffering wife, Alice, who has to put up with his stupid schemes all the time.

A common closing scene is Alice sitting dejected at the kitchen table with her back to Ralph murmuring "How could you?" because he's done it again: some hairbrained scheme that backfired. Ralph is rapidly walking back and forth behind her, arms waving, trying to explain what went wrong this time, how sorry he is and so on. His mouth is moving a mile a minute—but nothing is coming out. Nothing's coming out because he just can't come up with an excuse. There are none. For all the gesticulation and mouth movement, he was silent

So it is in this parable. Instead of seeing a wrathful and unbalanced king berating an innocent passerby we now see a sad, dejected host, full of anguish, saying, "How could you? How could you? After all I have done for you, you're here without grace!"

The king is to the man what Alice is to Ralph. "How could you?"

And suddenly we catch on. Suddenly we see ourselves in the parable. That is to say, there is the King, Jesus, who has been so caring, so forgiving, so excessive in his love, so persistent in his call to repentance. He has surrounded us by his providence, taught us by his Church, nourished us by his flesh, offered his living word, enticed us by his saints, coaxed us by his spirit, hunted and pursued us in a million ways by that unrelenting love of his.

He has told us more than once through many stories that we are the son or daughter of the prodigal father, the coin of the housekeeper, the lamb of the shepherd, the chicks of his gathering, and the feet of his washing. After all of *that*, what explanation will we be able to give for our ultimate failure to become a garmented saint? None. We are silent.

As with each Lent, we see this theme replayed in a garden. There are two people facing each other at a distance: Jesus the Master and his invited disciple, Judas. Judas goes up to Jesus and kisses him, the prearranged signal of betrayal.

And Jesus, like the king in the parable, is stunned. "Judas, friend, do you betray the Son of Man with a kiss?" He continues, "Judas, how could you? All that I have done for you, taught you, showed you, shared with you, broke bread with you. Why, last night I even washed your feet—why have you come here without the garment of grace? Answer me."

But Judas was silent.

On Good Friday, after the veneration of the Cross, the doleful "Reproaches" or "Lamentations" are chanted, alternating between the recurring questions of a hurt and puzzled Jesus and the silence of a guilty people. The theme is once more replayed. Listen to some of these liturgical Lamentations:

> My people, what I have done to you?
> How have I offended you? Answer me!
> I led you out of Egypt, from slavery to freedom,
> But you led your Savior to the cross.
> My people, what I have done to you?
> How have I offended you? Answer me!
>
> For 40 years I led you safely through the desert.
> I fed you with manna from heaven
> And brought you to the land of plenty;
> But you led your Savior to the cross.
> My people what have I done to you?
> How have I offended you? Answer me!

For your sake, I scourged your captors and
their firstborn sons
But you brought down your scourges on me.
I opened the sea before you,
But you opened my side with a spear.
My people, what have I done to you?
How have I offended you? Answer me!

I led you on your way in a pillar of cloud.
But you led me to Pilate's court.
I bore you up with manna in the desert,
But you struck me down.
I gave you saving water from the rock.
But you have me gall and vinegar to drink.
My people, what have I done to you?
How have I offended you? Answer me!

And so it goes: "Answer me. Answer me!" But there is no answer. Like the man at the banquet, the bus driver in the kitchen, we remain silent in our guilt.

Our intriguing gospel, then, is not about capricious punishment. It is about divine yearning and divine frustration. It's about abundant grace ignored, and Jesus' sadness that it was. It is about his accusing love and our dreadful silence.

Ultimately it is, above all, an invitation to fall down, Peter-like, strike our breast, and say, "I am a sinful, garmentless person. Lord Jesus, clothe me anew!"

3RD SUNDAY OF LENT
CYCLE A
JOHN 4:5-42

12

The Deep Well

That was a long gospel! And I even read the shortest version I could find. But it's a very visual one. We all have our favorite Jesus icon: Jesus as the Good Shepherd, Jesus standing in the boat stilling the waves, and so on. But I want to suggest that the image in *this* gospel is not only more powerful than we think but more urgent than we realize.

It's two archenemies meeting. It's hot. No, it's parched. The apostles are off to buy food in a local village and Jesus eases onto the rim of the well, anticipating a cool drink. Over the small mound from the west comes a woman from Samaria. She's carrying two buckets balanced on a rod across her neck. She stops, not only to relieve the throbbing rubbing pain but to assess what she sees: it's a man.

Not only a man but, from his attire, she can tell he's a Jew. She's of a mind to turn around and go back, but she knows he can easily outrun her and do what he wants with her. "Besides," she says to herself, "this is *my* well, and if he thinks I'm going to run away then he's mistaken. I can handle myself. I'll go to the well and, after a few well-aimed insults, he'll leave."

But he doesn't—and there we are with our tableau, our icon, our frozen image: all alone in a desert, a chance meeting between two people who hate each other and who have for a thousand years.

You got that picture in your minds? OK. Now let's begin.

Fast forward to today, and I invite you to go to the movies with me and test your memories. Let's start off with the movie, for various reasons both praised and criticized, *Driving Miss Daisy*. You recall the plot: two protagonists Miss Daisy Werthan, an elderly haughty Jewish woman, played by Jessica Tandy, and Hoke Colburn, an African-American chauffer played by Morgan Freeman, represent two people as opposite as you can get: two races, two religions, two genders, two people from different sides of the track who, by an act of fate, are thrown together.

We watch grace unfold as the slow grinding process of the years lead this white and haughty matron, now elderly and sick in a nursing home, to grasp the hand of her self-effacing chauffer and declare, "Hoke, you're my best friend." A complete turnaround. A conversion. A lesson. The gospel replayed.

In another classic movie, *The Defiant Ones*, Noah Cullen, a black man played by Sidney Poitier, and Joker Jackson, a white bigot played by Tony Curtis, are handcuffed together by a sheriff with a warped sense of humor. They escape a Southern prison. The sheriff cynically tells his men not to look too hard for them as "they will probably kill each other in the first five miles." Despite their mutual loathing, the prisoners must endure each other's company and we watch as, in time and through terrible episodes, mutual regard begins to replace the loathing.

The movie's closing scene has the two men, one wounded and the other too exhausted to run anymore, waiting for the posse. The sheriff eventually finds them laying on the ground, the black man singing defiantly and cradling the wounded white man in his arms. Hate had turned into love. Two people at a well.

Then there's *In the Heat of the Night*—most of you recall it—an African-American lawyer from Philadelphia, Virgil Tibbs played by Poitier, finds himself in a Southern town where he comes into conflict with a redneck police chief, Bill Gillespie played by Rod Steiger. We all watched as their mutual hostility eventually turns into mutual respect, leading at the end of the movie to a scene in which the police chief, with a smile, says to Tibbs as he boards the train home: "Virgil, you take care now."

With these movies in mind you can easily see that today's gospel is nothing more nor less than another version of the same compelling theme: two antagonists have met at a well, one is a Jew and the other is a Samaritan. As if ethnic barriers grounded in generational hate and mistrust weren't enough, one is male, the other female. The encounter, as you heard, did not start off well as they spar and trade insults, but eventually something is broken open and they meet on the common ground of compassion and love.

It won't be, by the way, the last such encounter Jesus has with an "enemy." There is that gospel incident where Jesus and his disciples are on their way south to visit Jerusalem, but they have to go through Samaritan territory where the Samaritans won't let them pass. The disciples are incensed and demand that Jesus send down lightning to destroy those wicked people. Jesus just shrugs and says, "No, we'll just take the longer way around them." To drive home his point—and to drive them crazy—when the disciples get to their destination, Jesus tells them the parable of the *Good* Samaritan—to them an oxymoron if there ever was one.

And, since we are so close to Passiontide, what about the Crucifixion where a totally innocent man has been falsely accused? He is hanging on a criminal's cross in unspeakable agony, hears insults hurled at him by the calloused enemies who put him there. But rather than shouting an ever-escalating tit for tat, he prays, "Father, forgive them. They know not what they do." He would not condemn a whole people for the mistakes of a few. He had broken bread with too many he admired and loved.

Speaking of that, let me bring you forward to our times. There's a man named Jonathon Stalls—a man with a mission. He is the founder of Walk2Connect, which promotes long-distance walking programs for individuals, groups, and neighborhoods to raise money for good causes. Back in 2010, Jonathon himself completed an 8 ½ month, 3,030-mile walk across the United States, generating half-a-million dollars in small loans to low-income business people around the world.

It's his comments about his encounters that are germane. He says, "My journey was one of profound growth, connection, and authentic transformation. My journey across the country was made possible by the hospitality offered at the homes and dinner tables of 120-plus 'strangers' in communities across America. I met families, partnerships, single mothers, college students, communes, public officials, all of whom varied in political, religious, racial, sexual, and economic ways."

He continues, "In time, my capacity for any form of certitude of what I thought was right or wrong started to fall away. My firmly held prejudices and judgments began to dissolve when the very people I disagreed with invited me and my dog into the warmth and intimacy of their homes. I found my self-imposed barriers crashing over and over."

"At the end of absolutely every homestay, I walked away convinced that people, in their core, are good, that we share a common journey of wanting to love and be loved, that we want to feel safe, comfortable and connected, that we want to belong, somewhere, that maybe our fierce, unyielding prejudgments is a form of fear, being afraid of the unknown, afraid to be wrong, afraid of truly trusting and letting go."

I think these images, these reflections, are so important, so needed in our time and we Christians should listen up; let me state what you already know: never have we been so divided, so polarized. Never has our conversation—if you can call it that—been so nasty, hostile, vile, mean-spirited, uncivil, and violently hateful. We don't talk, we *shout* over one another! Today, "Us versus Them" not "We the people," is the norm. We're not at the movies anymore. This is *reality*. To put a fine point on it, whether Trump is your president or whether you declare he is not, whether you're for or against global warming or any other contentious issue, today's gospel image of two people at a well must continue to speak to us.

Embrace that image, hug it to your Christian heart. Lock it in your imagination: an ethnic Jew talking with an ethnic Samaritan. A woman conversing with a man. A hated enemy sharing refreshing water with a hated enemy in a parched land. An odd couple whose civility and charity wind up scandalizing small-minded apostles.

The image reminds us Christians in a politically fractured and spiritually parched land that it's time *we* caused scandal by being different. It urges us, Jesus-like, to tone down the rhetoric, replace walls with bridges, and be peacemakers and bearers of reconciliation.

This won't be easy, but have confidence. Persevere. Yes, the divisions are deep but the well is deeper.

3RD SUNDAY OF LENT

CYCLE B

1 COR. 1:22-25

13

The Man on the Donkey

As we approach Holy Week, our most sacred time of the year, it sometimes helps to have a mantra, a symbol, or an icon as a focal point of prayer and meditation to deepen our experience.

One that comes to mind is from a wonderful book I read a long, long time ago when I was in college, H.M.S Prescott's *The Man on a Donkey*. It was one on those fascinating and memorable books that sticks with you, and that ruminates a long time. This is what I suggest to you as a mantra: The Man on a Donkey. Yes, Jesus on Passion Sunday getting astride a donkey and entering the city of Jerusalem with his disciples through the East Gate, the direction of the rising sun and light, amidst the cheers of the crowd. Try to picture it: the slow procession, the noise, the crowds, the hustle and bustle, the smells and traffic of Passover time.

It was not lost on Jesus, nor the crowd, that what was happening was a deliberate obverse of what happened just three weeks ago. Through the West Gate of the city, the direction of the setting sun, of darkness, came a mighty procession of armed Roman soldiers. It was expected. It was Passover time with its throbbing tourists, simmering resentments and hidden revolutionaries ready to throw off Rome's occupation. A show of force was needed to keep order.

At the end of the soldiers' procession came the Roman governor, Pontius Pilate, seated on a fearsome horse, full of Rome's power and might.

The two processions could not be more different: The Governor on the Warhorse, and The Man on the Donkey. Later in history, people would ponder who was the greatest, whose message of power and peace would prevail, but for now the procession began.

It was hard for the entrenched bureaucracy to swallow what was going on that Palm Sunday but word had spread about The Man on the Donkey. He was, the people said, a healer, teacher, leader, something of a celebrity and so they couldn't do much about it, but the bureaucrats seethed underneath and they plotted together and so, even as the crowd waved its branches and shouted its hosannas, the shadow of the cross looms in the background. Knowing this, nevertheless, the Man on the Donkey rode on.

He listened to the cheers and saw the excitement of the crowd, and the old Tempter came back for a last attack and whispered in his ear, "Look, they love you. Give them what they want. Just say a few negative things about Caesar that will raise your numbers at least a dozen points, make a few extravagant promises that no one expects you to keep and they will take you by force and make you king." He heard these flatteries. He ignored them. The Man on the Donkey rode on.

From his perch, he turned his head to either side and spotted his chosen apostles. They were positively giddy, grinning like the Cheshire Cat. At last, those three years with Jesus were paying off. He was coming into his own and they would be high officials in his kingdom. As he looked at them, the Man on the Donkey became distant and sad. On the one side, he saw Thomas who would not believe, Judas who would soon betray him, and Peter who would not only deny him three times but would also loudly boast that even if everyone else would abandon him, he would not.

He saw James and John who had asked outright for a place on his right and left when he did come into his kingdom and, when challenged that they were asking for more than they realized, they declared that they would stick by him, again, one at his right and the other at his left. And Jesus knew that when the time came he would indeed have someone at his right and left, but it wouldn't be James and John. It would be two total strangers, two thieves.

Jesus glanced at the other side and saw the rest of the apostles enjoying the moment, and yet he knew that not one of them would be around when he needed them most: not in the Garden of Gethsemane, not on the way to Calvary. The Roman soldiers would have to commandeer a stranger from Cyrene to carry the cross because there was no apostle present. They had all fled. Yet, knowing all this, The Man on the Donkey rode on.

He looked at the crowd. It was *hosanna* now. By the end of the week it would be *crucify him*! He knew that, too. But the Man on the Donkey rode on. Finally, he scanned the crowd once more. He seemed to be searching for someone. And then he found the one he was looking for. In one brief, terrible moment *our* eyes locked as if we were the only ones there.

And there we have it. We have our mantra, our symbol, our icon to ponder, to embrace, to pray over.

There's the frozen moment of contemplation when the eyes of The Man on a Donkey and our eyes meet: we with our fidelities, sacrifices, virtues, kindnesses; with our compromises, betrayals, sins, and contracted hearts. The brief, piercing look from Jesus is not condemnatory. It is invitational. Finding such compassion too much, we avert our eyes as The Man on the Donkey rode on.

Why? He knew what really lay ahead of him. And he did not welcome it. Rejection, pain, death was not the cup he would have chosen for himself. He had no martyr complex. He did not willingly seek to die. But the Man on the Donkey rode on.

So, again, why? He had told us already: "Greater love has no one than this: to lay down one's life for one's friends." Yes, Jesus came to take on every human weakness, every human condition: misunderstanding, pain, betrayal, rejection, spite, revenge, innocent suffering, humiliation, hate and death itself and nail these things to the cross, showing us dramatically that these are forever destroyed and they are not the last word. Crucified love is the last word. Yes, love is why The Man on the Donkey rode on.

Our Passiontide image: we, in the crowd, looking up and finding Jesus looking at us from his humble four-footed throne. It's a moment to behold, cherish and plumb before the Man on the Donkey rides on.

5TH SUNDAY OF LENT

CYCLE C

JOHN 8:1-11

14

Sin

I'm going to talk about sin this morning. I thought you'd be thrilled about that. Brings back stereotypes of hellfire and brimstone and bible thumping preachers, doesn't it?

But not really. Not anymore. Like so many other things, we have domesticated sin. It's no longer a word of accusation. It's a badge of honor. It's no longer a no-no with the wave of a stern finger. It is yes-yes coupled with wink-wink and snicker-snicker. It's no longer a deterrent. It's a come on.

Desserts are sinfully delicious. In the movie, "The Music Man," Professor Harold Hill prefers the sadder but wiser girl of the scarlet letter over the virtuous girl. Virtue is dull and boring. R-rated is no longer a warning but an advertisement. Sin is where it's at. No place ever boasts of being Virtue City, but Las Vegas brags of being Sin City. No question, virtue is out because it drains all the fun out of life and the sourpussed, constipated, fundamentalist clergy are definitely not welcomed in the public square except as comic relief.

Besides, sin is obsolete in a world of pop psychology. Years ago, a best-selling book was Philip Rieff's "The Triumph of the Therapeutic." He was dead on. People don't sin anymore. They don't need absolution. They need therapy. They don't need the priest. They need the psychiatrist. They lie, steal, cheat, defraud, rape, punch, and kill because of imbalanced hormones or because their parents fed them gruel instead of Cheerios, or because they were so poor they had to live with only six TV channels.

Well, that's a little simplistic. Let me state quickly that emotional and mental health has made great strides because of science, along with the men and women who have developed the arts of therapy. We owe them a great deal. It's just that this is not the whole story, and healing is not only a matter of the right pill and the right diet and the proper adjustment but something deeper in the spirit as well. I'm suggesting, therefore, that the old word *sin* be resurrected because, unlike the neutral words of our culture, it reminds us that life is fundamentally a moral affair.

Anyway, to continue our reflection, I think sin got a bad name not only because modern society has embraced a mechanical world instead of a spiritual one, but also because it became just a surface category. Older Catholics here remember the examination of conscience lists they checked off before they proceeded to the five steps to make a good confession. Let's see how good your memory is: The five steps to a good confession are: examine your conscience, be sorry for your sins, have a firm purpose of amendment, confess your sins to the priest, and be willing to do the penance the priest gives you. How did you do?

Examining your conscience meant running through the check lists of the three theological virtues, the four cardinal virtues, the six Commandments of the Church, the seven spiritual and corporal works of mercy, and the Ten Commandments. We were big on numbers in those days. See what you young people missed? Not only did you miss the challenge of navigating all those steps and lists but also the challenge of finding a priest who was deaf or foreign—or, if you were lucky, both!

The problem here was that sometimes preoccupation with the mechanics derailed what sin was really all about. It wasn't an item on a list. It was the ebb in the flow of life. It was a detour on the way to the full love of God, an attitude, or an off-the mark act. Indeed, the word *sin* originally meant, "missing the mark." Sin is something that goes deep into the soul. It taps into the tendency we have to mess up, that tendency Christianity has called Original Sin. Sin is a pattern thing, something that pulls us down, or aside and backward. It's made up of the rhythms of small compromises, betrayals, self-interest, pride, and omissions.

People don't realize that, which is why good people sometimes say, "I go to confession, but I don't know what to say. I don't go around killing people or mugging to sell drugs. I lose my temper, curse sometimes, have impure thoughts, but that's about it."

But that's so anemic, and so shallow. No wonder there's no progress in the spiritual life. But sin is deeper and broader. It's that which threads through us, the inner stuff that rises up and breaks out in our speech and attitudes, the product of our inadequacies. Sin is the code name for the protection of our egos, the broadband of our fears, jealousies, and pride. This is the kind of sin we must confess.

To be more specific, one is confessing not only the sin, but sinfulness itself. Sin, for example, is finding it hard to say 'I love you' to people who need to hear this and hear it often. Sin is the failure for being sorry, truly sorry, for what I said, for what I did that was hurtful, unjust, unfair, or fraudulent. Sin is the rash judgments of this or that person whom I tore down because it was the only way I felt I could rise up. After all, if he or she goes up, I must come down and my frail ego must rebalance that.

Sin is the jealousy I feel because I have not yet discovered the serenity that comes from detachment of ego and attachment to God, and I should confess that lack. I should confess my overwhelming desire for recognition, status, and superiority because I have not followed Jesus and his words to become like little children. I have not come even close to washing feet as he did as I have passed up opportunities for charity.

I still harbor unforgiveness despite Jesus' telling me to love my enemies and pray for those who hate me. Sin, in other words, is failing to framework my life within the revelation of God in the life and death of Jesus Christ.

I remember many years ago, a woman came to confession. I heard her come into the box, but she said nothing. After a while, I asked, "Are you there? You wish to confess?" She said, "I need time because I have something terrible to tell." So, I waited, wondering what awful deed she had to reveal. After a long time, she cleared her throat and said, "My besetting sin is that I have made myself the center of the universe." That was probably the best confession I ever heard. No checklist. No simplistic, off-the-cuff peccadillo. She went right to the heart of the matter. She confessed not an item, but a process, a journey detoured away from full love to self-centeredness, a missed mark, a failure to love as Jesus does.

Well, people don't go to confession much anymore, certainly not the young who, raised on the notion that everything is relative and no one can really say Hitler was a bad man—they have a hard time saying anything's a sin. And maybe too many things were labeled sin, which really were not.

But sin is real and there is a sore need to see the world in moral terms. Our challenge as Christians is to use Jesus as our moral slide rule, not somebody's churchy list. When we do, we will move away from our childhood line of "I disobeyed my mother" to the adult question of attitude towards others and the world, to my moral place in it, my obligation to improve it and my failures to do so, to my subterranean lack of wholeness.

And, to this extent, confession becomes not just a place to deposit checklist items. It is an encounter with Jesus. It is bringing attitudes and patterns to the wonderfully merciful Lord, to the Healer of souls. It is a humble act exposing at once my egotism and my need for redemption.

It is the place to strike our breasts and express that gospel truth as simply and sincerely as we can, "Oh, God, be merciful to me, a sinner. I made myself the center of the universe instead of you."

5TH SUNDAY OF LENT
CYCLE C
PHILIPPIANS 3:8-14

15

Knowing Jesus

In 2005, the American Film Institute asked some 1,500 film artists, critics, and historians to come up with a list of the most famous movie quotes. Here are the first ten. See how many movies you can guess.

> "Frankly, my dear, I don't give a damn."
> "I'm gonna make him an offer he can't refuse."
> "I coulda had class. I coulda been a contender. I could've been somebody, instead of a bum, which is what I am."
> "Toto, I've got a feeling we're not in Kansas anymore."
> "Here's looking at you, kid."
> "Go ahead, make my day."
> "All right, Mr. DeMille, I'm ready for my close-up."
> "May the Force be with you."

Most of you, I suspect, could and did identify the movies where the quotes came from. You probably also even knew the stars who said them. It's a tribute to the power of our cultural icons and mass media.

Because I'm a preacher, this introduction leads me to remark that we Christians have our quotable celebrity. "Love your neighbor as yourself," for instance. We know of Jesus Christ Superstar. After all, he's the most significant person in history. We hear his name in and out of church and see his image in art, precious and cheap, and a good portion of the world, like ourselves, carries his name: Christian; but the question today is, do we know him, say, as well as we know our favorite pop star? What does he mean to us? *How* do we see him?

Most of us, I suspect, see him probably through the official eyes of the Church through the readings we hear when we come here. We know him after layers of theologians, scholars, commentators, popes, councils, synods and creeds have gotten through with him: you know, God from God, Light from light, consubstantial with the Father—Trinity, Incarnation, transubstantiation—all accurate but not very warm or personal. But do we know him the way people did before there were gospels? We wonder, what was the first witnesses' impression of Jesus?

Let's try. Imagine for a moment that you and I were transported back into time in the early 2nd century and found ourselves sitting in the shade of some palm trees among some old timers who knew Jesus or whose parents, relatives, and friends did and who passed on stories about him. And we ask them, "What was he like, really like?" "How did you see him?" And suddenly we get a whole barrage of mixed comments tumbling over one another. Listen to the competing voices and let the images they conjure up flow through your minds in slow motion:

We see him weary, shouts one, as when he is tired and sits down at a well and winds up talking to a foreign woman. Another chimes in. We see him when he has his good days—the time Peter affirms him as Messiah—and when he has his bad days - the time Peter denies even knowing him.

We watch him making enemies while at the same time instructing his followers to forgive and pray for them. We see him full at a Pharisee's banquet and hungry in Satan's desert. We see him as only human when he gets exasperated with his opponents and calls them names, and other times we see him as more than human such as when he raises up Lazarus or blazes on the Mount of the Transfiguration. It is said, says one, that he showed such a fearful face to the blind leaders of his time but such a beautifully compassionate face to the sinful, the bleeding, and the possessed.

He seems to know all things, comments one, yet it is said he grows in wisdom, age, and grace. "Grown in wisdom," sneers another, yet he goes and chooses twelve inept, unreliable losers for his close circle. Go figure. The litany goes on. He walks on water near Capernaum and falls to the ground in Gethsemane. He speaks of having twelve legions of protecting angels to guard him and yet he gets slapped around in Pilate's prison.

He says no to his mother at Cana, calls her "woman" and tells her to move on: his hour has not yet come, but he winds up making water into wine anyway. He speaks serenely of his Abba Father in prayer and screams at him on Calvary. He dialogues with powerful people like Nicodemus and eats with lowbrow publicans like Zacchaeus. He speaks plainly at one point and tells catchy parables with hooks in them at another. He rejoices at one time when he senses the Father's presence and cries when he knows loss: the death of his best friend, Lazarus. He openly accepts the titles of Lord and Master yet, like the lowliest of servants, he, "Lord and Master" washes the feet of his disciples.

He calms the waters of Lake Tiberius at a single word yet can't even carry his own cross by himself in Jerusalem. He lives in a world of occupation yet tells the Roman governor, Pilate, he is greater than he. He says his mission is only to the people of Israel and yet he lets a foreign Syrian woman shame him into curing her daughter. He's hard to follow.

The shouting gets louder as another says, "He touches disfigured and ritually unclean lepers and yet cleanses the Temple. He's anti-violence yet he dies by violence. He talks the talk of forgiveness and winds up walking the walk by giving it from the cross. He is promised two disciples on either side of his cross, but accepts two criminals."

He claims to be the Way and the Truth and the Life, but he dies. Resurrected, he calls Magdalene to himself by name yet tells her not to cling. He physically ascends with his body into heaven and returns mystically to earth in his gathered assembly, the Church.

And on and on tumble out the comments, and we can only think: What an amazing, unforgettable, complex person, this Jesus of Nazareth is! So compelling, so mysterious, so challenging. No wonder these people are so excited.

Their portrait of Jesus is a fascinating one and moves us beyond rote prayer, saccharine holy pictures and prefab images. We've got to get to know Jesus as they do, to know him as well as we know our adored movie celebrities. Having that desire is itself the first step. So, there is prayer, study, reading small bits of the gospels daily, and perhaps taking up Pope Francis's book, "Walking with Jesus."

And, finally, don't forget this practical advice: to know Jesus, check your company.

What I mean is, hang out at least from time to time with those who give you a glimpse of what Jesus might be like. I mean, if your daily associations are always with those folks whose lives consistently cut corners, whose everyday language is boringly crude and vulgar, who are only out to score, get the best deal by any means, never reach out to others, whose minds are full of consumption and celebrity, whose chief interest is themselves, then—well, you get the picture. We all need people in our lives to challenge us to something better, deeper.

To show what I mean, let me repeat a favorite story:

Several years ago, a group of computer salesmen from Milwaukee went to a regional sales convention in Chicago. They assured their wives that they would be home in plenty of time for dinner, but with one thing or another the meeting ran overtime and so the men had to race to the stations with tickets in hand.

As they barraged through the terminal, they inadvertently knocked over a table that supported a basket of apples. Without stopping, they all reached the train and boarded with a sigh of relief. All but one. He paused, got in touch with his feelings and experienced a twinge of compunction for the boy whose apple stand had been overturned. He waved goodbye to his companions, hopped off the train and returned to the terminal. He was glad he did. He could see that the ten-year-old boy was blind.

The salesman gathered up the apples and noticed that several of them were bruised. He reached into his wallet and said to the boy, "Here, please take this ten dollars for the damage we did. I hope it didn't spoil your day."

As he started to walk away, the bewildered boy called after him, "Are you Jesus?"

We've got to hang around or encounter people who sometimes make *us* ask that question. We've got to rub shoulders, so to speak, with Christ-like people who evoke St. Paul's wonderful words in today's epistle: "The Spirit himself bears witness with our spirit that we are children of God . . ."

Good prayer, good spiritual reading, and good company are a beginning for the process of getting to know Jesus. He's really exciting.

16

Bad Fridays

If this were Easter Sunday, you would expect words of justifiable joy. But it's the Sunday before the Friday we call Good and so you must expect words of sober sorrow, and you shall get them. For the fact is that on Good Friday in this year as the Christian world commemorates the suffering and death of Jesus, it cannot but help think of his continuing crucifixion in our dreadful times as Christians are being tortured, exiled and killed by Muslim and Hindu extremists. Christ continues to die a million horrible deaths in the Middle East, Asia, and Africa.

It is well-known to those who care that, during Easter time this year, churches in India had to step up security. They could not forget how Muslim extremists recently attacked a university in Kenya and specifically targeted Christians, massacring 147 Christian students. As one survivor said, "If you were a Christian, you were shot on the spot." Christians worshipping in Iraq and Syria live in nervous fear, as Easter time is ripe for ISIS assaults.

On April 3rd of 2015, Good Friday, the Shabab militant group ran through another university, letting go those who could recite verses from the Quran and killing those Christians who could not. Picture these students, all in the prime of their lives, terrified and fleeing among the gunfire, watching their classmates drop before them. Many students had voluntarily gone outside, having been promised safety and lay down in neat rows only to be shot in the back of the head. The militants were cruel and gleeful. As *The New York*

Times reported, "Students who hid during the attack said they heard their classmates whimpering as the militants taunted them. Then a single gunshot. Then silence."

Picture yourself there. Picture your university son or daughter whimpering for their lives and then being shot. All because they were Christian.

Last year, the Islamic State tried to kill and starve Christians in northern Iraq—never mind they have lived there in peace for many centuries. More than twenty years ago, Christians made up about twenty percent of the Middle East's population. Today it is about five percent.

The suffering of Christians under ISIS is well-documented by the United Nations who reports how they abduct Iraqi children and then sell them as sex slaves at the marketplaces while killing others by crucifixion or burying them alive. Crucifying children! Burying them alive! The cruelty is mind-boggling. It is interesting how our western secular world can only comment on its outrage and how awful things are. It cannot bring itself to use the "E" word, "Evil" for it smacks too much of religion, but that's what it is. Plain evil, "the devil like a roaring lion seeking whom he can devour" in St. Peter's words.

No wonder the patriarch of Jerusalem commented in his Holy Thursday homily that Iraqi and Syrian Christians are examples today of Jesus' humiliated love on the cross. It was no surprise that a Rome service was held for five Mexican priests and clerics from around the world who were killed for condemning organized crime and drug trafficking.

All this, as I warned, is not a pleasure to talk about, not the stuff of a pleasing homily. It's a bit too much. We glance at it—it's hard to ignore, there is so much of it—we put it out of our minds and quickly submit to the endless distractions that a secular marketplace culture provides 24/7 and which we have become accustomed as a way of life.

A nod, a shake of the head, feeling sorry but then speed, the hallmark of our society, hurries us on to the next entertainment, the next TV series, the next sports event, the next rock concert, the next after-Christmas or after-Easter sales and never leaves us time to mull over this, to identify with people our own age, whatever that is, who form the world's largest refugee cohort, fleeing with whatever they can carry, children who can't go to school, sudden martyrdom around every corner.

Not that we have to be morbid. No, we just need to have a greater awareness: awareness of how blessed we are, and awareness that much of the world is suffering, keeping them in our prayers, giving some time to aid, or donating the money diverted from the latest sweater fad when we already have twenty-five of them in our closet.

Yes, it's this awareness that is important, not to depress us, but to make us mindful of the world's pain, an awareness that underscores our solidarity with them, that asks us what we can do about it, that makes us Christians celebrate Good Friday with a new depth, makes us see Christ crucified anew, urges us to pity and prayer, makes us commiserate with our fellow Christians who wear that label as heavily as we take it lightly.

Perhaps we can take the example of Pope Francis who again this year on Holy Thursday washed the feet of twelve inmates, men and women, from Nigeria, Congo, Ecuador, Brazil, and Italy—as well as one toddler who was there with his imprisoned mother. The pope said to the 2,100 men and women held in the detention center on the outskirts of Rome, "I'll wash the feet of twelve of your brothers and sisters who represent all of you here today."

Perhaps we can do the same by showing some kindness to someone, giving some money to some charity, helping out at a local food pantry making them represent all those who are suffering and in need, making them a reminder that we must lift ourselves from our own concerns and become aware of our crucified brothers and sisters around the world. In prayer and charity, we must be present to those who are crying out, "My God, my God, why have you abandoned me?"

It's a start.

17

Easter

A widower had always been indifferent to his wife, really not very nice to her throughout their marriage. He never really paid attention to her while she was alive, but strangely one day he found himself missing her. So, he went to a psychic to see if he could contact his wife. The psychic went into a trance. An unearthly breeze wafted through the room and suddenly the man heard the unmistakable voice of his departed wife.

"Honey!" he cried, "Is that you?"

"Yes, my husband."

"Are you happy?"

"Yes, my husband."

"Happier than you were with me?"

"Oh, yes, my husband, much, much happier."

"Wow, then that heaven must be an amazing place."

"I'm not in heaven, dear."

It's good and proper to laugh in church on the Church's most joyful day, the day it celebrates the premise of that story: life after death.

Life after death. Think about it. It's Easter—the resurrection of Jesus from the dead prompts us to do so, to pause a minute. Do people really believe this anymore in a society of hard science, pop culture, and celebrity atheists? Apparently so. In Britain, according to the polls taken in the past few years, half of the people surveyed said they believed in an afterlife even though not all of them believed in God. Also, a quarter of agnostics think that death is not the end. It's the same in America.

What gives? Why do so many unbelievers believe in life after death? Moreover, since they do not believe in God, the Bible or Jesus, where does this belief come from? Why in our modern secular time is the supernatural, the afterlife, all over the place and why is Hollywood making gazillions from afterlife franchises?

There is the top-rated *The Walking Dead*. There is *Doctor Who, Lost, Sideways World,* and *True Blood*—you name it. On TV and in the movies, belief in the afterlife is rampant: angels, demons, zombies, witches, vampires, animated corpses, and most of you, I suspect, are fans of one or the other. What may be surprising, even for believers, is that both in the Old and New Testaments, there is precious little about the afterlife - the Hebrews didn't believe in it—and New Testament references are real but meager.

Yet—there it is, as we said, all over our music, movies, TV, video games, computer games, books - one thinks of the best sellers, "Heaven is for Real" about a little boy's trip to heaven and back, and a similar book, "The Boy Who Came Back from Heaven"—novels, comics, and so on. These multiple venues are blissfully unaware that they subconsciously draw their images from Christianity's deep interest in angels and spirits during the first millennium of its existence, from Christian medieval art and literary works such as Dante's *Divine Comedy* or Milton's *Paradise Lost*. Whatever the ancient source and the modern franchises, after centuries of "rational" thinking and the intellectual elites' mockery of everything religious, there remains a deep, nervous, renewed backdoor flirtation for the afterlife.

Why? Because the afterlife calls to people—even unbelievers—to garner some kind of meaning out of life's difficult questions, out of life's unfairness: something has to be evened out somewhere. For all our modern skepticism and noisy atheism, there's an innate common instinct that says that if there really is nothing beyond this world, then that makes death the final authority of our lives and makes meaninglessness the norm of existence and we rebel against that.

Instead, we continue to have a strong intuitive deep sense that dying is a dying *into* life rather than simply away from it. We have a sense of the continuation of life, that the immaterials of faith, hope, love, generosity, sacrifice, and beauty are impervious to change and corruption. For many, in fact, the very persistence of our longing for something more is proof enough of this "something more's" eventual happening. So, in a perverse way, people need all those undead folks to keep this truth alive.

If all this weren't enough to tease us, there are those common mystical experiences that so many people have that hint strongly at something more, something beyond. For example, the publisher of all things, *Skeptic* magazine, recently told the story of his wedding day and how his bride dearly wished that her deceased grandfather could be there to give her away. Suddenly, the grandfather's long-broken radio, which they had never managed to fix, came on for that one day and then never worked again. The experience shook him up.

A young un-churched man tells of a retreat to which his girlfriend had coaxed him into going. There the people started praying for him. He recounts, "It doesn't feel necessarily like electricity, but it feels like your whole body would be, like, touched by some kind of extreme power and you're just shaking, like you just can't handle all this stuff that is being poured into you, and all they're saying is 'Come Holy Spirit, and fill him with overflowing' . . . I felt like there was somebody else in me, like, dwelling . . . and I was just overwhelmed in it."

Or, to tickle our Catholic fancy, how about Pope Francis? To those in the know, *Pope* Francis is not the same person as *Cardinal* Bergoglio. During his fifteen years as the Archbishop of Buenos Aires, yes, he *was* committed to the poor, evangelization and simplicity, but he was no superstar. Far from it. He rarely appeared in public. He was shy and boring when he did. The cardinal simply did not sparkle—so much so that, concerning Pope Francis, his only living sibling exclaimed, "I don't know this guy!" What happened? A noted author of a book about the pope tells this story:

Over Christmas 2013, the pope made an appointment with an old South American friend, a cardinal. His friend came into his modest apartment and, referring to his now exuberant and spontaneous public image, said point blank, "You are not the same man I knew in Buenos Aires. What happened to you?"

According to the cardinal, this was Francis' answer:

"On the night of my election, I had an experience of the closeness of God that gave me a great sense of interior freedom and peace and that sense has never left me."

Many people have similar experiences though they do not tell anyone lest they get taken off to the funny farm. But they happen, and happen often, and they make us think twice.

All these things are the reasons why we celebrate Easter and why we proclaim in the Creed, "He suffered death and was buried and rose again on the third day . . . and I look forward to the resurrection of the dead and the life of the world to come." Amen.

Amen. But I'm not finished. Sorry. One more thing. Concerning the afterlife, I think that sometimes we get tripped up by our modern media. We have too often bought into the cartoon concepts of heaven, you know: sitting on fluffy clouds, strumming a harp, and wearing a gold crown and, after all, we're much too sophisticated to believe all that stuff. We no longer realize that these are metaphors from the past: the cloud, like the presence of God, conceals and reveals; music is the nearest thing we have to ecstasy; and gold is the one metal that does not rust, hinting at heaven's eternity.

Anyway, the next time you watch *The Walking Dead* or dress up like one of the undead, realize that you're subconsciously flirting with mystery and playing games with things you're afraid to talk about openly.

And the next time when your faddish atheist friends tune into their favorite zombie show, you can secretly recognize their hidden wish for living beyond death, a rebellion against nothingness and their unwitting testimony to St. Augustine's oft-quoted words, "You have made us for yourself, O God, and we are restless until we rest in you."

So, we restless folk are here today on Easter to declare our faith in the Resurrected One, who said, "I am the resurrection and the life. Whoever believes in me will live forever"—and to gratefully re-embrace St. Paul's soaring, powerful words:

> no eye has seen
> nor ear heard
> nor has it even entered into the human heart
> what God has prepared
> for those who love him,

. . . words more than sufficient to cause me to wish you, with a full mind and heart, a Happy Easter.

2ND SUNDAY OF EASTER
CYCLE A
JOHN 20:19-31

18

The Wounds on Christ's Body

A little housekeeping, state-of-the-union reflection today, so, as Margo Channing, a.k.a. Betty Davis, said in "All About Eve," Tighten your seat belts.

There's an ancient legend that says that the Devil, Master of Disguise, tried to get into heaven by pretending to be the Risen Christ. He took with him his demons disguised as angels of light, and had them cry out the traditional first part of the welcome psalm that we sing at the Easter Vigil: "Lift up your heads, O ye gates of heaven, and lift up your doors, and the King of Glory shall enter!"

The real angels looked down on what they thought was their King returning in triumph from the dead. They in turn shouted back with joy the refrain, "Who is this King of Glory?" The Devil then made his fatal mistake. He opened his arms and spread his palms and declared, "I am!"

The angels immediately slammed the gates of heaven and refused to let the imposter in. They saw right away that he was a fake: there were no nail marks in his palms, no gash in his side, no holes in his body. The imposter had no wounds of love and no wounds of hate, and no signs of suffering.

This story reminds us that, in spite of pictures and statues we see of the Risen Christ with holes in his hands, side and feet, in spite of the gospel stories where Jesus appears to his bewildered disciples and shows them his wounded hands and his side, in spite of his insisting that Thomas actually touch these wounds, in spite of the fact that he wears them to this very day in heaven – in spite of all this, we never think of Jesus with wounds, now healed as scars, that are like so many reminders of his journey among us.

If that's hard to accept—Jesus with wounds in his body—it's harder to accept that the same is true of his Mystical Body, the Church. Yes, there are not only the wounds the Church receives daily from haters and persecutors—everything she has once opposed is now legal: contraception, divorce, same sex marriage, abortion, and, soon, the right to die—but also the wounds that the Church itself inflicts. The Church which has given healing so profusely over the centuries is also the Church that has wounded over the centuries.

Today there are so many such people hurting in the Church. Some stay, some leave, no, *many* leave, have left—in fact, the last time so many Catholics left the Church was 500 years ago at the time of the Protestant Reformation. Today, former Catholics, including family members, as some of you sadly know, and friends, form the second largest "religious" group in the country. Or, let me put it this way: for every convert to the Church, six Catholics leave. (Imagine Costco losing six customers for every one that joins.)

It's a massive exodus, apparent from our less than full churches and the predominance of gray heads (like mine). In fact, surveys show that only twenty-two percent of Catholics attend Mass weekly; that means almost eighty percent don't. In the Brooklyn Archdiocese, attendance is between thirteen and seventeen percent. Catholics are becoming less engaged with Church. The Catholic demand for the sacraments has declined worldwide. The closing or blending of parishes that we are now experiencing, the closing of thousands of Catholic schools – in 1965 we had 10,000 of them, while today only 5,000 and that number is rapidly shrinking. There is the crisis of the clergy shortage. In 1990, we had 34,000 priests, and in 2014, just 26,000. Today we have some 16,500 active priests – statistics that translate as one priest for every 1,762 Catholics. Predictions are there will be twenty-five percent less priests in the coming years. All the way around, we are losing ground and are contracting dramatically.

We must mention that this plummeting is true of all religions trying to survive in the context of today's almost total religious illiteracy plus a very aggressive secularism, often legally reinforced. But Catholics, it seems, do have an additional burden to carry because many have been personally hurt by their own Church. Many Catholics who have left the Church have a "church" story within which lies a big bundle of hurts. They may cite a particular reason for leaving, but often it isn't the root cause. For example, some will say they have disagreements with some of the Church's theological positions, but after further discussion, they'll say they tried to arrange a wedding or funeral and the parish staff was unfriendly or uncooperative.

Or, to move to the second person, consider this litany:

> You were chewed out by a priest once when you were an altar server.
>
> You were horribly embarrassed by a priest's harsh reaction to something you said in confession, and you haven't stepped inside a Catholic church since.
>
> You were abruptly let go from the Catholic grade school where you taught for many years.
>
> You were just received into the Catholic Church at Easter but are now dismayed by the lack of fellowship and indifference of your new "parish family."
>
> You feel heartbroken because a priest you loved and idealized for years was shown to be living a double life of sexual and financial misconduct.
>
> You find your parish more a corporation than a community, more turned in on itself than outward towards others. You find it less than compelling with lackluster, boring liturgies, and poor preaching.

> You are a Latino Catholic who feels treated like a second-class citizen at your predominately white suburban parish.
>
> You experience same-sex attraction and feel conflicted about the Church's teaching on homosexuality.
>
> You are a woman who has experienced a Church dominated by male clericalism.
>
> You are an elderly Catholic widow who never receives a visit from any parishioners, much less your own parish priests.
>
> You were sexually abused by a member of the clergy as a child.

How does one remain faithful despite all of this hurt, all this decline on every level? What does the future hold for a shrinking Church—at least in Europe and America? In other places, like Africa, it is flourishing.

I think that the future holds a long recovery, a long and hard period of reformation, but still a recovery nevertheless, for our strengths are many: a massive charity, health care, and educational system; thousands of outreaches like St. Vincent de Paul societies and other groups; many small confraternities and Bible study groups; countless dedicated people helping the poor and needy; a rich tradition, and all the rest. There is much hidden vitality. There are also many small signs today of renewal that point to a new style of Church for the future, meaning a Church more fully determined to be less "Church" and more "Jesus," less pyramid and more circle. The prediction is that the Church, as in its first centuries, will be more lay orientated, using the gifts of the people in a shared and collaborative ministry with the clergy. As one writer puts it, "A Church of one billion persons and more than 200,000 parishes will not be revitalized by the action of a Pope and some 200 Cardinals. Rather, revitalization will happen only when a critical mass of engaged Catholics steps up and leads."

So, there you are, and there we are. This has been a less

than uplifting homily, hasn't it? But it's necessary now and then to do some in-house examination, however embarrassing, however hard to take. But we can't begin to renew ourselves until we know what the problems are, admit our failures, access our strengths, and plot our comeback—and a comeback there will be.

One thing is sure, however, so be forewarned. As I indicated, renewal is not going to come from above but from below, from you and from your baptismal gifts. When called like the prophets of old, be prepared to answer, "Here I am, Lord. Send me."

Alec, Fred, and Jesus

"The Ipcress File" is a great old spy movie in which the enemy side constructed a village so real that their prisoner, played by Michael Caine, thought he was living in Hungary: the language, the sounds, the food, the smells, the neighborhood were all there, while in reality, all along he was in a warehouse in England.

In another great movie, "36 Hours," wounded Intelligence agent, played by James Gardner, wakes up thinking he is in a convalescent village years into the future and recovering from amnesia while all the time he actually has been in an elaborate German movie set complex where, fooled into thinking he is living many years after the war, he would carelessly reveal secrets of the supposed past. He, like Michael Caine, also believed in the so-called reality so artfully constructed for him.

So do we. So do we. We are believers. We are die-in-the-wool believers in a world that others construct for us.

We all believe, for example, that while we personally have never been to the moon, others have and the moon landings are not an elaborate "Mission Impossible" hoax like the "Ipcress File" or "36 Hours." Yes, almost all that we know - physics, chemistry, biology, history, psychology, what's happening in the news and in the lives of our beloved celebrities - we take on faith. We readily believe every advertisement that promises a rich, glamorous, fat-free life.

Yet hardly anything we know comes from firsthand experience because we simply don't have time to verify everything. We *have* to trust others—the pilot who flies our plane, the plumber who fixes our sink, and the surgeon who operates on us. Notice we never ask to see their licenses. Again, ninety-nine percent of our lives are spent trusting others, especially if they are celebrity reporters, scientists, and hawkers—after all, how can you not believe sincere-looking Alec Trevett when he is selling you a rate-lock insurance loan or Fred Thompson who sells you reverse mortgages?

With so much trusting belief in our lives, so much unexamined certainty that things are what others say they are, we seldom heed the warnings of those old philosophers like Bertrand Russell who said, "The stupid are cocksure while the intelligent are full of doubt," or Voltaire who opined, "Doubt is not a pleasant condition, but certainty is absurd."

Despite these warnings, in matters of faith, in matters of religion, have you noticed that it's the new atheists who come off as totally confident and certain in the belief that, given enough time, research and money, eventually human beings will know everything about the universe and God will be declared officially dead. Really? This despite that every new advance in science upends the old certainties, despite the advent of Quantum physics which has turned everything upside down causing scientists to retreat to tamer terms like "reasonable probabilities."

In contrast to the certain atheists, it's the truly religious people who are sensibly not certain—at least those who are not terminally fundamentalist - because they know that they are creatures, not the Creator. It's the religious people who in fact are humbly comfortable not knowing all the answers because they know their limited minds cannot contain the unlimited God. They accept the premise that something can be real and true, but which can never be fully known.

Believers, therefore, embrace mystery—not in a blind simplistic way but in a thoughtful way. And, nourished by the imaginative life of ritual, art, symbols and stories as well as the intellect, they believe in God and trust that God will have the last word.

Such trust in turn inspires prayer, unending charity,

sacrifice, gratitude, forgiveness, and every day small heroisms. In this regard believers rightly note the many decent, noble, and generous unbelievers; but they also resonate very much with Nicholas Kristoff's words in a recent *New York Times* op ed article. There he wrote: "I must say that a disproportionate share of the aid workers I've met in the wildest places [around the globe] over the years, long after anyone sensible had evacuated, have been evangelicals, nuns, or priests. Likewise, religious Americans donate more of their incomes to charity and volunteer more hours, than nonreligious, according to polls. In the United States and abroad, the safety net of soup kitchens, food pantries, and women's shelters depends heavily on religious donations and volunteers."

All this because countless people trust in the Man from Nazareth.

But, with all this being said, it isn't easy, as we know, being a believer in today's world. In fact, it is hard. For three obvious reasons. First, modern life with its incessant speed and 24/7 distractions are extremely hostile to the interior life. Time is money and there's no time to think, pause, meditate or discern the presence of God. This lack of meditation, reflection, and study shows itself in our country that has lost its moral center.

Secondly, popular culture, with its allies of commercial television, moral relativism, manufactured celebrities, constant consumerism, loud-mouth best-selling atheists and a secular media that has emptied the public square of all religion, tend to make believers defensive and tend to suppress their public identity and commitment. With all that pressure, who's going to say grace in a public restaurant?

Third, believers, sensitive to mystery, know they must necessarily face doubt, however painful. Not being God who knows all, they expect doubt because life is an ongoing, uneven reality and faith, like everything else, has its lows and highs. They are mindful how easily personal tragedy, life's unfairness, scandals, and massive horrors can shake belief. Doubt is a heavy cross they experience at different times—even the clergy among them.

An example: recently the prestigious Anglican Archbishop of Canterbury publicly said that, at times, he questioned if God was really there. This provoked the usual gleeful juvenile comments from the atheists snorting that, see, even an archbishop isn't sure if the whole religious thing isn't a fraud. But the Archbishop, like us, has his reasons to doubt: his firstborn, a seven-month-old baby girl, was killed in a car accident. As a teenager, he had to take care of his alcoholic father.

And who can forget the posthumous revelation that Mother Teresa was tormented with gloom and life-long doubt as she struggled to believe in God? They are in good company. Believers cannot forget Jesus crying out on *his* cross, "My God, My God, where are you? Why have you forsaken me?" On the other hand, neither can they forget the Easter mystery of the resurrected Jesus breathing out "Peace be with you" to the dejected, grieving, perplexed apostles.

So, the words "I believe" mean that, not knowing everything, "I trust." And remember, it's not an odd thing to do: to have trust in Jesus as the way, the truth, and the life—not when people freely have trust in Alec or Fred.

Yes, we *are* a nation of believers. It all depends whom we trust.

We have opted for Jesus.

Live the Questions

About two years ago, the English comedian and atheist, Stephen Fry was interviewed on TV and the host said to Fry, "Suppose it's all true, and you walk up to the pearly gates and are confronted by God. What will you say?" Fry responded with words we have in our hearts but are afraid to say out loud: "Bone cancer in children, what's that all about? *How dare you?* You create a world where there is such misery. That's not our fault?...Why should I respect a God who creates a world that is so full of injustice and pain?" Oh, oh. It's what the philosophers call the theodicy conundrum: How can there be a good God with so much evil in the world? Why doesn't God step in? Why *do* the innocent suffer? Or, from ordinary people like you and me, we ask these questions:

> Why am I suffering from cancer?
> Why are some of us capable of child abuse?
> Why can't we have wisdom when we are young and would really benefit from it?
> Why earthquakes?
> Why the evil brutality of ISIS?
> Why do you allow Boko Haram to kill hundreds of innocent women and children?
> If you're really there, why on earth don't you prove it?

Everyone has questions like these, one way or another. They're a part of the human condition. We're all hurting and, like the Hebrews of old, dying of hunger and thirst in the desert, we cry out many times on our collective life's journey, "Is God with us or not?" Yes, this is a question we ask especially in times of tragedy or deep sorrow such as the loss of a child, the teenage fatal car accident, the divorce, the daughter on drugs, the death of a spouse, or at an Alzheimer's diagnosis.

Yes, where was God at those tragic times? Why doesn't God answer? "Oh, God," we plead, "give us a sign." And if God did, then we could put up with anything but there is no answer, no sign, only emptiness and numbness. And so, there we are: perplexed to say the least, torn between faith and the evidence.

Two responses:

One, maybe there *are* no answers and we, puzzled and angry, just have to live with it. Period. We have to accept the atheists' conviction that life is meaningless and absurd and make the best of it.

Or two: maybe there *is* Someone higher than us who knows the answers. In that case, how do we work around this?

We start with the head, and ponder some thoughts about the absent God and our problem with it. Part of our existential frustration lies in our makeup. We, as a human race, crave knowledge. We are curious by nature. We are driven to know answers and are frustrated when we don't have them. As a result, we are irritated and rebellious when we are forced to realize that, no matter how brilliant we are, the truth is that we are a limited species. We are unhappy with those limitations.

Satan knew that and played on it. As the crafty and primal tempter, he said to Adam and Eve, "Go ahead, eat it. The only reason that God forbade it was so you would not be equal. You would be like God." It was a lie, of course. The fact is, if the human mind could fully understand God, then God wouldn't be God any longer but instead a figment of our imagination. God would be small enough to fit into the human mind and that's not very big at all.

In Mary Rakow's offbeat book, *This Is Why I Came*, she tells the story of a lapsed Catholic named Bernadette who has come back to Mass after an absence of many years. Her faith was once a comfort to her but it hasn't been for a long time. She is angry, afraid, and doubting. On Good Friday, she decided to go to confession. She says to the priest, "I don't feel I am committing a sin that I can't believe in God anymore. I can't will it. What happened happened. But I really wish it would change." To which the priest responds, "It's not a sin to refuse to believe in a God who's too small . . . To doubt the God you believe in, is to serve him. It's an offering. It's your gift."

Perhaps, then, one of the discomforts behind our questions is that we carry a distorted image of God and that we are incapable of understanding everything, much less why innocent people suffer, and we chafe under this limitation. We subconsciously resent not being masters of the universe. Anyway, the bottom line is that there will always be some darkness of unanswered questions because we are intractably finite.

With that bit of pride taken care of, let's go to the heart, to this bit of wisdom: If we don't have all the answers, and never will, we must learn to live with the questions.

The poet Rainer Maria Rilke said it well when he advised, "Be patient toward all that is unsolved in your heart and try to love the questions themselves . . . Do not now seek the answers which cannot be given you because you would not be able to live them . . . live everything. Live the questions . . ."

What does he mean by this cryptic "live the questions?" It means to enter into a relationship with the questions rather than trying to confront them. It means to engage them spiritually, for questions can take us deeper into the meaning of our lives when we live and are in dialogue with them and the people around us. It means that when we live the questions, we are in dialogue with life itself. In other words, we are seeking to measure our lives, not by the answers we don't have, but by the questions we do.

Ken Brewer, a poet who died a few years ago of pancreatic cancer, might help us here. He wrote:

> I measure my life in family
> Who speak through tears,
> Who serve me meals on a wicker tray,
> Who pray and love and float.

I measure my life in the pine birds
Who entertain me in feeders outside my
window
And Gus, the schnauzer,
Who curls next to me in bed
I measure my life in friends
Who do not know my sins,
Who hug my shrunken body,
Who break open my heart with words.
I measure my life in cancer
That has taught me how to measure my life.

This doesn't answer anything, but it enters us into the world of the compassionate. It measures life by a community of caregivers, hospice workers, family, friends, meal-makers, card-senders, well-wishers, huggers, prayers, Eucharistic ministers, and small newly-appreciated beauties. Most of all, living the questions puts us in the company of the suffering Jesus who, on Calvary, asked, "My God, my God, why have you forsaken me?"—only after his death to say serenely in the Upper Room, "It is I, do not be afraid."

Look: we are a pilgrim people. There *will* be mystery. There will be the big, the personal, the haunting questions. The unbelievers will agonize the questions but will the believers live the questions and in the living let them spawn faith, hope, and love?

4TH SUNDAY OF EASTER
CYCLE A
JOHN 10:1-10

21

Scandal

Let's talk this morning about the elephant in the sanctuary even though, I suspect, you'd rather not.

Into the already poisoned atmosphere of the clergy sexual scandals in the Catholic Church and its unconscionable cover-ups comes recent news of which most of you are aware, an allegation of sexual abuse by the pastor at St. Martha's in Point Pleasant, a parish where for six years I was weekend help and where today I continue to celebrate Mass every week on Thursdays and Friday.

An allegation of sexual abuse has been brought against him, an accusation quite public—on TV and within the *Star Ledger*, the *Asbury Park Press*, the *Monitor*—of which he is innocent until proven guilty, although the opposite policy seems to be operative in the press.

Then last week there was the exposure of Archbishop Jozef Wesolowski, the Vatican's papal Nuncio to the Dominican Republic. It was particularly shameless and revolting. He sexually preyed on poor shoe shine boys—a sick and evil man.

These revelations have resurrected the embarrassment, anger, total disgust, a deep sense we have of the hurtful betrayal by the Catholic Church and have raised again the often-asked questions: How could you ever trust the Church again? and Why would you even stay in a corrupt Church like that? I remember the last time some man asked me that last question, I inquired, "What is your profession?" He replied, "A lawyer," and what startled me is that he said it with a straight face. You know the old saying concerning lawyers, "It's the ninety percent that give the other ten percent a bad name!" I don't mean to be hard on you lawyers out there, just to point out that every trusted profession—doctors, teachers, coaches, CEOs—have their share of scandals. But that doesn't excuse the horrific scandal in the Catholic Church. We have to come back to our question: In the light of such scandals, why stay? Why do you stay?

Why do *I* stay? Let me answer that in many ways. I stay because of a story my mother told me. She came over from Italy as a small child and brought many old sayings and stories that served as moral lessons for us.

One day my brother, sister, and I said something critical about our pastor—nothing nasty, just a comment. Mom overheard, pulled us aside and sat us down and told us this story, this parable. One time when the weather was boiling hot and the humidity was suffocating, the apostles, who were walking along with Jesus, were complaining to him. "Lord, it's terrible! It's so hot! We're dying of the heat! Can't you do something about it?"

Just then, suddenly, from around the corner on the road where they were, flowed a stream of the most beautiful, clean, cool, clear blue water. The apostles went crazy. They got on their knees, splashed the water on their faces and drank till their hearts' content. "O, Lord, how cool! How refreshing!" Then they got up, walked a bit and turned the corner. Imagine their surprise when they saw that the cool clean, refreshing water was coming from the mouth of a dead dog! Ugh! What a story! It took us a while—a couple of years—to get the point of the story and it is this:

Grace does not depend on the agent, the source . . . Jesus and his message can be constricted but not extinguished by his followers, or by his ministers. He can and will still send forth living waters no matter the source, good or bad.

A famous man named Frank Sheed, about 50 years ago, put it this way. Listen:

"We are not baptized into the hierarchy; do not receive the cardinals sacramentally; will not spend an eternity in the Beatific Vision of the pope. Sixteenth century Bishop

John Fisher could say in a public sermon, "If the pope will not reform the curia, God will." A couple of years later, he laid his head on Henry VIII's block for papal supremacy, followed to the same block by Thomas More, who had spent his youth under the corrupt Borgia pope, Alexander VI; he lived his early manhood under the worldly Medici pope, Leo X and died for papal supremacy under Clement VII, as time-serving a pope as Rome ever had.

"But none of them ultimately matter. Jesus Christ is the point. I myself admire the present pope [Pius XII], but even if I criticized him as harshly as some do, even if I sometimes find the Church as I have to live in it, a pain in the neck, I should still say that nothing a pope or a priest could do or say would make me wish to leave the church, although I might well wish that *they* would leave."

"Israel, through its best periods as through its worst, preserved the truth of God's oneness in a world swarming with gods, and a sense of God's majesty in a world sick with its own pride. So with the Church. Under the worst administration, saddled with the worst scandals, we could still learn Christ's truth, receive his life in the sacraments, be in union with him to the limits of our willingness. In awareness of Christ, I can know the Church as his mystical body, and we must not make our judgment by the neck's sensitivity to pain."

He's got it right. That's why you and I are here this morning. I think people have an instinctive appreciation of this truth. No one—no pope, no priest, no bad Catholic—can completely erase the face of Christ, stop his endless spiritual and corporal works of healing, mercy and forgiveness, or undo his mission.

I stay because I know that:

For every clerical predator, there is a
Vincent de Paul
For every exploiter, there is a Dorothy Day
For every profit-at-any-price-manager,
there is a Francis of Assisi
For every coward, there is a Maximillian Kolbe
For every uncaring individual, there is a
Mother Teresa
For every bad pope, there is Pope Francis.

I stay because I see every day that grace is still amazing, that renewal is larger than sin, faith is stronger than scandal—just as it was in the time of its weak founding fathers: denying Peter—that "Satan" of today's gospel—betraying Judas, unbelieving Thomas, ambitious James and John—and yet it survived because Jesus was and is the center, not any of them.

I stay because I realize that Jesus is simply too strong, too "risen," too present, to be undone by a new set of Peters, Thomases and Judases.

Finally, I stay because of you, because hurt by the publicity, wounded by a breach of trust, plagued by doubt, or scandalized by betrayal, you still come here to worship, receive Jesus' sacraments, learn from the scripture, share the bread and wine and try to make a difference.

Yes, it may be hard to stay but to quote spokesman St. Peter from when Jesus asked the disciples, after a particularly trying day and when people found him a bit too much to accept and took off, "Will you also go away?" Replied Peter, the one who would later eat his words, "No, Lord, for we have come to believe that you have the words of eternal life."

I stay because I believe that too, because the words of eternal life, despite those who would mute them, can still be heard in the Catholic Church.

So—you ninety-seven percent lay Catholics, remember that you also are the Church, not just the clerical three percent. You are here to help it rise again, and it is my privileged task to help you do so.

Thank you for letting me try.

Spotlight

The movie, "Spotlight," tells the story of the *Boston Globe* reporters who first broke the news of the widespread sexual abuse of minors by priests and the cover up that went along with it. Its revelations prompted a tsunami of stories of similar abuses and cover-ups elsewhere. Eventually the Catholic Church would pay some four billion dollars in damages. The *Boston Globe* capped a Pulitzer Prize for its efforts.

The movie, disturbing and graphic, is a well-made, well-directed one with great performances and garnered the Best Picture of the Year award. It refocuses the world's attention on one of the worst scandals of the Catholic Church, a scandal that, like a scarlet letter, will forever be branded on its forehead.

The Church that boasts itself as one, holy, catholic, and apostolic now has another mark to announce, an old one that reaches way back into its history: *ecclesia semper reformanda*, the church always in need of reform. It's important to remember this old axiom, and that its roots go way back—and I mean *way* back to its beginnings. Which is to say, how did the Church handle scandal at the start? And there *was* scandal, big time, right at the beginning because, to paraphrase Jesus, scandal, like the poor, is always with us. We know this because, although the temptation was to cover up and slide over some terrible deeds, the early Church let them hang out in public. It started immediately with the chief honcho, the big man, the appointed leader of the apostolic band. We are so used to it that we have lost the ability to realize what a shameful, hurtful, cowardly act this was: to deny Jesus, and to deny him three times at that. "I know not the man!" he spat out, and then there was that awful cock crow. The deed was done and Peter slunk away scarlet-lettered forever.

And the remaining eleven? One of them betrayed him, another would not believe in him, and two boasted they would always be at his right and left but did not show up at Calvary where Jesus had to settle for two thieves. Three of them slept in the garden when they should have comforted him, and all of them, every one of them, fled and left Jesus in the lurch when he needed them most. All this dirty laundry the early Church hung out for all to see, and we don't know what the reactions were, whether people taunted Thomas for his weak faith, or called the others cowards, or whether some vulgar clod stood outside Peter's house at night and made cock crow sounds.

What we *do* know is that the failures, shame, and scandal did not stop them. They regrouped, went back to basic Jesus and his message, and wound up giving their lives for him. They didn't and couldn't undo the sin, the weakness, or the public failures. They couldn't wipe the slate clean. They couldn't erase the blot, but they could renew their love for Jesus and spread his gospel. And they did. They did.

So that's where we are. The Church today is not the glory Church of popes and power or politics. It is one, less-than-holy, catholic, and apostolic in the most basic sense. For it *is* the Church of the imperfect apostles. It is the Church of modern day Peters who will never forget the cock crow, but who know we must move on, with our scarlet letter showing, to live the gospel.

And, then, postured in our more humbled mood, we need to reflect and embrace what in fact that fallible group, the "Terrible Twelve" as we might call them, began, what this Catholic Church of theirs, in its best moments, has achieved. Just take our own country, never mind the rest of the world, over the past 2,000 years. Do you realize, for example, that one out of six Americans gets their health care from a Catholic institution, or that one out of five Americans living in poverty is served by Catholic Charities?

Do you know that Catholic schools are the largest providers of private K-to-12 education in a country with more than two million students, and the largest provider of private higher education enrolling more than one million students? Or that the national Catholic graduation rate is 99.4 percent of high school students? And that of these graduates, 84.9 percent go on to college compared to 39.5 percent of public school graduates?

Do you know that the Catholic Church is the largest settler of refugees in the country? That U.S. based Catholic Relief Services serves nearly 100 million people in need in 93 countries? The society of St. Vincent de Paul serves over 14 million people in need in the United States each year?

Bottom line: The Catholic Church—Peter's Church—is and has been the most important nongovernmental source of social good in our nation, and almost no one knows it. And it all started with a weak man who caved in under pressure. Yes, our enemies will never let us forget. Yes, they will continue to make rooster calls outside our homes and brand us as intractable sinners. But, as St. Paul, reviewing his own life as hater and persecutor of Christians, with Stephen's blood on his hands, wrote: "By the grace of God I am what I am and his grace has not been unfruitful in me."

The movie, "Spotlight"—it's our cock crow—has shined its light on the Church's shame—as it should. Caught in that spotlight we have our choice: to despair like Judas, flee and leave the Church like the others or, chastened like Peter, repent and continue to scatter the seeds of renewed faith; it is a second-chance hope and incalculable widespread charity that everyday comforts and helps countless numbers of people throughout the world, making Jesus present every day.

We're a *Pilgrim* People, as Vatican II called us, clearly with mud on our feet and dirt on our clothes, but we march on; despite always being in need of reform, much good has been done and remains to be done. Rubbing shoulders with Peter, let us go forward.

23

Home

Let me begin by sharing two similar and true stories. One Friday afternoon at his office, a man and his co-workers were talking about what they planned to do that evening, the beginning of the weekend. Several of his co-workers shared how they planned to meet various friends and hit some of the trendier nightspots in the city. The man, happily married for over twenty-five years, shared rather timidly that he and his wife planned simply to order in some pizza and watch a movie together. "That must sound so boring to you," he volunteered.

"Not at all," volunteered one of the young single women in his office. "We all do the things we do—restaurants, nightclubs, and the social scene—only so that sometime and, God-willing, sooner rather than later, we can be where you are now, content at home on a Friday night with pizza and a movie and someone to make a home with." Ah, someone to make a home with.

Second story. Spiritual writer, Fr. Ronald Rohlheiser tells of the time he was teaching a class at a university. He had assigned a book by Christopher deVinck which spoke movingly of the joys he found in marriage with his wife, children, and his home. It was only a week or so into the class that a thirty-something young woman walked into his office with deVinck's book and tears in her eyes. "Father," she said, "I have lived a hot-blooded youth and have slept my way through a couple of states, always thinking I was somehow finding and tasting life. But what I really want is what this man has! A home, someone to love me, a place of that kind of comfort."

Home. We all are looking for home, for a home to build, for someone to make a home with, to share life with, someone who does not exploit us but loves us and whom we can trust. Right now, let's save for another homily what "home" can mean for singles like myself, and today let's focus on the home called marriage.

The drive to find a good marriage starts early. The columnist David Brooks, for example, takes a look at online dating and the way some of the sites ask their clients to rate the other's attractiveness. Looks dominate online dating and the most attractive people get the most interest. When they get around to texting or tweeting each other, then the surveys reveal the most common words and phrases used. For men it's *good bro*, *ps4*, *my beard*, *in nba*, *hoopin*, and *off season*. For women, popular phrases include: *my nails done*, *mani pedi*, *retail therapy*, and *my belly button*.

These common exchanges reflect not so much shallowness as much as they reflect the consumerist values of our marketplace culture. This implies that seekers are basically shopping for a commodity, an ornament, not a person and so image over substance, appearance over reality, the wedding over the marriage become everything.

As Brooks comments of these online daters, "They pay ridiculous amounts of attention to things like looks, which have little bearing on whether a relationship will work." He's right because research shows in fact that these matching sites really don't click because what really creates a relationship can't be expressed in data or photographs alone. If the only questions asked are, "Does this choice serve *me*?"; "Will my partner fulfill my needs?"; "Can I assert my rights in this relationship?"; "Will he or she honor my autonomy, my private space?"; "Will my partner respect my personal boundaries?" When the measurement, the criterion, the focus of marriage is wholly on the individual, relationships cannot root. The individualist criteria, the sovereign "me" of each partner, like oil and water, can never mix into a lasting marriage.

Marriage success is made infinitely harder in our society that is so fiercely dedicated to such individualism. Intimacy has been undermined by a media that has created and celebrates a nation of consuming Peter Pans: the hook-up, no-responsibilities, forever- young adolescent, the engaging, swinging and non-committed fun person, the eternal 45-year-old boy with his backward cap and video games; the eternal girl, Tinkerbell, sculpted, cosmetic-ed and implanted, not ever, God-forbid, identified with being an elder or a grandparent with body fat or stretch marks.

Peter Pan and Tinkerbell never make the transition to adulthood no matter what their chronological age. They are eternal romantics—good looks, good sex—whose personal fulfillment trumps everything else. The idea of being content at home on a Friday night with a pizza and a movie and someone to make a home with escapes them.

Still, the truth is, married or single, we are all called to be an adult, an elder, a bearer of tradition, a shaper of lives, a provider for the next generation of roots and wings: roots to be grounded in, wings to soar.

Yet, it *is* hard for an advertising-saturated people to stop *thinking* in individual terms and start *feeling* in rapport terms, in mutual terms. People really need to explore if there is something deeper beneath the surface here between two people, something more that can grow. The real issues in a relationship are the issues of values, of purpose, and mostly, of goals larger than themselves. The real survey question, never asked, is how do we score on service to family, to others, to God? In good marriages, there is a sense that marriage only works when both realize that the relationship comes first, the needs of the partner are second and individual needs are third. The mature couple has the "Covenant" mentality, a vocational awareness, and a sense that they, together, are called to serve a larger purpose and that their individual needs take second place.

With a deep sense of having a vocation, they are intent on overcoming the proud ego. For them love is not going to go away even when they go through the normal episodes of failure, confession, apology, or forgiveness as they seek to love each other precisely at those times when there is nothing lovely about either of them. As an old-timer told me, "In my time you didn't throw away things that were broken. You fixed them." And you can only "fix" a marriage if you have a larger goal, a sense that your relationship is not about itself but about service to others, a covenant, a sacred call to serve others.

Couples who declare that they only need each other, who seek lifestyles dedicated only to their own needs, will soon suck each other and society dry. Again, they need, as we all do, something more than themselves or, as we said, goals larger than themselves to which to dedicate their mutual love that will wither without these goals.

In other words, when calculation gives way to vulnerability and people begin to move from selfishness to service, the roots of real love begin to take hold. When marketing alone and the superficial trendy attributes promoted by a surface society are set aside, and things like purpose, the needs of each other and a mutual dedication to something larger than themselves replaces them, then love has started to grow.

Couples know love has rooted when at one magical moment they realize that the "I" has become "We," and the "We" becomes "Them." They have made it home.

Afterlife

In Britain, according to the polls taken in the past few years, half of people surveyed said they believed in an afterlife even though not all of them believed in God. Also, a quarter of agnostics think that death is not the end. It's the same in America.

What gives? Why do so many unbelievers believe in life after death? Moreover, since they do not believe in God, the Bible or Jesus, where does this belief come from? Why is the supernatural, the afterlife, all over the place and why is Hollywood making gazillions from afterlife franchises?

There is the top-rated *The Walking Dead*. There is *Doctor Who, Lost, Sideways World, True Blood*—you name it. On TV and in the movies, belief in the afterlife is rampant: angels, demons, zombies, witches, vampires, animated corpses—and most of you, I suspect, are fans of one or the other.

What may be surprising, even for believers, is that both in the Old and New Testaments, there is precious little about the afterlife—the Hebrews didn't believe in it—and New Testament references are meager. So where does our current belief in the afterlife come from? It's everywhere: in our music, movies, TV, video games, computer games, books—one thinks of the best sellers, "Heaven is for Real" about a little boy's trip to heaven and back, and a similar book, "The Boy Who Came Back from Heaven"—novels, comics, and so on.

These things in turn subconsciously draw from centuries old medieval art and literature, mostly from Dante's

Divine Comedy, Milton's *Paradise Lost*, and Christianity's deep interest in angels and spirits during the first millennium. Whatever the ancient source and modern franchises, after centuries of "rational" thinking and the elites' mockery of everything religious, there remains a deep, nervous, and renewed backdoor yearning for the afterlife.

Why? The answer is that this fascination with the afterlife helps people—even unbelievers—garner some kind of meaning out of life's difficult questions, out of life's unfairness: something has to be evened out somewhere. For all our modern skepticism and noisy atheism, there's an innate common instinct to rationalize that if there really is nothing beyond this world then death the final authority, making meaninglessness the norm. We rebel against that.

Instead, we continue to have a strong sense deep within ourselves that death is a dying *into* life rather than simply away from it, a sense of the continuity of life, that faith, hope and love, generosity, sacrifice, and beauty are impervious to change and corruption. For many, in fact, the very persistence of our longing for something more is proof enough of its eventual happening. In a perverse way, people need all those undead folks.

Yet it is strange; while the afterlife is a subconscious wish for non-believers, it is the official doctrine for believing Christians although it seems to be of minor interest to them. They don't talk about it much, and liberal Christians, in fact, find the afterlife an embarrassment even though we pay homage to it in our Creed: Jesus rose from the dead, ascended into heaven and will come again to judge the living and the dead and he will rule over an endless kingdom.

There's more to deter us. Profoundly conditioned and shaped by modern media, we have too often bought into the cartoon concepts of heaven and hell, you know: the fluffy clouds, the harp, the gold crown, the union-suited, tailed and horned devil and his pitchfork, and we're much too sophisticated to believe that stuff.

We never realize that these are metaphors from the past: the cloud, like God himself, conceals and reveals; music is the one universal reality that binds us; gold is the one metal that does not rust, hinting at heaven's eternity; the devil's pitchfork is for shoveling coal into the fire, itself a metaphor for suffering and separation.

But, worse than that, profiled consumers that we are, we bring to our concept of heaven our culture's worst illusion, namely, that we are the center of the universe, the very thing that caused us so much trouble on earth. We want to know if our dogs go to heaven. Will my hair return, my blemishes evaporate, my stretch marks disappear, or my waistline go back to when I was sixteen? Will my marriage literally be one remade in heaven? Will the food be gourmet, the accommodations elegant, the golf links perfect, or the sex great? In short, heaven will be all about me and my comfort, only writ large. If that's the case, we're back to square one, and heaven will be hell.

But Christ's explosive love in emptying himself at his death and his resurrection ought to be a means of freeing us from precisely that kind of thinking, that kind of self-centeredness which has been the source of so much of our suffering and unhappiness. If the afterlife is nothing more than domestication, a projection in Technicolor stereo of our paltry lives, what kind of heaven, what kind of happiness are we talking about?

When Jesus talks about many rooms in my Father's House, he is not talking about my Sandy-restored house I lived in on earth. He is talking about his *Father's* house where our restless hearts rest in that perfect Love that has always yearned for us.

Anyway, the next time you watch *The Walking Dead* or dress up like one of the undead, realize that you're subconsciously flirting with mystery and playing games with things you're afraid to talk about openly. When your faddish atheist friends tune in to their favorite zombie show, you can secretly recognize their hidden wish for living beyond death and a rebellion against nothingness.

But for you who are here, remember your roots. Remember the one who said, "I am the resurrection and the life. Whoever believes in me will live forever"—and St. Paul's soaring paean "that no eye has seen nor ear heard nor has it even entered into the heart of humankind what God has prepared for those who love him."

The afterlife is both radically different from and better than the special effects. It deals with an eternal life and love we can't even imagine.

Charleston, South Carolina

Daily Mass goers, at this time of the year, are being exposed in the first readings to the saga of Abraham and his clan, and they will hear bits of the story each day until they complete the cycle filled with outsized personalities like Sarah, Lot, Isaac, Jacob, Esau, Miriam, Aaron, and Moses. Each day, then, the first reading takes a piece of the Hebrew foundational story and unfolds it.

Sunday church goers will miss all this, but let me tell you that the two basic themes which make up the foundational identity of the Hebrew people emerge from the readings: first, God has chosen them as his very own—they are a Chosen People—and, second, God has made a special covenant with them by giving them the land of Canaan. Henceforth, they are Yahweh's people and will remain so *provided* they keep the terms of the covenant, which means in practice that they must do Yahweh-like things: take care of the orphan, protect the widow, pay a just wage, honor the land, and enact justice.

Their history, recorded in the Bible, is an ebb and flow of fidelity and infidelity to this covenant. And each time they fail, each time they're down in the pits and are about to disappear as a people, they know that to survive they must return to their roots. They must take a second look at their very flawed heroes, revisit the ancient stories, and rediscover once more who they are and start all over again.

At Passover, the youngest asks the eldest, "Why is this night special?" and the elder retells the story that started it all, reintroduces the people who were there at the beginning in the hope of imitating them, of recapturing the first fervor. The message is: when times are bad, go back to the source, go back to the heroes, revisit the pristine story.

We still do that in many homely ways. Harper Lee, for example, wrote her famous novel, *To Kill a Mockingbird*, and introduced us to the noble Atticus Fitch whom she had modeled on her own lawyer father. In the novel itself, she has Atticus' son, Jeb, inherit her father's watch as a reminder of his heroism and what he stood for and what he might imitate.

Mary Ann Evans, whom we know under her pen name George Elliot and who gave us the novels *Silas Marner*, *The Mill on the Floss*, and her masterpiece *Middlemarch*, used her own unlettered father whom she adored as a model for her noble male characters. She kept his wire-rimmed glasses on her desk as a reminder of him and his values. If she was tempted to stray, a look at those glasses brought her back.

The point is: when we lose our way, go back to the inspirational source.

Note how Pope Francis did this. Startling everyone at his election, he took the unexpected name Francis, after Francis of Assisi, the man of poverty, the man of peace, the man who loves and protects creation and the environment. He did this because he was keenly aware, as indeed was his savvy audience, of the Francis story and Francis' conversion in the broken-down church of San Damiano outside the gates of Assisi, how Francis heard a voice telling him, "Go, rebuild my church which, as you can see, is falling into ruin."

And Pope Francis and everyone else knew exactly what that meant. Christ's church of the 21st century was broken, falling into ruin. Scandal, clericalism, inertia, being out of touch was creating the world's second largest religious group: ex-Catholics. The Church needs rebuilding. Pope Francis understood that we, too, needed to revisit our foundational story, go back to Francis of Assisi, who went back to Jesus, who forgave sins.

Such a fundamental forgiveness happened recently. In June of 2015, we as a nation got an example of exactly what the Pope meant, of exactly what being radical meant. In one more of our nation's terrible dark massacres, a young twenty-one-year-old white male killed nine black people who, with others, were gathered in a historic Christian church in Charleston, South Carolina for bible study.

Once more, the nation was horrified. The police quickly caught the young man and a few days later, as the world was watching, he was in court facing the survivors and families and friends of the ones he slaughtered. The TV cameras were rolling as each black person spewed out their grief, their hurt, their shock, their profound loss, their anger - and each one, struggling with pain and tears, ended up forgiving that hate-filled young white man! Eventually, as a Christian parish they *all* forgave him.

They forgave him! And it made such an impact on the nation for there it was out in the open: that foundational Christian story in all its primal toughness, angst, and full implications were there for all to see. On worldwide TV, Jesus' words were rolling over and breaking through our culture of high-tech, special effects revenge—yes, there were his words for all the world to hear: "Love your enemies. Pray for those who persecute you." There, too, loud and clear, hanging on South Carolina's Calvary, was Jesus' pitiable agonizing voice to his executioners, "Father, forgive them."

And *that* brought us back to Christian basics. This is what the pope with the name of Francis had in mind. Let's revisit our foundational Jesus stories with its heroes and villains. Let's call so-called Christians who defraud, cheat, abuse, hate other races and nationalities, and tell them they're part of the problem and they're not true to the Jesus story. Let's read a few lines of the gospel daily to catch a different rhythm of life. Let's see Jesus as he was before we tamed him. Let's watch him touching the untouchable leper and remember that if Mother Teresa could do the same, so can we.

Let's look at our too-muchness and see what we need

to give to the poor because Jesus said that the one who has two coats should give one away. Let's ask God—if we can't bring ourselves to do it (and that's understandable) to offer forgiveness to the wretched one who hurt us badly in the hopes we may be able to do it ourselves someday.

Let's reconsider that Jesus agenda on giving drink to the thirsty—physically and morally—food to the hungry, and our presence to the sick and imprisoned. Instead of posting "Wonderful Me" on Facebook, let's strike our breast and cry out with the man in the Temple, "Oh God, be merciful to me, a sinner!" and announce ourselves as in need of God.

It's all there in *our* foundational story. The pope named Francis reminds us that God has chosen us through Jesus. We, you and I, have a baptismal covenant with God. But we've strayed as a Church and so we are in great stress. It's time for us to imitate our fellow Christians in South Carolina who brought us dramatically back to our identity.

There's a little mantra I adopted many years ago to help me focus on the basics of ministry. It's the fourfold direction:

> Gather the folk
> Tell the story
> Break the bread
> Share the event.

So far, I have done the first three. After you go out the door, the rest, "share the event," the hard part, is up to you.

The world needs a sign like the one our fellow Christians of South Carolina gave. You are that sign. Let's get back to basics.

Miguel Pro

Half a dozen years ago, a report on religious freedom revealed that seven out of ten people in the world are unable to freely live out their faith. It also found that Christianity is the most persecuted religion in the world, with at least 200 million suffering from discrimination.

It was always so back to Peter, Paul, Stephen, Agnes, Felicity, and countless others. Think of the French Revolution that killed clergy and religious, and which turned the cathedral of Notre Dame into the "Temple of Reason" with prostitutes lolling on the altar. Think of the priests' holes (little secret closets) hiding priests in late medieval England. Think of the Nazis, imprisonment, and the death of thousands of Polish priests. Think of the Soviet Union's forcing of godless atheism on millions. Think today how in the very cradle of Christianity, the Middle Eastern Christians are being persecuted and fleeing in great numbers.

This was the same situation in 1900's Mexico when the government launched a fierce persecution of the Catholic Church. This is where our story of a brave priest, Miguel Pro, a stand-in for so many like him, begins.

Miguel Pro was born in 1891 in Guadalupe, Mexico. He was a precocious, high-spirited, risk-taking child. He was quite close to his older sister and when she entered the convent, he began to feel a call to become a priest. But that would wait. There were girls and the expected career of managing his father's successful business. Eventually, like Francis of Assisi, he gave it all up and entered the

Jesuit novitiate in Mexico when he was twenty years old. He was there until 1914 when it became intolerable. Just four years earlier, the government had unleashed a tidal wave of persecution against the Catholic Church, and it was quickly becoming more severe. Accordingly, along with other Jesuit seminarians, Miguel had to flee to the United States to a Jesuit house in California and, from there, in 1915 he was sent to a seminary in Spain where he remained to continue his preparation for the priesthood. He was ordained in Belgium in 1925.

Miguel suffered from severe stomach problems and underwent several operations. Still, his health did not improve, and so his superiors felt that it would be better for him to return to Mexico despite the ongoing persecution there. He returned in the summer of 1926. Restrictions against the Catholic Church had grown even more severe. Catholics were not allowed to teach in schools. Public worship was forbidden outside of churches, religious organizations could not own property, clergy and religious were forbidden to wear their roman collars or habits in public, and priests who criticized the government were subjected to five years of imprisonment. Since the churches were closed, Miguel went into hiding to secretly minister to the Mexican Catholics, both spiritually and physically, especially the poor. Hunted by the secret police, like Sherlock Holmes he donned many disguises. Sometimes he was a beggar, sometimes a police officer (so he could bring Communion to death row Catholics), and sometimes he was disguised as a businessman.

Eventually he became a wanted man when he and his brother Roberto were falsely accused of a bomb attempt against the Mexican president, although the one who was involved in the attempt testified that Miguel and Roberto had no part in it. Nevertheless, the brothers were betrayed. Roberto was spared but Miguel, because he was a Catholic priest, was sentenced to death by facing a firing squad without any legal process. On November 23, 1927, at his firing range, he stretched out his arms in the form of a cross, forgave his soon-to-be executioners, refused the blindfold, and died shouting, "Long live Christ the King!"

The president had the execution photographed and

spread the pictures on the nation's front pages as a warning to others, but the pictures had the opposite effect in rallying the opposition. We can still view these photographs. We can see Miguel kneeling in prayer before his execution. We can see him standing against the fence with his arms outstretched. We can see a saint.

He was beatified in 1988 by Pope John Paul II who, ironically, 54 years after Miguel Pro's execution, visited Mexico. I say ironically because the laws were still on the books and the pope, in all his papal garb, was technically forbidden to enter the country. He was welcomed by the president and wildly cheered by the people.

Miguel Pro: a witness to the faith like the countless others in both the past and present. I just thought that I'd share his story to remind us that our faith is still being bought at a great price.

CYCLES A, B, C

27

Ascension

"Grandpa, what happens when you die?"

Grandpa explained it as best he could. Still puzzled, the boy asked, "Does that mean you won't be here anymore?"

Grandpa nodded, "Yes, that's true."

"Does that mean you won't be able to play catch with me anymore?"

"Yes, it does."

"Does it mean you won't be able to fly a kite with me anymore?"

"Yes, son, it does."

"Does that mean you won't be able to take me fishing anymore?"

"Yes, it does."

"Well, Grandpa, when that time comes, who is going to do these things with me, if you're not here?"

The wise grandfather explained, "When that time comes, it will be time for you to do those things for another little boy."

The Feast of Ascension is the official statement that says, "the time has come."

Yes, it was the time for Jesus to physically go to the right hand of the Father and it was time for his disciples physically to be Jesus' voice, his hands, his feet, his presence, his Church.

It took time for them to absorb the meaning of it all, to wrestle with second thoughts about whether they were up to the task. *Could* they let go of everything they thought was necessary to walk into a different future? Could they be another Christ? With such musings in their hearts they just stood there numb as Jesus disappeared until they were brought back to earth with the angel's sharp words: "Why are you looking up to heaven? Get on with it!"

So, unsure and hesitant, they trekked off to the Upper Room to await the Spirit who would be their guide and comfort—the Spirit they would sorely need, when, as all their spiritual descendants would soon learn, misunderstandings, betrayals and failures would shake them to their core. Still, as history has shown, by the help of the Spirit, they would repent, renew and recover each time to reaffirm their mandate and get on with being church.

So again, Ascension celebrates this transition from Jesus to the apostles to us. As Jesus said in the first reading, "You will be my witnesses to the ends of the earth" and in the gospel, "Go, therefore, and make disciples of all nations." So here we are today, their heirs.

The 16th century mystic, St. Theresa of Avila, put it this way:

> Christ has no body but yours,
> No hands, no feet on earth but yours.
>
> Yours are the eyes through which he looks
> Yours are the feet with which he walks to do good,
> Yours are the hands with which he blesses the world.
> Yours are the hands, yours are the feet,
> Yours are the eyes, you are his body.
>
> Christ has no body now but yours
> No hands, no feet on earth but yours,
>
> Yours are the eyes with which he looks with
> Compassion on this world,
> Christ has no body now on earth but yours.

Let me move forward five centuries and tell you how it works today—or rather how an 86-year-old nun I know, a Sister of Saint Joseph of Chestnut Hill, Sister Rita Scully, makes it work.

A little background: When she was young back in the 1940s she used to take the train to downtown Philadelphia for a part-time job at Bonwit Teller, a very upscale store. There, she modeled dresses. She also used to dance at St. Benedict's Catholic USO. This was during World War II and the USO was a place where servicemen on leave could relax and dance.

Once, a nun asked her to conduct a weekend dance workshop at a Catholic grammar school some distance away, and so during that time she had to stay at the local convent and that's where she felt the call to become a nun. The part-time model and ballet dancer became Sister Rita Scully.

Anyway, not long ago she took on a new challenge. She still loves to travel to downtown Philly and goes to Mass when she's there at St. Joseph's parish that is, in fact, a few decades older than the United States itself. One day she was dipping her hand into the holy water font to bless herself when a woman sidled over and whispered, "Sister, you really don't want to use that font. Last week I saw a homeless man rinsing out a pair of filthy socks in it." I would have recoiled saying "Ugh!" But Sister Rita's reaction was, "Well, there must be people who need socks," and so a new ministry was born at that holy water font.

Sister Rita now buys pairs of socks and puts a pair in a plastic bag along with a list of places where a homeless person could get a meal and a list of job referrals. Eighty-six-year-old Sister Rita travels Market Street, and whenever she sees a homeless person hands him or her a bag. She says that by the time she gets to 9th Street, she's all out of socks, and that adds up to about one homeless person per block. It also adds up to where, post-Ascension, Christ can be found right now. She is his eyes and ears, hands, and feet.

Or, as an old Quaker story puts it: by accident a lady happened in on a small Quaker congregation. They were all sitting in silence as Quakers are wont to do. "When does the service begin?" she whispered to the man sitting near her. His answer: "As soon as the meeting is over."

Jesus has gone to the Father. Ascension says, *Let the service begin.*

Remember

"You loved them even as you loved me."

An image: Daddy's squatted down holding his little toddler daughter. Mommy's a few feet away, also squatted down, with her arms extended. They're coaxing her to take her first steps. She repeatedly starts and stops, falls and gets up, but little by little she stumbles into mommy's waiting arms and her parents are full of encouragement, praise, and love.

Love. But think about it. They love her when she falls and when she stands. They love her when she fails and when she succeeds. They love her when she moves her sturdy legs, and they love her when she moves her crippled legs, and they even love her if she was born with no legs at all.

The fact is that they love her unconditionally, period, and nothing she can do or fail to do can alter that fact. Their love does not depend on her performance. She can't earn it or deserve it or thwart it. She can't turn it off or turn it on. She can't stop or start it. It's just a given, just there.

And here we have the basic, fundamental principle of the spiritual life, its very foundation. For the same is true of God. God loves us completely, fully, and totally at all times. There is nothing we can do to stop or start it. We cannot earn God's love or make ourselves deserving of it. It is out of our control. It is there and never ceases being there.

That, as I said, is the basic foundational truth of the spiritual life and we forget it to our great harm. That's why, for centuries, the mystics held that the greatest sin in the world was forgetfulness. Yes, forgetfulness. To forget that one was freely loved, that one could not bargain for or shut it down, was the source of all evil.

And understand this, too: all those Lenten penances, all those prayers and sacrifices, all those self-denials, were never meant to bribe, coax, buy back or regain the love of God that was always there. Rather, like clearing a thicket to get to the beloved's cottage, our prayer and penances were meant to hack aside and pluck out whatever obstacles led us to forget in the first place, that led us to forget that we were always and forever, without space or hesitation, in good times and in bad, sound or crippled, with virtue or with a thousand vices of the soul, beloved of the Father.

If we remember who we are, we will act like who we are.

Once we get rid of the childish notion that we have to earn God's love, say so many prayers, do so many deeds to be worthy of it, once we put aside the pernicious heresy that our sins, no matter how horrid or unspeakable, can cancel it, then we will begin to respond with a life of love. Then, too, we can be immune to the arrows and slings of life.

I am saddened that so many of our youth, especially those not given any religion by their parents, are susceptible to hurt and depression because they do not know this truth. Their identity is extrinsic rather than intrinsic, that is, their identity depends on how many "likes" they get on social media. When they post, they wonder if they will get a lot of hits or become popular. Or will ridicule of them go viral, sending them into a tailspin of depression? Will they wind up a celebrity, an "in" person or a miserable nerd? Social media is a mixed world. Listen to this. A stunning report issued in 2016 revealed that an unprecedented number of deaths from suicides for children ages ten to fourteen had caught up with their death rates from automobile accidents. Yes, suicides for this age group are up alarmingly. Far more boys than girls killed themselves but, note this, the increase for girls was much sharper.

The reasons are complex, but social scientists point to two causes. One factor is that, as they say, "social media is girl-town" meaning that they are into it in ways boys are not. Girls dominate platforms like Facebook, where they daily receive validation (or not) from their peers and see where they stand in the pecking order. Popularity or unpopularity is quantified. In the old days, you knew who your friends were and what they were doing after school. Now social media assigns numbers to those things—and everything's public. In the past if you wore the wrong clothes or did some stupid thing, only a limited number of people would know what a nerd you are. Now your humiliation is public, gone viral and that can be very, very destabilizing.

The second thing is that girls, like boys, reach puberty earlier. Today's twelve-year-old girls are yesterday's sixteen-year-olds—which means they are becoming young women when they are least equipped to deal with the changes, and that may be why girls experience depression at twice the rate as boys in adolescence. Both boys and girls are living in a fast-paced, hyper-sexed relativistic world and are taking more medications than ever before.

Some resort to sexting—sending nude photos of themselves—because they think they don't have something more substantial to offer the world, and so in effect announce what you see is what you get when, sadly, they don't realize that what you *don't* see is a more basic truth: that I am beloved of God. I am more than what appears on Facebook, more than looks, more than popularity and money, more than a body. If only we could get them to remember that I'm not what I do. I'm not what other people say about me. I'm not what I have. My spiritual identity is not rooted in the world or the things the world gives me. My life is rooted in the fact that God loves me.

Do they know this? If not, why not? Who did not teach them? Do they know of the trials of some of the saints? Do they know, for example, of the great black scientist Booker T. Washington? He was called to the Washington Ways and Means Committee in 1921 to give an account of his work with peanuts. Being a black man, he was left for last. He was shocked at the unprofessionalism of the committee, the lack of attention, and decorum as members sat with their feet on the desks.

Anyway, when he was finally called as he went up the

aisle, someone called out, "Hey, nigger, I suppose you have plenty of peanuts and watermelon to keep you happy!" He blanched. As he went up the aisle further, another shouted, "Down where I come from we don't accept any nigger's testimony and I don't see what this fellow can say that has a bearing on this committee."

Twice he was called what we delicately call the N word. Washington was deeply hurt and was ready to turn right around and go home, but just listen to what this good man wrote in his autobiography. Quote: "Whatever they said of me, I knew I was a child of God." He went on to give his speech and, in fact, was so engaging they wound up extending his talk to several hours and ended with applause.

And I think, can young people say they know they are a child of God? Addicted as they are to the social media and its tyranny, do they know that they have a deep resource to draw upon, the ultimate negation of vicious words? Do they grasp that they are beloved by God, that they are more than their images, that with all their human limitations and mistakes, they are the objects of the unearned love of God? To return to our opening, they are loved whether they have two good legs, two crippled legs or no legs at all, they are loved.

Whatever else is ever said of them, they are, as we are, fundamentally children of God, and God has a mission for them. Can they—can we—remember that?

St. Paul summed it up best when he wrote, "Who will separate us from the love of Christ? Will anguish or distress or persecution or famine or nakedness or peril or the sword? . . . No, in all these things we conquer overwhelmingly through him who loved us. For I am convinced that neither death, nor life, nor angels, nor principalities, nor present things, nor future things, nor powers or height, nor depth - nor, as we would interpolate—backbiting, nor shame, nor malicious gossip, nor putdowns, nor the social media—will be able to separate us from the love of God in Christ Jesus our Lord." (Romans, 8:35-39)

My message today: Remember, beloved, who you are.

Pentecost

Preachers on this Pentecost Sunday will say a lot of good things about the Holy Spirit, about this being the Birthday of the Church and so on, but I want to share with you a different image to think about, to cherish, when we mention the Holy Spirit. Think of the Holy Spirit as "The Last Word" or as Surprise with a capital "S."

As in today's gospel where the dejected disciples were gathered: their leader executed as a criminal, their hopes dashed, their dreams scattered, their hearts full of fear. The last words they knew were death, disappointment, and disaster. But, in a flash, all these words suddenly became next-to-the-last words. The last word was surprise as Jesus comes through closed doors and breathes "Shalom." The last word was the Holy Spirit, the Lord of Surprise.

Later, gathered in another Upper Room and not knowing where to go, what to do, awaiting something or other—they knew not what—they were startled when tongues of fire descended upon them and they received the Holy Spirit who renewed them.

And so it would go: the Holy Spirit came to be known as the Last Word, the One who with great regularity, in the worst of times, in the depths of misery, surprises everybody by raising up people who advertise its presence. In the 13th century when all was wickedness and chaos, along comes Francis of Assisi. Then there's Dorothy Day in the bowery, Charles de Foucault in the desert, Damien in the leper colony, Mother Teresa in the slums of India, Thomas Merton in Greenwich Village, and a reformed alcoholic priest, Mychal Judge, in the Twin Towers debris of 9/11.

And there are today's stories. Let me share a few.

In 1977, some may recall, there was an awful blizzard that blanketed the East Coast, leaving three feet of snow, icy roads, and downed power lines. Buffalo was hit particularly hard. Dennis Morrison's future mother-in-law, Ruth, was at her friend's house playing bridge. Used to Buffalo weather, she left, and got into her car to go home. When she found her street blocked, she left the car and decided to walk home.

Then a stranger appeared, warning her that the path to her home was too dangerous to walk alone. He guided Ruth around fallen trees and power lines and got her safely to her front door. No one knew this man and he was never seen again. Ruth swore it was her Guardian Angel.

Then there's a blogger named Hallie Lord who shares these words. "In a sense, life has matured us to a far greater degree over the past decade than I ever could have imagined. Life poured six babies into our hearts. Life asked us to trust him and each other as we wrestled with a decade of financial hardship. Life asked us to travel from state to state as we sought the place in which the earth would invite us to put down roots; and Life said, 'I know this is hard, but love each other anyway.' And we did. Imperfectly, of course. I cringe when I think of the things I've said and the damage I caused, but my husband had remained emphatic that forgiveness and love rule our home. He has taught me to leave the pain behind and march forward with him, hand in hand."

Then she adds these Pentecostal words: "There are moments in life when God lifts you up and gives you a moment of ecstatic clarity. These are the moments that give all those crosses meaning and reveal their goodness." The Spirit has breathed again.

Finally, there is the priest they used to call Father Dollar Bill. That wasn't his real name, of course, which was Father Maurice Chase who was a long-time priest and fund raiser for the Archdiocese of Los Angeles.

He earned his nickname, as you might suspect, by giving out dollar bills. He was in his nineties when he died a few years ago. When some people said that his dollar bills really had no long-term impact he would reply, "I'm just trying to give them hope, to give them a sense of dignity."

The "them" he referred to were his Skid Row recipients. How they missed him when he was gone. "He was just a glorious man," said one woman. "He was always there," another said. "He will be missed, not because of the dollar. Because of what he gave spiritually."

Father Dollar Bill loved the poor and he looked forward to his weekly trips to give them a boost. But I love what he said in his old age. He said these Pentecostal words, "God has given me the happiest part of my life at the end."

Yes, all the episodes of his life, all his shortcomings—and his death—whatever, were never the last words. The Spirit of surprise, who saved the best part for last, was.

On the night before he died, Jesus knew his disciples would be devastated, crushed, wounded. He tried to prepare them for the horrors of the next day and the depressions of the days that followed. He said many comforting words, but among his best were his promise of the Holy Spirit who would be the Last Word, and the Lord of hope and surprise.

We all have our histories of loss, betrayal, disappointment, sickness, old age, unbelievable hurt, life's unfairness, death - but all these are all next to the last words. The last word is the Holy Spirit who will make all things new again.

Ordinary Time

Ode to Happiness

A story. A true one. Adbu Rahman was the caliph of Cordoba in 10th century Spain. He was an absolute ruler who lived in complete luxury. Here's how he assessed his life:

"I have now reigned above 50 years in victory or peace; beloved by my subjects, dreaded by my enemies, and respected by my allies. Riches and honors, power and pleasure have waited on my call, nor does any earthly blessing appear to have been wanted to my felicity. I have diligently numbered the days of pure and genuine happiness which have fallen to my lot: they amount to 14."

An unhappy man like so many today. That leads us to ask, what makes people happy or unhappy?

Circumstances surely are determining to some extent: discrimination, lousy job or boss, poverty and loneliness, but there are other and deeper explanations for unhappiness. One is the wrong-headed but incessant message of the consumer media culture that the pursuit of fame, wealth, and pleasure will bring happiness yet the truth is that, like the pursuit of alcohol by the alcoholic, such a pursuit actually prolongs unhappiness.

Take fame. Researchers checked the success of some college graduates in reaching their goals. Some had "intrinsic" goals such as deep, enduring relationships with others, with God. Others had "extrinsic" goals such as achieving reputation or fame. The researchers found that intrinsic goals were associated with far happier lives. The people who pursued extrinsic goals experienced more negative emotions, such as shame and fear. They even suffered more physically.

Then, of course, there's the well-known paradox associated with fame. Like drugs and alcohol, once you become addicted, you can't live without it. But you can't live with it either. I once read that celebrities have variously described fame as being in an animal cage; a toy in a shop window; a Barbie doll; a public façade; a clay figure; or that guy on TV. Yet they can't give it up.

Still with all these constricting drawbacks people seek it and some, especially teens, aspire to become celebrities as their goal in life. We see this all the time. So, what we get is reality television in which ordinary people—clothed or naked—become actors in their day-to-day lives for others to watch. Why? To be noticed, to be wanted, to be loved, to walk into a place and have others care about what you're doing, eating, or thinking.

Then there's Facebook, YouTube, Twitter and the like where you can broadcast the details of your life to others, chalk up your "likes" to perfect strangers. It *is* a good way to stay in touch with friends but it does tempt fame-seeking—and research shows that can make us unhappy.

After all, people don't post pictures of themselves yelling at the kids, having a bad hair day, having a hard time, or not being part of the in-crowd. No, people post pictures of themselves partying, hiking, smiling, hanging out, and having fun. They build a fake life—or at least an incomplete one—and then share it. In turn, people consume the fake lives of their social media "friends." So, they spend part of their lives pretending to be happier than they really are and gazing at others who seem much happier than themselves. By contrast, you're not having such a good time. You can wind up depressed.

Then there's money and material things. Money no doubt does relieve stress in cases of true need, but when it becomes an end in and of itself then it only brings misery. Research shows that people who rate materialistic goals, like wealth, as top priorities are more likely to be depressed, anxious, and drug users. Physical ailments often beleaguer those who set their sights on intrinsic values.

Then, finally, there's sex. Thanks to a 24/7 soft and hard-core media, early hook-ups, sexting and texting, non-stop sex on TV, casual encounters, routine infidelity—all seem to usher in a new liberated heaven on earth of pleasure and unending happiness. Not to mention that, from an evolutionary perspective, it works because we get to pass on our DNA—although such sex is usually recreative rather than procreative. Mother Nature does not care about whether this routine makes you happy or not as long as you pass on your genetic material.

But as far as happiness and unhappiness go, time after time research shows across the board that for men and women alike to claim true happiness, the optimal number of partners is one. I think of basketball great, Wilt Chamberlin, who boasted of having sex with thousands of women and lamenting he would have given it all up for just one who would truly love him and whom he could love.

As for material things, they always have a short shelf life. They satisfy for the moment but fade in time, and we always want more. Consumerism drives our lives and, in the end, re-routes and consumes them. Fame, money and pleasure, sought as an end in and of themselves, each conspire to make people live out that deadly motto, "Love things, use people."

And we see this sort of thing every day: people are physically, emotionally, and financially manipulated and used—and both the exploited and exploiters are unhappy.

So much for that.

At this point, we who are here are suddenly beginning to grasp the obvious countercultural truth that the gospel of Jesus Christ radically inverts the formula. He preaches, "Love people, use things." Which is to say, put aside selfishness and pride and seek to gain the strength to love others. Love your neighbor as yourself.

This means, be wary of the materialism that so infuses our lives and winds up giving us a false identity by defining who we are by what we have. Be wary of a media and a multi-billion dollar advertising industry whose only goal is to convert wants into needs. Be wary of fame at any price—the price of ignoring or having no time for loved ones. Attend, really attend, to Jesus' words, "What does it profit a person to gain the whole world but lose one's soul, one's very self, who and what we really are, and what we are meant to be?" Yes, we all want admiration, fame, and pleasure and that's ok as long as they are byproducts and not goals.

Back to Adbu-Rahman. He never achieved happiness, never knew the right formula. He invested his whole life in power, money, and pleasure. He loved things and used people and only got 14 days of happiness out of his 50-plus years. We are Christians. All I want to say is that, by definition, we should do better, infinitely better. That means re-orientating our lives, making up our minds to invest in getting our priorities straight by determining to use things and love people, not the other way around.

Recall this biblical snapshot: The young man asked Jesus, "Master, what must I do to be saved, to be happy." Jesus responded, "Love God with all your being and your neighbor as yourself" and then, to illustrate, he went on to tell the world's most famous parable: the nameless Good Samaritan, the enemy who loved his enemy and, in giving away his money to pay for his recuperation, made him a friend.

His creed? People first. Things second. *That* in God's eyes, and in human experience, is happiness.

5TH SUNDAY, OT
CYCLE A
ISAIAH 58:7-10

31

The N Word

Today will be a bit different. The opening entrance antiphon of today's Mass will be our guide: "Have mercy on me, O Lord, for I cry to you all day long." This means you're in for a somber reflection rather than a feel-good-homily, a little consciousness raising for troubled times.

I want to talk about the N word.

How's that for an opening sentence as you tighten up wondering what's coming?

The "N' word. We readily know what we mean by the N word here in America. It's a word so freighted with bad memories, that in the public schools, for example, it has been excised from Mark Twain's classic, *Huckleberry Finn*. It's a word, a racially loaded slur that brings distain and punishment when uttered aloud.

But the terrible N word I want to talk about belongs to another part of the world, the Middle East. That's the place, you cannot help but know, where today Christians are literally being enslaved, tortured, beheaded, and crucified in their ancestral homes, the place of massive killings creating today's vast unending waves of immigrants fleeing the religious genocide. The radical Islamic State, or ISIS, is systematically exterminating Christians simply because they *are* Christians. It has left a trail of unspeakable horrors in its march through Syria and Iraq—videotaped beheadings, ritualized rape, the routine use of poison gas, grisly torture, and murder.

But note this—to further their terrible crusade, wherever ISIS goes, Christian homes are marked with the large Arabic letter "N." If the N word *here* is an insult, *there* the letter N is a death sentence. For fanatics the N letter is the Muslim definition of contempt for Christians. It stands for Nazarene, so named after Jesus of Nazareth. Yes, the N word in the Middle East has a new horrifying meaning. It's a new deadly house symbol that marks Christian households—the Nazarenes—for extermination. If the N letter provokes disgust here, the letter N word strikes terror in the Middle East.

As an aside, let me mention that here in America we also have our own massive intellectual and cultural forms of Christian persecution that seek—somewhat successfully—to exterminate religion and moral values, that condition us from remaining faithful to Jesus of Nazareth. But here it's done so entertainingly, so pervasively, that we don't even notice the large invisible N marked on our homes.

In the Middle East it's out in the open. It's happening especially in Iraq, a civilized country, once the home of the great Babylonia Empire, fabulous Baghdad, the Book of Jonah's Nineveh and the great lawgiver Hammurabi. The persecution of Christians there is unending. One particularly black day was in August 6th of 2014 when an ISIS offensive in the north broke out leaving thousands of Christians dead or homeless. Priests and sisters were tortured.

This offensive drove an estimated 120,000 Christians into exile inside the country and 600,000 outside the country into refugee camps in Turkey and Jordan and elsewhere. Their lives are miserable and so desperate are they and others like them to escape that they have become prey to unscrupulous smugglers who have no regard for human life, only profit as the Office of the UN's commission of Refugees lamented. Bundled in cars, vans, and trucks, this human cargo often winds up dead like the 71 recently found asphyxiated in a truck in Austria or the 2,500 lost at sea this year.

ISIS also invaded ancient Mosul, one of the largest Christian communities in the world, where they once lived peacefully with Muslims until the fanatics took over, and they murdered or expelled all the Christians with the aim of enforcing their interpretation of Islamic law. During that assault, venerable Christian churches and monasteries were destroyed, centuries-old Christian manuscripts were burned, sculptures smashed, paintings mutilated and scores of Christians were killed in the most terrible way by flogging, beheading and crucifixion. A year later, the Islamic State bulldozed Mar Elian, a 5th century Christian monastery in southeastern Syria containing many irreplaceable treasures—a part of their barbaric strategy to eradicate any semblance of Christianity.

Elsewhere in the Middle East there has been the same scenario. For example, the Christian population of Turkey, home to so many of St. Paul's visits and early Christian churches, and where the first Ecumenical Council of the Church, the Council of Nicaea in 325, was held, is evaporating rapidly from twenty percent to less than two percent today. Once Christians made up 84% of the population in Lebanon, but only thirty percent live there now. In Bethlehem, only the slimmest remnant of Christians survives. The vast birthplaces of Christianity are disappearing, and Christians are being persecuted as never before.

Today these persecuted Christians are refugees like the Jews were back in 1948 when they were purged from the Middle East. But the Jews had a place go to, the new State of Israel. The Christians have nowhere to go and must beg asylum wherever they can, often at great peril to their lives.

Sad to say, the secular West has largely ignored the plight of the Christians coming up with only a few hundred visas for the thousands and thousands of refugees seeking asylum. The *Catholic News Agency* reported on August 5th 2015 that "since October 2014, 906 Muslim refugees from Syria were granted U.S. visas while only twenty-eight Christians were given the same."

Pope Francis has added his deep concern. He said, "Today we are dismayed to see how in the Middle East and elsewhere in the world many of our brothers and sisters are persecuted, tortured, and killed for their faith in Jesus . . . They are today's martyrs, humiliated and discriminated against for their fidelity to the gospel. The Church must not forget or abandon its exiled children."

But it largely has. The Patriarch of Iraq lamented, "We feel forgotten and isolated." He said, "We sometimes wonder, if they kill us all, what would be the reaction of Christians in the West? Would they do something then?"

A good question. The point of my little lecture to a congregation of comfortable Christians, is that we should not forget our brothers and sisters of ancient roots, who at this very moment, are suffering physically as well as emotionally for the faith. Nor should we forget that our Lord and Master, Jesus, along with Mary and Joseph, were also once refugees fleeing a wicked king out to kill them, and lived several years in a foreign land. He lives on in these people.

End of reflection.

I close with a suggestion. Pray, of course, but also in solidarity raise your consciousness by going online and tapping in the words, "Aid to the Church in Need." This is a worldwide Catholic relief group. There you will find updates, information, stories of heroism and forgiveness and, most of all, how to help.

The loaded N word is back. Remember, it is a word of shame in the West, but it is a death sentence in the Middle East, that place today which continually prays:

"Have mercy on me, O Lord, for I cry to you all day long."

5TH SUNDAY, OT

CYCLE B

1 COR. 9:16-19, 22-23

32

Emil Kapaun

Today's 65 million refugees—the largest number since World War II—the horrific tortures and killings of ISIS who bury alive and crucify children, the oppression in Ukraine, Korea and Africa, religious persecution, ethnic cleansings, global suffering and injustices, are massive and appalling. Yet, against this background every tragedy, every age, has its small voice of protest, its heroic resistance, its determined love in a climate of hate, its ray of hope in time of despair. Among the million such unsung heroes, as an example of what goes on, let me share the story of a brave man, a brave soldier, a brave man, soldier, and priest, Father Emil Kapaun.

The son of Czech immigrants in a small town in Kansas, Kapaun enlisted in the army during WWII and was dispatched to the Southeast Asian theatre of war, where he soon gained a reputation for just appearing wherever the fighting was.

He returned home, received a masters in education from Catholic University, and then went on to become a parish priest in Pilsen Kansas. But it wasn't enough for him. Kapaun re-upped for military service in 1948. As a result, after the Communist invasion of South Korea, he wound up being among the first American troops who hit the beaches and pushed their way north through hard mountains and bitter cold.

Then Chinese forces entered the war with a massive surprise attack—perhaps 20,000 soldiers poured down on just a few thousand Americans. In the chaos of dodging bullets and explosions, Father Kapaun was seen racing between foxholes, out past the front lines and into no-man's land, dragging the wounded to safety. When his commanders ordered evacuation, he chose to stay in Korea. Kapaun resumed his constant presence under unbelievable hardship. Even when enemy fire rendered his jeep inoperable, he took to riding a bicycle along the front lines. One of his fellow prisoners, Ray M. Dowe, Jr., later wrote in *The Saturday Evening Post* in 1954 about the chaplain's rides:

"Helmet jammed down over his ears, pockets stuffed with apples and peaches he had scrounged from Korean orchards, he'd ride this bone-shaker over the rocky roads and the paths through the paddy fields until he came to the forward outposts. There he'd drop in a shallow hole beside a nervous rifleman, crack a joke or two, hand him a peach, say a little prayer with him, and move on to the next hole." It was no surprise that Chaplain Kapaun was awarded the Bronze Star in Korea for heroism in August 1950 for running through enemy fire, dragging soldiers to safety.

But eventually he was captured uninjured by the Chinese military in 1950, after refusing to leave wounded soldiers. On one occasion, he pushed away the weapon of a Chinese soldier standing over an American with a broken ankle, and the two were taken on the Tiger Death March to a North Korean prison camp, Pyoktong, with Kapaun carrying the solider for a time. On that terrible march, when other prisoners stumbled he picked them up. When they wanted to quit—knowing that stragglers would be shot—he begged them to keep going.

Kapaun was inventive and tireless. He turned old shirts into bandages, and snuck out to wash old bandages and old garments for the suffering. Among the dying, Capt. Emil Kapaun traded his watch for a blanket at a North Korean prison camp—and cut the blanket up and made it into socks for fellow prisoners.

Among the men he was called "The Good Thief," delivering stolen food retrieved on trips inside guards' areas. He recited American menus for starving prisoners, and led officers in "America, the Beautiful" and the national anthem "God Save the Queen" for Brits in the camp. He fixed leaking water pouches with the burned down soles of rubber boots and became, in general, a huge pain for Chinese guards trying to indoctrinate the prisoners. When guards would ask, "Where is your God now?" he would reply, "Right here."

The guards continued to ridicule his devotion to his Lord. They took his clothes and made him stand in the freezing cold for hours. Yet he never lost his faith. At night, he used to slip into huts to lead prisoners in prayer, saying the Rosary, administering the sacraments by offering three simple words, "God bless you." One of them later said that, with his very presence, he could just for a moment turn a mud hut into a cathedral.

That spring, he held an Easter service. As the sun rose that Easter Sunday, he put on his purple stole and led dozens of prisoners to the ruins of an old church in the camp. And he read from a prayer missal that he had kept hidden. He held up a small crucifix that he had made from sticks. And as the guards watched, Father Kapaun and all those prisoners—men of different faiths, perhaps some men of no faith—sang the Lord's Prayer and "America the Beautiful."

"That faith," wrote one survivor, "that they might be delivered from evil, that they could make it home, was perhaps the greatest gift to those men; that even amid hardship and despair, there could be hope, amid their misery in the temporal they could see those truths that are eternal . . . Looking back, one of them said that is what kept a lot of us alive."

"He joked with the soldiers and said prayers for them, and held them in his arms like children as delirium came upon them," Dowe wrote in 1954. "But the main thing he did for them was to put into their hearts the will to live. For when you are wounded and sick and starving, it's easy to give-up and quietly die."

Kapaun fell ill in the spring of 1951. Thin and frail, he began to limp with a blood clot in his leg. And then dysentery, then pneumonia. That's when the guards finally saw their chance to get rid of him. They came for him over the protests of the men who loved him. The guards sent him to a death house, a hellhole with no food or water to be left to die of starvation.

And yet even then his faith held firm. "I'm going to where I've always wanted to go, he told his brothers. And when I'm there I'll say a prayer for all of you." And then, as he was taken away, he blessed the guards, "Forgive them," he said, "for they know not what they do." Despite an apparently improved condition, guards took him away to a dingy, dark building to die alone. "Tell them back home that I died a happy death," he shouted. Two days later, he died. His body was taken away, his grave unmarked, his remains unrecovered to this day.

Kapaun was declared a "servant of God" by the Catholic Church, considered a precursor to sainthood.

President Obama, on April 11, 2013, posthumously awarded Father Kapaun, age 35, the Medal of Honor. He said, "This is the valor we honor today—an American soldier who didn't fire a gun, but who wielded the mightiest weapon of all, a love for his brothers so pure that he was willing to die so that they might live."

Among the wicked ones it's good now and then to remember the quietly heroic lovers.

7TH SUNDAY, OT
CYCLE A
MATTHEW 5:38-48

33

Violence

That gospel is, as you heard, Jesus' take on violence, his puzzling radical take I might add: Offer no resistance to one who is evil when everything in us tells us to fight back? We're no doormats. Turn the one cheek when one strikes us on the other, or when the movies din us with special-effects revenge in Technicolor? We're men and women of action and reaction! The quick kick in the gut, the fast gun, the explosive, the graphic torture. No wimpy "other cheek" for us is the media message.

Love your enemies, those SOBs? Actually *pray* for the scum who are persecuting us? They don't deserve it. Literally, to hell with them.

Yes, this is a tough countercultural teaching, almost impossible to follow, yet the fact is Jesus *is* preaching non-violence and we Christians find ourselves wallowing in violence day in and day out, year in and year out, and it hasn't solved one blessed thing but keeps on escalating: the Ukraine, Sudan, Egypt, Syria, Venezuela, Nigeria, our own USA and, to narrow it down, my own state as the publicized violence and murders in Camden, Newark, Asbury Park, Lakewood, and Patterson remind us.

Last week, for example, the *Asbury Park Press* had an article about a young man, 25, being sentenced to life imprisonment for murder. His name is Carl Holdren of Lakewood, a high-ranking member of the Blood's street gang affiliate, "Sex, Money, Murder." He killed another rival gang member. His nickname is "Killa," and he was indicted along with Qumer "Tragedy" McClendon, Valdo "Soldier Boy" Thompson Jr., Zackery "Zoo" Butts and Darnell "D-Nell" [death knell] Stovall.

All are in their mid-20s and will spend most of their lives in jail, a violent place. What a waste. What a loss. But violence, notice, is their self-adopted name—killa, soldier boy, death knell—and violence is their game. It may be theirs, but it's definitely not Jesus Christ's.

One wonders how they got to such violence, why they advertise it with their names, their violent video games, violent TV, the avalanche of violent movies that fills our screens? Unemployment? Prejudice? Poverty? But not all poor, unemployed people are violent. One suspects broken homes led them to forge artificial gangs for the family they needed but never had. One suspects drugs.

Whatever, Jesus weeps. After all, they're only eight or nine years younger than he was when he was violently killed. Anyway, to be more emphatic, take note that Jesus did walk the talk as we say. When he and his disciples were going through Samaritan territory—an enemy gang's turf—and his followers asked him if they should call down fire and destruction on them, Jesus said no, skip the violence and let's go a roundabout way.

Soon we'll be into Lent and its terrible passion. We find that in the garden, when some hothead pulled out the violent sword Jesus ordered him to put it away. *That's not who we are*, he said. That's not what we're about. Those who take up the sword will perish by the sword. We find him before three violent men, Caiaphas, Pilate, and Herod. "Have you no answer?" they asked. He didn't. He was silent. No threats, no invective. He knew that these violent people would not understand his non-violence.

When the soldiers tortured him, he did not strike back but instead absorbed it all, took it all in, determined to break the cycle. Violence would go no further. It would stop with him.

When the crowd, the high, and power brokers jeered at him on the cross, he did not curse them but took their toxic words into himself, into his deep self, into his absorbent love. The Prince of Peace prayed for his violent executioners because he was determined to stop the cycle of violence. It had to stop or somewhere else it would go on and on.

For a while, you know, people actually listened to him. In fact, so profound were Jesus' teaching and example that, for the record, for the first few centuries Christians were forbidden to join the military.

Anyway, his teaching and example are at the heart of Christianity—we can't excise them—and we are obliged to measure ourselves against them, to act in accordance with them, as a test to see whether we are disciples or just followers.

Let me share a true story.

My story, told to me by an Irish friend, is from the penal law days in Ireland when the British forbade the open practice of the Catholic faith and forbade Catholics to assemble. It was the days of the hedge school teachers: the catechists who gathered the children in the thick hedges and secretly taught them their catechism, and the days of what was called the "priest holes," a little cupboard under the staircase where the priest hid—very much like Harry Potter living under the staircase. Remember the letter sent to him from Hogwarts? Remember the address?

> Mr. H. Potter
> The Cupboard Under the Stairs
> 4 Privet Drive
> Little Whinging
> Surrey

That was the priest's residence. The priest never knew when the cupboard door would be ripped open and he would be executed.

Anyway, the story: One morning in Donegal, a farmer herds his four black cows along with one white one into a corral. This is a code, a sign, to his fellow Catholics as to where Mass will be held at noon: this sign of four and one means a particular hedge under a hill. The people casually drift away from their work before noon and assemble silently around a rock where the Mass will be celebrated.

The priest is forty years old. He gets halfway through the Mass, but just after the Consecration, when he lifts up the Host, he is drilled between the eyes with a bullet from a British soldier on the hill. The priest falls down dead and the host flutters into the mud. The usual raid then ensues and several men are arrested, and the priest is buried in a pauper's grave. The soldier is a man aged forty. He has a young son about the age of ten. The soldier finishes his year of duty in Ireland and goes home to Bristol. His son turns out to be a scholarly lad and, in time, goes to a university and then into the ministry. At the age of thirty the boy is an Anglican curate, with all his future smiling before him and there are many who think he will be archbishop of Canterbury before long.

But something happens to the boy and he grows more and more interested in how Anglicanism grew from Catholicism. This, of course, is a dangerous road and his superiors frown upon his inquiries, but he persists. By the time he is thirty-five, he makes the break and converts to Catholicism. Five years later he is a Catholic priest, much to the immense dismay of his father.

One night the father, a bit in his cups, terribly frustrated and angry, loses his temper and tells his son something he has never confessed to a soul, not even to his late wife, the boy's mother: that he shot and killed a priest just as the priest raised the Consecrated Host. The son is horrified and covers his face with his hands as the father, shouting, says he never regretted that shot for an instant, and that he never made such a fine shot before or since, and that the priest and his fellow conspirators got what they deserved, just that, only that, exactly that.

A month later, the son, having researched the annals of the constabulary for the incident visited the village and asked its oldsters where hedge Masses were held in the dark days. He finds the rock under the hill and gathers the villagers one morning and finishes the Mass that was interrupted thirty years before by a bullet.

When Mass was over, he and the villagers bury an unconsecrated host and a bullet in the earth by the rock, and then they all trail along back to the village.

Bury the bullet. No more violence.

It was Mohamed Gandhi who said that if we keep on practicing an eye for an eye and a tooth for a tooth, we're going to wind up with a blind and toothless universe. And he was right. We are in a world that is blind and toothless and, as a result, it is violent verbally, physically, and sexually.

Maybe Jesus foresaw all this when he taught that loving your neighbors but hating your enemies won't cut it. No, pray for the unworthy no-goods. And why? Because this way you will be like your heavenly Father who lets his sun shine on the bad and the good indiscriminately.

In other words, if for no other reason—and listen to this—if for no other reason than this, imitate the way my Father treats you, sinner that you are. Yes, he will treat us as we treat others. It's his golden rule. Think about that. That should be motive enough to put away violence, to bury the bullet.

8TH SUNDAY, OT
CYCLE A
1 COR. 4:1-5

34

The Three Stages of the Spiritual Life

Spiritual writer and Benedictine nun, Sister Joan Chittister, reminds us that the spiritual life is a process which usually—and hopefully—progresses in three stages from one level to another.

The first stage is compliance. This is the stage of the minimal, the rule-keeping. Being spiritual in this stage depends on keeping the official lists of do's and don'ts, of keeping count and fussing if the count is off or you are forced to skip a First Friday or novena day, or a break or a rule of the Church. This is the penitent who confesses missing Mass because she was sick in bed with the flu or in a car accident and was in the hospital for a month; the penitent who forgot it was Friday and accidentally ate meat—as if anyone could commit a sin by accident.

The drawback at this stage is that we really don't make choices. We simply do it or we don't. We conform or rebel. We do what we're told and call ourselves holy for having done so. We do everything we're told, but never ask whether or not what we're doing has anything to do with the Beatitudes or real life.

The second stage of the spiritual life is a giant step that moves beyond mere compliance. It is awareness. It has to do more with becoming Christian—becoming Christ-like—than it does with going through the rituals of being Christian, as important as they are. It's more internal. It's an attitude.

This stage of spiritual development awakens in us the awareness that our role as Christians is to witness to others a life of personal integrity and moral honesty, that our role to help make the world a just and peaceful place. We are not simply to make ourselves paragons of churchy correctness, examples of organizational piety but disciples. To put it another way, at this second level of the spiritual life we come to realize that although God began the process of creation, it is our responsibility to complete it. In other words, we begin to conceive of ourselves as having a calling, a vocation. We were put here for a purpose beyond simply consuming and building the good life for ourselves.

So in our own small way, we begin to build bridges rather than walls, we try practicing forgiveness, to go out of ourselves for the sake of others, for the sake of the world, rather than simply rewarding ourselves gold stars for being regular observers of ancient rituals. We seek to live beyond the pleasure principle.

In short, this second stage of awareness consists of the realization that, however humble our station in life, we matter and are called to give an account of our lives. We are called to make a difference. We sense that. We embrace it. We have a holy awareness that we are important in God's scheme of things, and that's a good spiritual place to be in.

Finally, the third stage of the spiritual life is transformation. This, I think, is the level of the saints. Here we begin, as St. Paul wrote, slowly but surely, to put on the mind, the values, the attitude, of Jesus. "Put on the Lord Jesus" were his words. In short, we begin to think like him, to see like him.

We begin to adopt an inner sense of what it means to be honest in a world of bribery and deceit by cutting corners or being number one; what it means to be just in an unjust world, meek in an arrogant one, humble in a domineering one, accepting in a prejudiced one, and compassionate in an oppressive one.

We begin to see the world as Jesus sees it. Though we may be unaware of it, with all our limitations and failures, we're moving towards the transformation into being what the ancients call the *Alter Christus*, another Christ.

Let me share the stories of two people who moved beyond the rules, two people who couldn't be more different, one a minister and the other an SS guard.

Louis Saunders was a Disciples of Christ minister and pastor in Texas. He was serving at a church in Fort Worth when he learned that the most hated man on earth at the time was going to be buried in his town. The man was Lee Harvey Oswald, who had assassinated President Kennedy and who had in turn been killed by Jack Ruby. Saunders knew that Oswald's mother was a Lutheran, so he called around to arrange for two Lutheran ministers to conduct the service. They weren't sure they should comply. After all, this man had killed the President. Think of it! But Saunders coaxed them into it. Everything was put in place and, when the day arrived, Saunders stopped by the cemetery to observe.

When he got there, he found out that the ministers, fearful of being exposed to potential snipers, had backed out. The small, forlorn and impoverished Oswald family went over and asked Saunders to fill in. He struggled with stages one and two as we might say—would he be breaking the rule to bless such an unblessed person? Then, too, the Oswald family was of a different faith. Could he have any part of them? But he became aware that something deeper was calling to him and he responded. He had no ritual, so from memory he recited the 23rd Psalm and then at the end simply added, "Mrs. Oswald tells me that her son, Lee, was a good boy and that she loved him. And today, Lord, we commit his spirit to your divine care." Short, simple, transformative.

As we said, there was no one in the country more hated than Lee Oswald. No one had anything good to say about him except his mother—and the Reverend Louis Saunders and, of course, the God who came into the world to reclaim sinners.

An Auschwitz survivor: "You know everything was terrible in Auschwitz. There was no food, there was no water; there was cold, you didn't know whether your father or mother were alive. I worked in a factory. One day it was almost Christmas and the snow that fell was like a table set for guests—it was so white and beautiful. And, of course, we had to work inside starting at 5 o'clock in the morning and finishing 5 o'clock at night, and not having food or anything we need. The foreman was watching us every minute, making sure we were making every ammunition part that was supposed to be made. And then the foreman looked at me and called me over."

"I was terrified. I was sure I was going to be punished because all the way walking over to him, the SS man is there smacking his whip against his hand. You don't work fast or you don't do work like it's supposed to be done, they beat you. I was 15 years old and my legs were shaking. I am trying to tell him, please don't hurt me. Please, I will work faster. And the foreman says to bend over and I feel he is about to beat me when he whispers, 'Here, take this bread. Put it under your coat and go out fast.'"

"The SS man was standing behind him and he saw the whole thing. He should have followed protocol and turned me and the foreman in, but, amazingly, he did nothing. He also put his life on the line to give a child a chance. Have you any idea what a slice of bread meant? Could you imagine that I am starving? Instead of beating me, the foreman gave me bread and the SS guard gave me a pass. Both gave me life."

Beyond compliance to rules, beyond awareness, there was a grace-filled moment when both foreman and soldier did the transformative thing and traversed the stages of the spiritual life. God was present and a life was saved.

8TH SUNDAY, OT
CYCLE C
LUKE 6:39-45

35

One by One: A Patchwork of Stories

An election or two ago, *USA Today* ran a series of articles on what Americans are worried about. After all the comments about employment, jobs, the economy, the terrible wars, violence, the persistent and basic concern was about values, moral values, about how the country is basically soul sick: so rich in things but poor in people, so near to self, so distant from community, so strong on "me" yet so fragile on "us." The impression is that as a nation we cling to shadow over substance, personality over character. We are awash in celebrities, smothered in advertising. Responsibility for one's actions, respect for others, fairness, and integrity are values that were missing. In short, people felt the moral center is not holding.

Unfortunately, these sentiments haven't changed over time. And I could launch into all kinds of long sociological and theological explanations that would put you to sleep. Instead, in search of an answer, I am going to tell you a half-dozen stories about real people. People are always the best homilies.

A woman once wrote that when she was ten she found a brown wallet. There wasn't any money in it, but she was savvy enough to know that when she returned it she would get a reward. She could hardly wait. All day she called the number found in the brown wallet, but there was no answer. Finally, her dad relented and drove her to the owner's address. It was a modest military housing unit with a torn screen door. As she rang the bell, her dad took three $20 bills and tucked them into the wallet. She remarked that it turned out that her reward was getting to see one of life's true heroes in action. She still remembers and tries to live that memory.

When Michael Keaton, whose real name is Michael Douglas, won the Golden Globe award as best actor for the film *Birdman,* he delivered a memorable speech that focused on his family,

"My name is Michael John Douglas. I'm from Forest Grove, Pennsylvania. I'm the son, seventh child—of George and Leona Douglas. And I don't ever remember a time when my father didn't work two jobs. When my mother wasn't saying the rosary, or going to Mass, or trying to take care of seven kids in a rundown farmhouse, she was volunteering at the Ohio Valley Hospital where I was born in a hallway. In the household in which I was raised, the themes were pretty simple: work hard, don't quit, be appreciative, be thankful, be respectful. My best friend is kind, intelligent, funny, talented, considerate thoughtful . . . He also happens to be my son, Sean. I love you with all my heart, buddy. This [holding up his award] is for all those people." Do parents ever realize the great privilege, the awesome responsibility, they have? Love of God, respect for others, forgiveness, and what really matters are lifelong messages they are forging every day. Faith, hope, and love begin with them as no other.

For example, growing daughters eleven-year-old, Rosalie Elliot, a spelling champion from South Carolina was asked at the fourth national spelling bee in Washington to spell "avowal." However, her soft southern accent made it difficult for the judges to determine if she had used an 'a' or an 'e' as the next to last letter of the world. The judges deliberated, listened to recording playbacks but still couldn't determine which letter had been pronounced.

Finally, the chief judge put the question to the only person who knew the answer. He asked Rosalie, "Was the letter an 'a' or an 'e'"? Rosalie knew by now the correct spelling of the word but without hesitation she replied that she had misspelled the word and used an 'e.' As she walked from the stage, the entire audience stood and applauded her. She did not win the contest, but she had definitely emerged a winner that day.

No mystery where she learned that.

The incident I'm relating happened a dozen years ago when, on Christmas Eve, a stressed-out Christine Basney was raising four children, studying in college, and working in a small Michigan country story when Richard Heath walked in. Heath bought a scratch-off lottery ticket and won $100. He asked for the winnings in two $50 bills, then he gave one to Basney and one to another co-worker as holiday gifts.

Fast forward ten years later. Basney, now a registered nurse, walks into a patient's room to introduce herself. She was surprised to see it was Heath. They both recognized one another. "As soon as I saw him, my eyes welled up with tears . . . I told him that Christmas, 2002 had been the roughest one ever for me and that $50 went a long way. I was deeply honored to be caring for him. I never forgot how kind total strangers can be"—here's the spiritual zinger—"and I have tried my hardest to be as kind as the lottery man."

That's how love works: it isn't taught. It's caught.

A few years ago, an unemployed mother of three, Jessica Robles, attempted to steal $300 worth of groceries from a supermarket in Miami. She was caught. It just so happened that police officer Vicki Thomas arrived at the scene and asked Robles her reason for shoplifting. She responded that she did it to feed her three kids. Instead of taking her to jail, the cop gave her a notice to appear in court on a misdemeanor charge. But then Officer Thomas used $100 of her own money to buy groceries for the Robles family. She delivered them herself and witnessed the joy on the kids' faces that they actually had something to eat. When the story spread around, another $700 was donated for the Robles family and soon a local business owner hired Robles for a job.

Just as greed and selfishness spread from one to one, so do kindness and generosity.

Finally, there's George Shuba of Youngstown, Ohio—a less than average baseball player with the old Brooklyn Dodgers. So why, when he died at 89 in 2014, did he rate a long obituary in *The New York Times*? Because way back in 1946 when a baseball player named Jackie Robinson, the first black player in the history of organized baseball, made his debut with the Montreal Royals, he hit a homer. When he ran the bases, George Shuba did what so many of the others were unwilling to do so—greet him with a warm handshake. That was witness.

If our country has lost its soul, it's because too many lives have not been enfolded early on with the moral embracers we call parents, family, friends, neighbors, community, and public icons. But where it happens, we have fathers with compassion, actors with gratitude, kids with integrity, strangers with heart, officers with pity, and ball players with courage.

As a result, hopefully kids will grow up to be politicians who put the common good before vested interests, CEOs who put people before profit, legislators who put justice before party and media moguls who put human dignity before exploitation.

The moral to all these stories is that restoring our national soul begins with us, one by one. Not the government, not education, not even the Church can match that. They can only support us one by one. One by one, need I say, is you and I, and we are here beseeching God's Spirit to grow in us.

11TH SUNDAY, OT

CYCLE C

LUKE 7:36 - 8:3

36

307

Let's start off with a bit of Christian trivia: you're probably generally aware that at different times Jesus asked some questions, like, "Who was neighbor to the man who fell in with the robbers?" or "Who do people say that I am?" or "Will you also go away?" "Could you not watch one hour with me?" Most remember these.

But did you know that he asked 307 of them? Yes, in those four short gospels Jesus asked 307 questions . . . 307! Remember his first recorded words are a question, "Did you not know that I must be about my Father's business?" And his last words were a question, "My God, my God, why have you abandoned me?" Furthermore, people who like to count things tell us he in turn was asked 183 questions and answered less than ten of them. Jesus obviously prefers to ask questions than provide direct answers

No mystery here. Jesus was a first-century Jew and so he stood in the tradition of the old vaudeville exchange: "Why does a Jew always answer a question with a question?" Response: "Why shouldn't a Jew always answer a question with a question?" Jesus was part of his culture and times, which means that less than one percent of the population could read or write, which means that storytelling—parables - were the common means of conveying thought and wisdom, and that questions were the ordinary means to stimulate storytelling and extracting wisdom. Think of Aesop, Socrates, the Hebrew prophets, and the Zen Masters.

Tanya and Ezidio were Buddhist monks who, after a pilgrimage, were returning home. It was the monsoon season and so, as they approached a familiar stream, it was flooded. Standing there in distress was a lovely maiden afraid to forge the raging waters. Tanya kindly offered to carry her across, which he did and she was grateful and left. But Ezidio was brooding to the extent he could no longer hold his tongue. "Tanya," he accused, "Why did you carry that maiden across the stream? You know we monks do not look at women much less touch them, especially beautiful maidens such as that one?" Tanya replied with a question, "I put her down on the other side of the stream. Are you still carrying her?"

Wisdom.

So, to today's gospel. As you heard, while Jesus was dining at Simon the Pharisee's house, a woman described as a sinner crashes the party, falls at Jesus' feet and begins to bathe them with her tears and dry them with her hair. Because she is known as a sinner, the Pharisees and other people of that polite company have nothing to do with her. Upright people act as if she does not exist. These conventions are so strong that Simon simply assumed that Jesus must not recognize that she is a sinner. He concluded he does not see her for who she is because, if he did, he too would treat her as invisible.

It is in this context that Jesus asks, "Do you see this woman?" A probing question. The woman is right in front of them, but that does not mean that they all see her. Simon sees only what sort of woman she is. Jesus does not see a *sort* of woman. He sees *this* woman. He sees not what she is, but what she can be. He means, "Do you see this woman, really see her? Yes, she is a sinner but she can be much more. Can you see beyond to redemption, repentance, or renewal? Can you see her as loved by my Father?"

The heaviest burden in this life, bar none, is not to be seen, to be passed by, dismissed, pigeonholed, not noticed, to be accounted as having little or no worth. We all desperately crave to be seen, to be validated, and counted as worthy. When we are not, we either withdraw or act out sometimes in very destructive ways.

An insightful youth worker made it one of his goals to

make the kids feel truly seen. So, if someone is in a funk and grumpy, he will say, "He just wants to be seen in his unhappiness." If someone dropped out of the group, he would say, "I don't think he felt seen here." People will go to extremes to be seen, to be noticed, especially by the significant people in their lives.

Three stories, one funny, one with a bite, and the third the gospel retold: The young woman had just gotten engaged. She was all excited, eagerly waiting to show off her ring at the office. She arrived and, waving her hand all around, made a big show of taking off her coat. No one noticed. Later she stood in the room talking animatedly, waving her ringed hand all around, but again no one noticed. Finally, later on she said out loud to no one in particular, "Whew, it's hot in here. I think I'll take off my engagement ring!"

Hey, notice me!

Then there's the man who relates, "We had a power outage at our house. My PC, laptop, TV, DVD, iPad, and my new surround sound music system were all shut down. Then I discovered that my phone battery was flat and, to top it off, it was raining outside so I couldn't play golf. I went to the kitchen to make some coffee and then I remembered this also needs power. So, with nothing to do, I sat and talked with my wife for a few hours."

"You know, she seems like a pretty nice person." There's a whole subtext in that story!

Finally, this woman: I grew up knowing that I was different and hated it. I was born with a cleft palate and when I started school my classmates made it clear to me what they saw: a little girl with a misshapen lip, crooked nose, lopsided teeth, and garbled speech. When they would ask what happened to my lip, I'd tell them that I'd fallen and cut it on a piece of glass. Somehow it seemed more acceptable to have suffered an accident than to have been born that way. I was convinced that no one outside my family could love me.

There was however a teacher in the second grade whom we all adored—Mrs. Leonard by name. She was short, round, happy—a sparkling lady. Annually, we would have a hearing test. I was virtually deaf in one of my ears, but when I had taken the test in the past, I discovered that if I did not press my hand as tightly upon my ears as I was instructed to, I could pass the test. Mrs. Leonard gave the test to everyone in class and finally it was my turn. I knew from past years that as we stood against the door and covered one ear, the teacher sitting at her desk would whisper something and we would have to repeat it back, the usual things like, "the sky is blue" or "do you have new shoes?"

I waited there and, to my surprise, heard those words which God must have put into her mouth, those seven words that changed my life. Mrs. Leonard said in her whisper, "I wish you were my little girl." Then and there I knew that she saw me, not as misshapen and imperfect, but for what I truly was: a beautiful child of God."

Let me end and sum up the gospel message with a reference to that old wonderful movie, *The Enchanted Cottage*—still replayed at times on TV. Robert Young plays a war pilot horribly disfigured by shrapnel, and Dorothy McGuire plays a homely maid. They meet at the remote cottage to which Young has fled. He hides in his room, keeps away from the public because he is so repulsive. She retreats to the cottage because she has so often been rejected by the soldiers at the local canteen, soldiers who approach her from the back and flee when she turns around and they see her face.

Two misfits thrown together. Gradually they begin to tolerate one another and then slowly, fall in love. One golden moment after an argument, she runs to her bedroom, falls downward on the bed and cries and cries. Chastened, he comes in to talk to her, to say he's sorry and gently turns her over. When he does, she is radiant. She is beautiful. And when she dries her tears and looks at him, he is handsome.

From then on when the other characters in the movie see them, the camera shows the old disfigured, homely faces they actually have, but whenever they look at each other, the camera shows them as beautiful and handsome. It's then they discover the secret of the Enchanted Cottage—and the gospel: love transforms.

"Simon, do you see this woman, really see her?"

12TH SUNDAY, OT

CYCLE C

GALATIANS 3:26-29

37

The Church in Conversation with AA

Recently I had lunch with a friend, a devout Catholic who is in recovery.

"It's hard when we read the Big Book and get to Bill's letter about clergy," she said. "The Big Book," she explained, "refers to the Alcoholics Anonymous handbook written primarily by AA co-founder Bill Wilson. He writes that, over time, he came to accept, and actually admire, some of them." Then she sighed, "When we get to those lines, almost everyone in the room groans."

The groaning indicates that some members—many?—had less than happy memories of clergy or organized religion. In fact, for many of those who attend the meetings with my friend, and her brothers and sisters elsewhere, AA and other 12-Step programs have become their default church.

This "church," I learned, is a blend of many faces. In this church, you'll find victims of clergy abuse who, as you can imagine, can barely force themselves to enter a *church* basement where the meetings are held. There are those who have felt spiritually starved in what they experienced as a cold, judgmental, and unforgiving Church culture. There are those whose memory is one that is less dialogue and more monologue, one of being talked to rather than of being talked with in conversation. And there are those who feel isolated by the lack of welcome or superficial greetings among those in the pews.

I asked my friend about this. She laughed and commented, "If I had a dollar for every person who has asked me, 'Why can't the Church be more like AA?' I'd be dining out every night." Too often, much too often, I thought to myself, she's right. I shudder at how righteous, rigid, or insensitive some clergy can be.

I know. I have another friend named Mohammed Almallah, a Muslim who converted to Catholicism. He is a devout, serious Catholic. Both he and his wife are truly pious and caring. They live their faith. When they had their darling daughter Rosalina, they went to the parish church to arrange for her baptism. The priest would agree on one condition: that they change their last name. "What kind of Catholic can she be with a Muslim name like Almallah?" he challenged. Fortunately, they found a priest who was more Christ-like.

So, maybe it is time for the Church to sit down and have a conversation with AA, to find out in what ways the 12-Steps answer deep spiritual needs which the Catholic Church can learn from the encounter? Can the Church begin to address its own sources of spiritual poverty with new honesty and compassion, and put on the mind of Christ as in St. Paul's wonderful phrase?

So, we start the conversation.

Church: Where do you think we ought to begin?

AA: First rule, come as you are.

Church: What do you mean by that?

AA: Well, there's no "dressing up" in AA. By this, I mean more than just a wardrobe, though this is a good place to start. When your people get ready for Mass, they tend to put on their best. This is as it should be. They should show some respect and reverence. But truth be told, they also do it to keep up appearances. They know that they will see and be seen. They tend to adopt the "dress code" of the church community of which they're a part. They dress up, and evaluate others on this basis of how they look. They carry in society's conditioning of being nice, proper people. They bring their cell phones and preoccupations, their surface responses, code of conduct and, most of all, their subconscious assumptions about goodness and decency. They bring their virtues. They don't know it but they are acting out of any kind of socially sanctioned script. For us, there's no pressure to put on a happy face, no need to calculate how many "likes" we get on Facebook. Not even a stiff-upper-lip attitude. No pretense. At a 12-Step AA meeting, it's quite the opposite. It's a meeting of the imperfect.

Church: Did this insight originate from Bill Wilson, your founder?

AA: Yes. Bill once told the story about the time in May 1935, when he was in the lobby of the Mayflower Hotel in Akron and a business deal had fallen through. He heard sounds of laugher and ice tinkling in the bar, and found himself thinking what he had not thought in over five months, "I need a drink!" But then, by some miracle, that impulse was pushed out of his mind by a completely new idea. "No," he found himself saying, "I don't need a drink. I need another alcoholic!" He began a series of phone calls until he contacted Dr. Robert Smith, another alcoholic who would later become co-founder of AA. Years later, Wilson would recall their meeting. "I knew I needed this alcoholic as much as he needed me. I needed this mutual give and take."

Church: What did he mean by that?

AA: He meant that only another similarly broken person could allow him to reveal his own brokenness without being ashamed.

Church: Hmmm . . . All right . . . So how does an AA meeting differ from going to church?

AA: In AA, people come as they truly are, people with their wounds and addictions and wretched experiences. They come with a life out of control, a passionate need to be sober for one more day, a deep dependency on God, a humble striking of the breast, whose prayer of "O God, be merciful to me a sinner!" is not a quotation but a cry.

Church: Go on.

AA: Struggle is the common ground that unites us. Regret is the common bond. Honesty, the common language: *I am out of control. I am hurting myself. I am hurting others. I need help. I need God.* "Good morning. My name is Joe, and I am an alcoholic."

Church: You're saying, only if we would be a Church like that: consciously an assembly of the broken. Otherwise we find it hard to appreciate that too often you have barely made it to Mass because you couldn't get in focus, or the kids were sick, or you had an argument with your spouse, or you're swamped with unpaid bills—only to be exhorted by us to copy the wisdom and perfection of the saints, most of whom were never married.

AA: Right. Don't the priests know that when we are vulnerable, tired, struggling, or just looking for the light at the end of the tunnel, even the parables can become the mountain too far to climb? Why do they focus on "goodness"—good behavior, good works, virtue, and aspiration when life, in fact, is often flawed, painful, complex, and difficult? When we are trying our best, the emphasis on doing even better can set us on the slippery slope from compassion and forgiveness to judgment and self-righteousness. It can leave us even lonelier than we were before.

Church: Anything else?

AA: Yes, one more thing. In AA, the people's voices are heard. There is no intermediary, no "expert," no high priest; in our AA "church," there's no judgmental attitude. Sharing one another's journeys, tales of tragedy and loss and resurrection are the profound gifts that the group gives its members. As a result, we discover in ourselves a wisdom and strength we didn't realize we possessed. We gain perspective on our problems and learn to bring them to a "Higher Power." In short, in recovery people are able to share their wisdom in a safe and supportive setting. I have to say, there is not much listening in the Church. Sorry about that.

Church: No! no! No need to apologize. Well, you've given me much to think about to forge better platforms and places where people can be heard, about how our homilies need to be about where the people are rather than where we are, and about how we must be learners as well as teachers.

For the people, too, at least those who *do* come to church, I guess we have to remind them that they have to come with a greater humility, a stronger sense of the need for a Higher Power, and a respect for the broken, perhaps even join them in a bit of breast striking.

AA: I'll drink to that!
Church: You can say that?
AA: Sure. If you can't laugh at yourself, you haven't fully recovered.

Loving in Weakness

"Therefore, I am content with weaknesses, insults, hardships, persecutions and calamities for the sake of Christ; for whenever I am weak, then I am strong."

So wrote St. Paul, never knowing that two thousand years later I would use his words to construct the homily you are about to hear—but I begin with this caution: it's going to be a sensitive homily, both to preach and to listen. That's because it hits on some tender spots for many of us here. On the surface, it's about dads—the kind of homily you would expect on Father's Day—but underneath it tells a deep truth for us all.

I start off with a tale told by a son, Father John Donato, an associate vice president at the Catholic University of Portland in Oregon. Here is his story. Listen.

I met my late father again two years ago at Christmas. I was visiting my mother, her memory now almost wholly faded and I opened an old box, and there were all the Christmas letters my father had written annually to my mother. They were married for 35 years, the last ten of those with my dad increasingly sick, but he wrote her a love letter every year. I sat there with his letters in my hands and was flooded by memories.

My dad was one of seven boys in a family of eight children. His dad had emigrated from Sicily. My dad was the quietest and perhaps the brightest of the children. He loved languages and relished learning new words. He was the only man I ever knew who read dictionaries for fun.

He was good at numbers and details. By age eight he had already purchased an accounting ledger and made entries in it for every penny he earned and spent. Naturally, he became a banker. His clients loved him.

He loved to fish and golf. He never swore, even on the golf course; he explained to me that vulgarity was for those who could not find proper words to express their thoughts and feelings.

He met my mother at a church dance shortly after the end of the Korean War. He was with one of his old high school flames when he encountered my mother at the dance wearing pink shoes. Both were fine dancers; they danced and my father, who had come with another young lady as his date, offered to drive my mother home. My dad's date was not pleased.

My mother quizzed her girlfriends about my dad—was he a good man? Did he come from a good family? Yes, and yes. My mother accepted my dad's offer. He fell in love with her immediately. He later said that when he came home that night he was ready to get married, start a family, and make his way into the world. My mother, however much she was also smitten, made him wait a respectful ten months, from meeting to marrying. A year later they had my older brother.

"If something should ever happen to you, I would continue, though as an empty shell of a man," my father wrote to my mother the first Christmas they were married.

I think my happiest childhood memories have to do with late afternoon when my mother would cook a simple and delicious dinner, bathe, and then emerge radiant and perfumed for dinner. My dad would walk in with the *Wall Street Journal* under his arm, and cigar and briefcase in hand. Frank Sinatra or Dean Martin sang as my mother kissed him. Sometimes they would dance for a few moments. She would often reach over during dinner and gently rub his neck. My dad's last Christmas letter to my mother ends with this question, "Do you really know just how much I love you for just being you?"

When I visit my mom now, with her memory wholly gone, she calls me Paul—my dad's name. I find that I am proud to be called Paul.

He was quiet and pensive with me. He was an oversized presence, sometimes causing me to lose my sense of footing and confidence yet he was patient with me, teaching me to throw and catch a baseball, ride a bicycle, bait a hook, drive a car, showing me how to steer safely out of a skid on snow or ice.

In my deepest memory, the furthest back, I am on the diving board, high over a motel pool. I am scared and enticed by the height. My dad and my older brother have been diving off the high board and now it's my turn. I tiptoe to the edge and glance down at the faraway pool, lose my breath, and gasp and squeal that I can't. I can't. My mother and brother both call encouragingly, but I look to my dad, and he nods and then I leap.

When I was fourteen, my dad had a stroke. After that he was mostly bedridden for the next ten years, until he died, not yet aged sixty. By age sixteen, I knew I wanted to be a priest.

My dad thought this a childish phase that would pass; he advised me, in no uncertain terms, to be a lawyer. We argued. We argued so bitterly that I fled the house once. I was gone for two whole days.

When I came home, exhausted and scared, my fragile father stood up from his couch with a face so sad and loving and told me that he loved me, and we would figure it all out and if I wanted to go to college and work towards being a priest, that was fine. And in the years after that, as he grew weaker and weaker, more often he would embrace me and kiss my cheek and whisper, *I love you, John. I love you.*

Now I know that he always loved me, but he was not strong enough to tell me so. Only in his weakness did he grow strong enough for that. And I love him, and I always will until the day comes when I can kiss him on the cheek and tell him, *I love you, Dad. I love you.*

A touching story.

On one level, the story embarrasses us men, and I apologize to my gender for telling it and making us all feel uneasy in front of others. It embarrasses us because it reveals the truth that, really deep down, we do love and feel but we find it hard to express these sentiments outright. It's a guy thing, and the women and children in our lives should give us some slack and try to understand us, if not appreciate us.

But it's the closing words of the story that should capture all of us, men and women alike. Listen to it once more: "Now I know that he always loved me, but was not strong enough to tell me so; only in weakness did he grow strong enough for that."

There you have the great spiritual paradox: when we are self-focused, self-controlled, self-made, riding high, in charge with our "got it made," "I'm number one" attitude; when we are "strong," we tend to ignore others and God. But when we are weak, put down, dependent, felled by loss, sickness, disaster, betrayal, shame, disappointment, our world falling apart then, at that point, we may be strong enough to say, "I love you," to family, to friends, and to God. We have to be down and out to see things differently. We have to experience need and vulnerability in order to be able to cry out, "O God, be merciful to me, a sinner!"

Many a person has found redemption in weakness. St. Paul, as we heard at the beginning, was one of them when he went from persecutor to persecuted and wrote, "For whenever I am weak then I am strong." Only in weakness can we grow strong enough to say *I love you* to those near-and-dear, and to God. Only when we turn down the noise of self-importance can we hear God. *Do you really know just how much I love you for just being you?*

5TH SUNDAY, OT
CYCLE A
ISAIAH 58:7-10

39

Résumé Versus Eulogy

Let's begin appropriately, with Jesus. Let's begin with his words that have become less forceful from familiarity. "See the lilies of the field. They neither spin or weave, yet not even Solomon in all of his glory was arrayed like one of these. Consider the mustard seed, the smallest of all yet it grows to be the greatest bush. She—the widow—gave more from her little store than those with great possessions. Unless you become like little children, you will not enter the kingdom of heaven. The one who would be master of all would do well to be the servant of all."

Let's give them new life as we tune into a David Brooks' column that asked readers the big question: *What is the purpose of life, the meaning of life?*

He received thousands of answers and he could not but help notice one common theme that kept appearing. It surprised him because he had expected the answer to the purpose or meaning of life to be the usual clichés hectored in annual commencement speeches. You know: dream large, fulfill your potential, make it big, catch the career, the world is waiting for you. Yes, the cameras are rolling for you and life's purpose is being there in the spotlight, endlessly repeating to the world what Norma Desmond said in *Sunset Boulevard,* "I'm ready for my close up, Mr. DeMille."

But to his surprise, many of his respondents came up with precisely the opposite formula: they found their life's purpose by pursuing, not the large TV camera, celebrity "got-it-all-made" cool lifestyle so dear to the media and image industry, but by pursuing the small things in life.

A lovely example: one respondent, a woman, said she once heard the story of a man who was asked by a journalist to show his most favorite possession. The man was proud and excited to show the journalist a gift he had been bequeathed: a banged-up tin pot he kept carefully wrapped in cloth as though it were fragile. The journalist was confused. What made this dingy old pot so valuable? "The message," the friend replied, was that "we do not all have to shine."

The woman said that this story resonated deeply. "In that moment," she said, "I was able to relieve myself of the need to do something important, from which I would reap praise and be rewarded with fulfillment. My vision cleared."

She went on, "I have always wanted to be effortlessly kind. I wanted to raise kind children . . . [I have found that everywhere] there are small, tiny, seemingly inconsequential circumstances that, if explored, provide meaning to life if one is generous and kind."

"I always wanted to be effortlessly kind and raise kind children." What a goal . . . a key. What a meaning and purpose to life!

Words like these always provoke a compulsive parenthesis from me. Sorry about that. And it is this: parents want their kids to do well—best résumés, best schools, best careers, best scholarships, best pay—and the kids get the message and stress out over grades, exams, and getting into an Ivy League school. They want to perform well to please their parents and score points with their peers. Nothing wrong with striving to do well.

What *is* wrong—painfully wrong—is that there is often no equivalent teaching and training that our students should do good, no matter what the school or career. To do good is to find the meaning and purpose of life in being effortlessly kind. It means that if ever doing well and doing good happen to collide, you choose the good. Now that's a purposeful life.

The landscape is littered with people who have done well but not good: doctors, lawyers, clergy, athletes, CEOs, politicians, celebrities—rich, successful people, provide daily fodder for the evening news of cheating, bribing, raping, or abusing drugs, people, and trust. They did well, very well. They just didn't do good.

On the other hand, a teacher writes, "Before class I sometimes would sit in the chair of a student who was having a lot of trouble and pray that I might be a blessing to him that day." For her, the small act of being a blessing to someone who needs it gave meaning to life.

One doctor writes, "Once I used to be one of the solid ones—one of the people whose purpose was clearly defined and understood. My purpose was seeing patients and 'saving lives.' Period. *Now* my purpose in life is simply to be the person who can pick up a phone and give you 30 minutes in time of crisis . . . I can listen to your complaints about your co-worker . . . I can look you in the eye and give you a few dollars in the parking lot. I am not upset if you cry . . . ."

One man wrote that his purpose in life became clearer once he began to recognize the 'decision trap' whereby the big decisions define your life. He says it's the small ones that count. So, he says, "I have a terrific wife, five kids, friends from grade and high school . . . horses, dogs, and cats. I have a small business that I started and have run for 40 years based on what I now call as the principles of Pope Francis."

One college student was driving after smoking weed and drinking when he was pulled over. He confessed everything to the cop, who saw that he was in college and bent over and whispered to him, "Don't let your friends get you into trouble you can't get yourself out of," and let him go. "My purpose in life," this student writes, "is to mentor, provide that whisper in someone's ear that changes their life."

"Not everyone can have a great mind, but everyone can have a great heart" is an old saying. Yet, in a secular consumer world we tend to over cultivate the mind and under cultivate the heart, and so we wind up, as Jesus noted, gaining the whole world but losing our true purpose and meaning.

To put it another way, in our lives there's the résumé and there's the eulogy. The résumé recounts a person's achievements. The eulogy recounts the person. It tells who he or she really is, why and how they counted, what they meant to certain people, what life meant to them, what they liked, or how they acted, loved, helped, and lifted up - or not. Our tendency in an image-is-everything-society is to honor the résumé that in turn is supposed to calculate and celebrate a person's purpose in life. We need badly to attend to the eulogy.

Jesus had the right idea when he spoke of taking the last place, giving drink to the thirsty, food to the hungry, comfort to the sick, hope to the imprisoned—the little everyday ways of being effortlessly kind, effortlessly holy. These are the little everyday ways of moving from résumé to eulogy.

To answer the question of how one begins to create a eulogy after years of creating an outbalanced résumé, let me end by taking you back to the old movie days when the talkies where just coming in. There was back then a very popular character actor named George Arliss, and he starred in the movie, "The Man Who Played God."

It was the story of a very talented and very wealthy musician but, alas, the worst possible thing that could happen to a musician happened to him: he began to lose his hearing. He was going deaf. Music was his whole résumé in life. It made him, he thought, who he was. He was lost, crushed, and became very bitter and cynical. As a result, not only did he turn his back on his friends but also on God. With no résumé, he became cruel.

Being rich, he moved into a penthouse and there he took lessons in learning how to read lips to compensate for his loss of hearing. From his penthouse window, he overlooked a park. He would look through a pair of high-powered binoculars and read the lips of people passing by. One day he concentrated on the lips of a passing young man whose lips were moving in prayer and determined what the young man was praying for and, being wealthy, he dispatched his butler to give the young man what he had been praying for.

On another occasion, he read the lips of a young

woman who was telling her friend about something that she desperately needed and, once again, he dispatched his butler to fulfill that need. And on and on.

This wasn't charity as you might think. No, each time he performed one of those services, the cynical musician would chuckle aloud at those benighted people who thought that somehow God has heard their prayer. He would raise his face to heaven and laugh at God because he found it absolutely humorous and laughable that he was deluding those people, that he was playing God yet he didn't even believe in him.

What happened in time, as you might guess, was that, doing all these kind things, meeting people's needs, the man who for years played God, *found* God and when he died and all was discovered, his résumé wasn't nearly as impressive as his eulogy.

15TH SUNDAY, OT
CYCLE B
MARK 6:7-13

40

Undercover Boss

Most of you, I think, are familiar with the TV show, "Undercover Boss." For those who are not, like those old wonderful classic movies *Sullivan's Travels* and *The Devil and Miss Jones*, each episode follows the CEO of a large company or corporation who disguises himself as an ordinary worker among his employees so he can listen in and find out what it's really like in the workplace, and what it's like to follow orders and do the dirty jobs.

For the CEO who never wants for anything, whose whole life is spent in the upper levels of society interacting with his peers at first class restaurants and golf clubs, who lives in splendid isolation, the experience is revealing and at times jarring. He meets employees of all stripes: the lazy and conniving, the hard workers, and reliable. He runs into managers both compassionate and cruel, sensitive and stupid.

Mostly he comes face to face with his employees' everyday lives: the mortgages, the illnesses, family struggles, and their aspirations and dreams often frustrated because of lack of opportunity and money. It's usually a very humbling, mind-changing and heart-moving experience for the CEO. Slowly he begins to see his employees, not as anonymous cogs in his company machine, but as people. He is shamed by some for their carelessness and indifference, yet overwhelmed by others whose loyalty, integrity, and faith he seldom has found elsewhere.

At the end, as in real fairy tale form where the kings

disguised as peasants, or angels as pilgrims, reveal themselves—think Richard the Lionheart in *The Adventures of Robin Hood* or the angel Raphael in the biblical Book of Tobias – he calls a company meeting and reveals himself as all the surprised folk exclaim, "Oh my God!"—especially his co-workers.

The CEO, now thoroughly chastened and humbled, confesses what he has learned as an undercover boss, tells them how he marvels at the dignity and goodness of people he has met. He promises from now on to see his company, not as a simple money-making machine, but as a collection of human beings—a family, a community—joined in a common enterprise.

He even calls into his office various employees he has met, good employees whose goals and dreams are temporarily on hold because they do not have enough money to realize them, and gives them thousands of dollars to pursue them. He's a changed man. His employees are changed people. Because of him they see themselves differently.

To the alert Christian, "Undercover Boss," needless to say, is layered with religious overtones and motifs. It begins with that first Christian wonder, professed automatically every Sunday, that God became man. "The Word was made flesh and dwelt among us." Yes, it is our faith that God, the Undercover Boss, would know our highs and lows, aspirations and limitations, joys and sufferings, and even our despairs and deaths. He would consort with tax collectors and sinners, forgive the fallen, touch the untouchable, and love the unlovable. His church would not be a corporation—though it often became that—but a Pilgrim people, a Communion of Sinners and Saints.

In today's gospel, Jesus moves his undercover strategy one step forward as he sends out his followers with ordinary dress and meager traveling items so they too would be on the ordinary people's level. Note the implication: without bread, bag, or money they become part of those in need. They were to preach the Good News by living the good news.

But, as history unfolded, something went wrong in both church and society as living in underground catacombs gave way to living in palaces, as sharing all things in common, as the Acts of the Apostles tells us, some equals became more equal than others. Over the centuries society itself became more stratified so that, for example, in our time, California has become a symbol of inequality because it's a state that has the most ultra-rich—people worth more than $30 million—and the worst poverty rate in America existing side by side—something never envisaged by the "Undercover Boss" who broke bread with the poor and sinful.

With all this in play, how can we not notice that today we have an unusual man, a pope, quite intent on playing the Undercover Boss—to the approval or the scandal of many. Yes, this extraordinary 78-year-old man with one lung, whose radiance and humanity has made him a world figure, has decided to live today's gospel and travel lightly among ordinary people.

You might recall that there were signs right away.

For example, the Pope-Watchers noticed that on the day of his election the new pope abandoned the red cape with the ermine trim, began his first papal address with "Good Evening" instead of a formal blessing, asked the people in fact to bless *him*, washed the feet of two women on Holy Thursday, one of whom is a Muslim, addressed the cardinals "my fellow cardinals" instead of "Your Lordships" chose not to live in the papal apartments but rather in the Casa Santa Marta residence inside the Vatican where he eats dinner in the company of lower-ranking priests and visitors.

The papal Undercover Boss has caught the world unawares, whether he's cleaning the feet of the homeless, or dialing up strangers and celebrities for late-night chats: Putin on Line 1, Obama on Line 2, JayZ on hold; convincing a self-described atheist like Raul Castro to give a second look at the Church, visits Naples and excoriates the Mafia corruption there in words only a former bouncer could use, quote: "Corrupt society stinks." He witnesses twenty marriages of some couples who were hardly paragons of traditional Catholic values and speaks to Texas evangelical pastors, telling them how he yearned for unity, embraces a severely disfigured man, celebrates his birthday by having breakfast with homeless people, and describes the Church as "a field hospital" open to all sinners. But it doesn't stop there, not by a long shot. Like Jesus in today's gospel, he has summoned us to follow him: to live more simply, to be aware of the poor and needy, to honor the planet; in a word, to pull back from our comfortable and isolated lives and become undercover bosses of justice, compassion, and charity.

The gospel has come full circle. There's nothing left for me to say except, on behalf of us all, pray:

"O God, merciful Lord, I'm not much but I'm yours. You have summoned me as you did your apostles. You have given me a task. I don't want fame and fortune as much as I want a sense of purpose, a sense that you have created me for that purpose. All that I ask is that you make me an Undercover Boss, comforting where I may, helping where I can, supporting where I'm able, being present where it counts. Amen."

16TH SUNDAY, OT
CYCLE B
MARK 6:30-34

41

Swapping Stories

"The apostles gathered together with Jesus and reported all they had done and taught." So today's gospel informs us. It was debriefing time. The apostles, recall, had been sent out with the gospel good news and now were reporting back their experiences—experiences of not only how they did, but what they saw, what they learned. "How did things go today?" Jesus was asking.

And so they sat there catching their breaths, bonding, and swapping stories.

In the spirit of the gospel, let me do the same. Let me share some simple stories that I came across since we last met as I was scanning the magazines and newspapers. Call this "Homily Lite" if you want—but maybe not as lite as you might first think.

For example, let's start with a throwaway item. Daughter texting to dad:

Daddy, I'm coming home to get married soon. So get out your checkbook. I'm in love with a boy who is far away from me. I am in Australia and he lives in Scotland. We met on a dating website, became friends on Facebook, had long chats on Whatsapp, he proposed to me on Skype and now we've had two months of relationship through Viber. Dear daddy, I need your blessing, good wishes, and a really, really big wedding. LOL, Lilly.

Dad's reply; "My dear Lilly. Like, Wow! Really! Cool! Awesome! Whatever . . . I suggest you two get married on Twitter, have fun on Tango, buy your tickets on Amazon, and pay for it all through PayPal. And when you get fed up with this new husband, sell him on eBay. LOL, Daddy.

A laugh, yes, but with a serious commentary about our times and the bumps on our spiritual journey.

More than 40 years ago, writes another woman, my husband and I lived on the first floor of his parents' home. We had four children—two budding teenagers and two younger tykes and so, needless to say, our living quarters in that two-bedroom apartment were pretty cramped. I had a younger sister who worked for a prominent investor as governess to his children. One day he came to our home to pick her up and saw our tight living arrangements.

"This is not good," he said to me. "These children need room to play and sleep without falling over each other. Go find a house to buy." I laughed, replied the woman, and said I'd be glad to do just that after I get rich. Without skipping a beat, the man shot back, "You find the house, then we'll talk." She couldn't believe her ears.

"That weekend," she continues, "my husband and I found a three-bedroom ranch house in a suburb about 40 miles outside of Chicago. And sure enough, this wonderful man made the down payment, which was about $3,000 and a lot of money in those days. We moved right in."

She reflects: "My gratitude to this man, now deceased, is never ending. Because of his generosity, my children were raised in a safe, clean, and fun environment with plenty of room to run around and play. I still say thank you to him, and I'm still living in the house."

The Good Samaritan story retold, I thought.

After her bartending job at a casino was over, Jill Bien boarded a charter bus for Chicago where she lives. About 35 miles into the 90-mile trip, Jill suddenly felt the bus drift to the right shoulder of I-94. The bus scraped the concrete barrier and veered back into traffic.

"Stop the bus!" she yelled to the driver, but his seat was empty and she saw him lying crumpled on the stair well floor. "Call 911!" Jill yelled to the passengers who were bouncing around in total panic. Jill then leapt into the driver's seat and grabbed the wheel. She finally turned the bus onto the shoulder of the road bringing it to a stop. Emergency personnel eventually arrived and took some 34 passengers to the hospital for minor injuries. (The cause of the bus driver's collapse hasn't yet been released.)

Despite lingering anxiety and bruises, Jill took the same bus back to the casino the next day. She was a hero when she needed to be, and I thought of Jesus saving his frightened disciples on the sea by calming the water and the winds.

This story is cousin to our first story—which means it too has a serious subplot: A man says, "We had a power outage at our house this morning and my PC, laptop, TV, ROKU, DVD, iPad and my new surround sound music system were all shut down. Then I discovered that my phone battery was flat and, to top it off, it was raining outside, so I couldn't play golf. I went into the kitchen to make some coffee and then I remembered this also needs power. So, I sat and talked with my wife for a few hours. She seems like a pretty nice person."

Maybe that brings a spiritual "ouch" or two.

Then there's this story from the well-known minister, Tony Campolo, who tells of the time he attended a funeral in an African-American church in the South and he was the only white person there. A young friend of his, Clarence, had died.

The minister was a powerful orator, speaking about life after death in such glowing terms, that Campolo said he wishes he would die so he could listen to him again. Anyway, at the end of his remarks the minister went over to the open casket and yelled at the corpse, "Clarence! Clarence!" with such authority that Campolo said he wouldn't have been surprised if Clarence had answered.

"Clarence!" continued the minister, "Clarence, you died too fast. You got away without us thanking you," and he listed all the good things Clarence had done. Then he said, "That's it, Clarence. When there's nothing more to say, there's only one thing to say, "Goodnight!"

Now picture this: the minister then grabbed the lid of the casket and slammed it shut with the sound ricocheting all around the church, as he yelled "Goodnight, Clarence, Good Night, Clarence 'cause I know, yes, I know God is going to give you a good morning!"

Then the choir sprang to its feet and sang, "On that

great getting up morning we shall rise, we shall rise!" and in a flash, all the people were up on their feet dancing and hugging.

Campolo remarks, "I knew I was in the right church, the kind of church that can take a funeral and turn it into a celebration. That's what faith is all about. It's about the promise of eternal life . . ."

I can't imagine any of our staid churches doing that. I can't imagine faith so vibrant, so colorful, so loud, and joyous.

Finally, this item I stumbled on: about a month before Rev. Martin Luther King Jr. was murdered, he singled out one of the many threatening phone calls he received. The caller said simply, "If you come here, we're going to kill you." He'd had life-threatening calls many times before, "But that night," he said, "for whatever reason, it shook me to my roots. I couldn't go back to sleep. I brewed some coffee. I drank the whole pot. I began to cry at the kitchen table, and I lost all my courage. I put my head in my hands and I thought, I can't do this anymore. I don't want to die." Then he added, "At that moment, I felt this strength in me that I had never felt before. I knew what do to, what I needed to do."

And I thought: another man quietly facing Calvary.

There we are: a half-dozen minor stories that happened to come my way these past weeks, with even the funny ones being commentaries on more serious themes, stories of unheralded generosity, heroism, faith and a sense of mission no matter what the risk—small thoughtful stories beyond the usual scandal, or violence and vapid celebrities we're used to. Stories that should prompt us to pray:

> "Lord, don't let me remain where I am.
> Help me to reach where you want me to be."

If we ever achieve that prayer, then some day *we* may wind up in someone's homily as a story to be retold as signs of God's presence.

16TH SUNDAY, OT
CYCLE C
LUKE 10:38-42

42

E.T., Don't Call Home
(at least not while you're driving)

There it is: one of those clever *New Yorker* cartoons: Two hip young executives - brief-cases, beards, tattoos, Brooks Brothers Suits—on a Wall Street pavement standing side by side but facing in opposite directions, each with his cellphone glued to his ear with one about to leave. The caption is, "Nice talking to you, Al."

The cartoon's zinger is that we can no longer communicate directly, face to face, with one another anymore, not without a mediating phone or gadget. This emotional and personal distancing has reached epidemic proportions. Let's look at our cellphones from three points of view: the psychological, the moral, and the spiritual. (Turn off your cellphones!)

First, the psychological. Let's set aside for the moment the oft-cited studies that show that people who use their cellphones excessively lose face-to-face communication skills and retreat into a virtual rather than real world. Instead, we'll focus on the addictive aspect of our smart and cellphones. There is a whole new industry to deal with it. Psychotherapists are increasingly warning us of the cellphone addiction and likening it to gambling addiction.

Today many corporations charter outdoor camps for their employees, camps that specialize in teaching them how to go through withdrawal, of living without 24/7 cell-phoning. Families and individuals are seeking help.

The writer Andrew Sullivan wrote an article that got a lot of attention. It was entitled, "I used to be a Human Being," and described what it's like to have your soul hollowed out by the web. There is also a new documentary called "Screenagers" that addresses how parents deal with the effects of excessive screen time on their adolescents.

In a PBS documentary, one teacher says, "In a career that spans 38 years, I have not seen any single diversion that so distracts students from reading, writing, thinking, and working. When the cellphone is in front of them, they are completely focused on it. When the cellphone is in the backpack, they are worried because they can't see it. On the first day of class, I tell them that if they can't go 57 minutes without checking their cellphones, they have a problem and need to seek professional help. They laugh. I laugh, but I know how true that is. Only when I tell them to take their cellphones and put them inside their backpacks do they understand how accurate my diagnosis is." He agrees that for some classroom tasks the cellphone is helpful, but even here the students are off elsewhere . . . . "Their bodies are in the classroom, but their minds are inside their cellphones," he says.

For all, teens and adults, the cellphone has become an addiction. The stats: 90% of Americans own a cellphone and many are addicted to their mobile devices. Think you're not addicted? You may be if you are—according to a Pew survey—among the 67 percent who check your phone or messages when your phone doesn't ring or vibrate. One survey found that we check our phones 221 times a day—about every 4.3 minutes and use it 80 times a day or 30,000 times a year. The average American adult spends five and a half hours a day with digital media, and the young spend about nine hours a day. A study of female students at Baylor University found that they spend ten hours a day on their phones. We just don't want to miss out on what's happening—no matter how banal or trivial. What *is* Kim Kardashian doing today? Somebody's posting messages on Snapchat that you want to know about. You click on because, according to psychologists it gives you a passing dopamine burst to swipe right or register a "like."

Then there are the telltale signs. Are you anxious when

you don't have your cell or smart phone, uncomfortable when you accidently leave it at home, restless till you get it, spend time on it when there might be better and more productive things to do? Do you feel the need to use it even when there's really no reason? Have you gotten what is called "text neck" pain, pain resulting from looking down at the phone or tablet too long? Excessive time with things reduces needed growth time with people. Studies show that the smart phone, so filled with instant information, lowers the need to think as the mind outsources more to the gadget. Why encode information when you can look it up? Studies also show that the smart phone distracts even when not in use. Just being present smart phones distract students and workers and affect their performances. There's clearly a dehumanizing process, psychological harm to think about here.

Second, consider the moral dimension. Lately all the press and news outlets have made front-page revelations that accidents and death by automobiles have skyrocketed. Cause? Distracted driving. Conclusion: phoning and texting is a sin, a serious one. Sin, oh, yeah, another new sin from an oppressive Church. No, actually this sin is ancient and pre-dates the Church. It is a violation of the old truism summed up in the two great commandments: love of God and love of neighbor.

That's it. To phone or text while driving in too many cases hurts, maims and kills your neighbor, not loves them. It's a proven statistic. One survey showed twenty-two percent of drivers using apps, forty-eight percent texting, and forty-three percent viewing phone maps while driving. The youngest drivers, not surprisingly, reported the highest rates of cell-related distraction, an alarming rate since the youngest drivers, even before the cellphones were invented, already had the highest crash rates. So, phoning and texting become a moral issue, plain and simple. Were you ever inclined to go confession, it would be listed way up there: driving distractedly, you played moral roulette with human life, did not love your neighbor as yourself. This is serious stuff. Distracted driving *is* a major moral issue not just a legal one.

Finally, and most profoundly, our love affair with our

gadgets is a spiritual issue. Hey, no finger pointing, but I, like everyone else, see people coming out of their cars and into the church vestibule fully engaged on their cellphones. Mass is barely over and their feet hardly out of the church proper when the cellphones are whipped out. Who knows, perhaps during those forty-five minutes the pope or the president called? What matter of worldwide import needs your attention? What if, while you were at Mass, Apple put out a new and wonderful smart phone and you missed the news?

I'm being facetious, but let's get serious, very serious.

At the beginning of Mass, cantors around the land announce something like this: "In deference to the sacred liturgy, please turn off all cellphones." Nevertheless, as we have noted, despite the announcement, we're at the point when we feel emotionally naked without our phones. We do suffer withdrawal if we don't have them.

But attend to this. Part of being human is to live the examined life for, as Socrates famously said, the unexamined life is not worth living. We know that our daily lives are in fact filled 24/7 with thousands of consumer messages, ranging from the trivial to the pornographic. We are manipulated and profiled down to our toenails. Consumerism and celebrity dilute our values and capture our allegiance. Every day, like polluted air, we ingest the banalities of TV and the emptiness of mass advertising. There is no time to examine one's life.

What's the current joke: After a short trip to Earth the Martian cosmonaut arrives back home and presents his superiors with a TV screen and a smart phone. "Sorry," he says, "that I couldn't capture and bring back any Earthlings, but I did better than that: I brought back two of their gods." Funny but true.

To avoid being conditioned into groupthink, into mere consuming units—and that is what has happened—we need to take time to slow down, to reflect, to respect Jesus' wisdom to come apart with him, to find out who we really are, what life is all about. The refreshment of soul, spiritual growth, and our deep spiritual heritage each require us to center down before an important encounter; we need to clear the mind, to cleanse the heart, and to be open to the Spirit. That's why vacations and retreats are important.

Sunday Mass, let me add, is also one such opportunity to do these things, however briefly. Don't bring the baggage with you to church. Entering the sacred liturgy with a distracted mind and heart is not ideal any more than when entering the highway. So, for the serious Christian, I propose a solution. For our parish, let's make an effort to leave our phones and gadgets in the car when we come to church. Let's be known as the parish who does that. Yes, come to Mass phoneless. Remember, even having them, as studies show, even if you do not use them, is a distraction. Be open to the Spirit. Your and my goal will be to achieve that and to encourage others to do the same.

Leave you cellphone in the car. Just as some families have courageously banned all cellphones from the dinner table, we will ban them from church. Leave them in your car. Give them a rest. Give yourselves over to sacred space and sacred worship with receptive minds and hearts.

And for those who want a step up—and it is that—leave all cellphones and gadgets home altogether. This way, after Mass you and the kids won't be racing to the car to grab the phone. Who knows? You might even have a conversation! And finally, for the deeply serious, look forward to giving up the cellphone for Lent or, as a good practical compromise, say, give it up for the Fridays of Lent, maybe even another day of the week. It's a start, the beginning of regaining your soul.

Bottom line: giving full praise for the gadgets that let workers gather knowledge, students conduct research, friends keep in touch, and grandparents rejoice in grandkids a continent away, let's also be mindful of the downsides and forge a new determination to make our gadgets servants instead of masters.

18TH SUNDAY, OT
CYCLE B
EPHESIANS 4:17, 20-24

43

Annie and Friends

It's the words from St. Paul in today's second reading that is our focus. His words, directed to the newly baptized Christians, are that from now on they cannot live as the pagans do. Rather, he says, "Put away your old self and put on a new self, created in God's way."

Lord knows we are inundated with the pagans: they are the stuff of our media, the scandals of our magazines, and the ones we try keeping up with. But I thought today I would introduce you to some non-front-pagers, some non-celebrities who took St. Paul's words seriously. Nothing thrilling, nothing spiffy, just some people you never heard of and won't again, but I just wanted you to know they're out there.

Take a convert of mine, Annie Wright, a teacher. When she died, her family found her precious old beat up scrapbook. It had pasted on its front page the very words of St. Paul from today's second reading: "Put away your old self of your former way of life . . . [and] put on a new self, created in God's way . . ." Apparently those words guided her life as her scrapbook was full mementos, letters, notes and lots of photos of family, friends and the people they helped over the years in the many food drives, home visitations, communion to the sick, walk-a-thons for charity, and so on.

Here's a typical entry under a photograph of her empty classroom: "Before class I sometimes would sit in the chair of a student who was having a lot of trouble and pray that I might be a blessing to him that day. I felt this was my calling, my "new self's mission."

Nice to know there are Annies out there.

Rick Kearney is a Catholic. He is also very, very rich. He is a self-made millionaire. But he's different. He doesn't own dozens of homes the size of football fields. He doesn't own a fleet of jets and cars. No, he spends all his money building housing, clinics, funding outreaches, soup kitchens, and opening shelters for the homeless in Tallahassee.

It all began when he saw the homeless scavenging for food in the trash and families sleeping in cars. *It should not be*, he thought, especially when he had the means to help them. Rick's a serious Catholic who says that he knows that at the end of the day he will be held accountable for what he did or did not do for the least of his brothers and sisters.

Rick Kearney, the millionaire, who refuses to live as the pagans do. Nice to know he's out there.

Then there's Tom Catena. He too is a Catholic, a doctor, a lay missionary from Amsterdam N.Y. Dr. Tom in fact is the only doctor at the 435-bed Mother of Mercy Hospital in the Nuba Mountains in Sudan, the only doctor among a half million frightened people on whom every day the Sudanese government drops bombs or shells, causing untold suffering and damage. The poverty, the chaos, the war is unending. The U.S. and other world powers have turned away their eyes and have abandoned the people of the Nuba Mountains. Dr. Tom is left alone to do what he can without running water, a telephone or so much as an X-ray machine. Try to imagine that.

Dr. Tom earns $350 a month, with no retirement or regular health insurance. So why does he do it? He is driven, he says, by his Catholic faith. Like Annie and Rick Kearney, Dr. Tom says, "I see it as an obligation, as a Christian and as a human being, to help." People revere Tom Catena, never want him to leave. Why? Not because he's the only doctor in the place but, more profoundly, as one Muslim put it, "He is Jesus Christ." Nice to have Jesus in the Sudan.

Finally, this odd one. It's the story of the discovery of a scrapbook of endless lists, letters, and photographs that lay hidden for years in the attic in England of 106-year-old man, a bland bachelor stockbroker from Hampstead,

England. It was found in 1988. The scrapbook contained lots of lists and photographs of children, and lots of letters to families around the world—and what a story they told.

So, to the man behind them. His name was Nicholas Winton—later *Sir* Nicholas Winton, much to his chagrin. Here's his story. This mild Englishman had gone to Czechoslovakia in 1938 for a holiday—the exact time, as fate would have it, that the Nazis invaded that country.

Unspeakable chaos, cruelty, and eventually concentration camps were not long in coming. Because Nicholas was a foreigner, desperate people for some reason thought that he might be able to help the increasingly orphaned and abandoned children to leave Prague and get to the West—the last thing he had in mind. Despite his protests and bewilderment, people began knocking at the door of his hotel in Prague at 6 a.m., and when he would get out of bed and open the door there would be shivering, starving, desperate children.

It was his moment of truth. He didn't have to respond to this unexpected intrusion into his routine life, but he did. So over time he began to make lists of the children, took their photographs, got them British Home Office entry permits—sometimes he forged them—found the foster families and organized their departures on trains by way of the Netherlands.

He went back to Britain and continued his work from there. Most of the children were Jewish and sometimes he had to place them with gentile families—whoever would take them. He got no help from the government, and even the U.S. would not help him in spite of his many letters to senators, congress, and President Roosevelt. But he knew marketing and he made it work. He knew he had to get the children out of Czechoslovakia and fast. They would arrive lonely and exhausted at Liverpool. By the war's end, he had saved 669 children.

The war ended. Nicholas Winton quietly put everything—lists, photographs, train schedules—into a scrapbook and stowed it in his attic, where it stayed for 50 years. He went about his life until the scrapbook was discovered. The media somehow got a hold of it, and one day he found himself on one of Britain's popular talk shows where, when he entered, the whole adult audience suddenly stood up and applauded him—and every one of them was a child he had saved.

In post war Germany, Nicholas Winton had the job of going over tons of army crates containing all kinds of stuff—books, china, silverware, trinkets, watches, wedding rings and so on that had belonged to the persecuted and slaughtered parents. He got the best money he could for them and sent it to Jewish charities. In his later years, he worked for a mental health charity and helped set up homes for the elderly. He got old, sick and at age 106 he died—an ordinary man.

There we are: Annie Wright, Rick Kearney, Tom Catena, Nicholas Winton—hardly household names, and you'll soon forget them—certainly no one you'll read about today, watch on television, or put on Facebook—but I thought I would mention them anyway and, in the midst of the latest shooting or drug bust or celebrity divorce, let you know not only are there such people out there lighting the moral darkness, but that we—you and I—should be numbered among them. That's the point, isn't it?

Through their stories we are reminded that, a la St. Paul, we cannot live, should not live, as the pagans do. We are reminded that we have put away the old self and our former way of life and put on a new self, created in God's way.

Bottom line: we know in our hearts that our names should be found in the litany that contains the names of Annie, Rick, Tom, and Nicholas.

18TH SUNDAY, OT
CYCLE C
LUKE 12:13-21

44

Sparking Joy

It has been said that moving is the seventh most stressful thing a person can do. I can testify to that when, motivated by illness, I began to move some four months ago. I was moving from my two-story, cellar-attic-annex-garage home to a much smaller apartment. My formidable challenge, in effect, was to try to fit a quart into a pint bottle.

The experience was chastening, an experience in humility when I realized how much "stuff" I had collected in 25 years, stuff hidden away in nooks and crannies, unused, unknown, stuff that largely represented "what dreams are made of" as Humphrey Bogart, alias Sam Spade, said in *The Maltese Falcon*.

I realized that my unthinking and casual accumulations were a triumph of the 24/7, ubiquitous advertising industry that continuously strokes our desires even if what we are made to desire is not what we really need or want. I recalled a passage in Billy Lynn's searing novel, *Billy Lynn's Long Halftime Walk*. Billy Lynn and his buddy soldiers, who have accidentally become heroes after surviving an intense firefight with Iraqi insurgents, are brought home for propaganda purposes at a celebratory ceremony at a Dallas Cowboys game. Still disorientated from the trip home, Billy looks at the wretched excess, the junk food, and fancy clothes obsession with celebrities, status, and money and he wonders when "America became a giant mall with a country attached." Rummaging through my endless archives of collected stories and articles, and coming across this one didn't help my mood either.

This man had written:

"I'm tired of the lies. I hear them daily, read them nightly, and watch them before I go to bed. They are so prevalent that I have a hard time knowing what is truth and what is fiction. Do cars really make you sexy? Are diamonds forever? Is a purchase the best way to show love? Is my worth tied to my waistline and my wallet? Am I worth loving based on my productivity or stature? I know that the answer to each of these is no. I know that these are lies, and yet I can't help but wonder. Somehow the father of lies is seeping into my subconscious and making himself at home."

Another saved article:

"What is it that we celebrate as a culture, as believers? One can celebrate love and honesty, mercy and forgiveness, justice and truth. On the other hand, a person may also celebrate power, prestige, greed, corruption and pride. But one thing is certain: "We become what we celebrate."

We become what we celebrate. Well, the message was clear: If we celebrate obsessive consumption and celebrity adoration and must-have clutter that advertises we are what we have, then we become so full of stuff that the personal, spiritual, and gracious things of life have no room left to take root much less flourish.

Anyway, as part of my reluctant conversion, I had to make decisions: save this, toss that. I had to make such decisions over and over, and over again, until I had gotten rid of at least three-fourths of my stuff. And when I got to my small apartment, I made two more sweeps and now, prompted by a book, am ready for a third.

A book. The book I'm referring to is one of the most currently talked-about books of the year. It is by Marie Kondo. Her book is, *The Life Changing Magic of Tidying Up*. She also has a new book called, *Spark Joy* with the subtitle, *An illustrated Master Class of Organizing and Tidying up*. Her philosophy is "have nothing in your house which you do not know to be useful or believe to be beautiful." So, she writes, only have possessions that spark joy by which she means that you should take up your things in your hands and feel whether they make you feel good or not. Go through your possessions, discarding the non-joy sparking items. As for the merely but necessarily functional things—say your colander—she advises respect their function, their utility, and get pleasure from that.

She is right on. To tell the truth, my house was starting to get to me. It was physically impossible to open drawers because so much was crammed into them. I found myself buying things I already owned because I couldn't find them. I had books and papers everywhere, and articles that I had compulsively saved or clipped out in the event I might use them in a homily someday. They were eating up my house space.

For example, I had boxes of stapled papers from Aetna, my secondary insurance. During my sickness, they came regularly every week and sometimes twice a week, proclaiming "This is not a bill" and showing pages of arcane, monopoly figures—$88,000 for this procedure, $42,000 for that and, the bottom line, you owe ten dollars sort of thing and warning me to save this for my records—until I had boxes and boxes of them, and until I decided to throw the boxes of clutter out. Let them arrest me.

The same with files of miscellaneous material—credit card bills, legal papers. And then there's the clothes I hardly ever wore, dishes and platters I seldom used. Did I really need a full set of Lenox dishes someone had given me? And so, it went. It was like sifting through an archaeological dig.

The most difficult category to tackle, as Kondo warned, was the sentimental things: letters from my mother, friends now deceased, invitations, reviews of my books. But I had to weed them out too.

The whole procedure was like an examination of conscience like you do on a retreat, like, I confess, hearing the gospel anew such as: "Be on your guard against all kinds of greed, for one's life does not consist in the abundance of possessions," and "be careful not to store up treasure for yourself, so much so that you wind up not being rich in what matters to God."

I was being forced to think that one over.

But something did happen. In the rigorous weeding and tossing out process, in the gifts to charity, in the chances I had to meet needy people, for example, those near homeless folk who were so grateful for the 3 beds I gave them, in the "emptying out" as St. Paul would say, in learning to live more simply, there was a certain freedom and I found that Marie Kondo, whether she knows it or not, standing in the strong Christian tradition, being right when she promises in her book, that keeping only what sparks joy will "not just transform your home but also change your life."

I end with an incident, from another saved article, concerning Joseph Heller, the celebrated author of *Catch-22*. He was once told about a hedge fund manager who had made more money in one day than he had earned from all his books combined. Heller replied, "Then I have something he will never have: Enough."

I'm learning that "enough" is a good gospel place to be. Make room for what counts.

19TH SUNDAY, OT
CYCLE B
1 KINGS 19:4-8

45

Elijah and the Upturned Cup

Poor Elijah. This prophet of God we met in the first reading had his moments. He intimidated kings. He performed miracles. He bested some 180 false prophets in a contest. But is seems his glory days are over and here he is, on the run. He is discouraged and depressed. The wicked queen Jezebel is after him to kill him. He's a low ebb of his life. Nothing's going right. He's given up.

So he treks across the desert, and plops down under a broom tree, which is actually a large desert shrub. Like a hiding animal, he's snuggled in among its branches, and there he asks God to take his life. He wants to die. He has nothing to live for.

But in the story, God does not summon dejected Elijah to the life hereafter. Instead, he nourishes him and summons him to the life here and now, yet it's a different kind of life and that's the key to the story.

Like you, I've met Elijah over the years. People who have hit bottom, are battered by life, depressed, discouraged and hurting, waiting for death, glory days way behind them,—the looks, the health, the money, the control are gone—addicted, feeling useless, crushed by a terrible mistake they made or deed they've done, dependent, alone and abandoned, sick and tired of being sick and tired. They want to die.

For them, for us all, the Elijah story offers three truths to ponder.

The first truth to grasp is to realize that sometimes the only way the Lord can call us to greater wisdom is by making our lives fall apart. When we were in charge or chartered our own path, we often ignored or marginalized life's deeper values. Sometimes relationships, friendships, family, love, not enough time together, not enough "I love you's," letting forgiveness slide or the mending of fences—all were put on the back burner in the pursuit of the career, which paid off handsomely in some ways but often left what really counts to wither and we are now emotionally, humanly, and spiritually poorer for it.

So now, hurting, weak, and powerless beneath the broom tree, we have a chance to ask: What is this weeping asking of me? What is this loss, this dreaded illness, this emptiness calling me toward?" What new, better truer directions can my life take? What values can I recapture?

Something like this happened to St. Augustine, who found himself at a low point in his life. Everything was collapsing. Though famous as a philosopher and rhetorician, his personal life was falling apart. His relationship with his illegitimate child and the woman with whom he lived was breaking up. He had troubling doubts about his pagan faith. He found himself to be near a nervous breakdown. In his famous autobiography, he wrote that one day he found himself all alone sitting in a garden, Elijah-like, under a tree where he put his head in his hands and sobbed like a baby. He wanted to die.

Until, like Kevin Costner in *Field of Dreams*, he thought he heard a voice whisper, "Take and Read. Take and read." Take what? Read what? So, he went into the house, picked up a Bible, returned to the garden, and opened the book at random.

Immediately his eyes fell on St. Paul's words, where he read, "Not in rioting and drunkenness, not in chambering and wantonness, not in strife and envying, but put on the Lord Jesus Christ and make no provision for the flesh and its weaknesses." He wrote, "No further would I read, nor needed I, for instantly at the end of the sentence, by a light, as it were, of serenity infused into my heart, all the darkness of doubt vanished away." From the ashes of his old life he found new life.

Who was more sick and depressed than the macho soldier, Ignatio, whose leg was shattered by a cannonball? End of soldiering, end of career. Several painful, failed operations left him useless and destined to a life of forever limping, leaving him depressed during his many hospital stays. Eventually he was left to ask the fateful question: What is all this loss, this suffering, asking of me? Is there something else, something more? He had no idea that one day at age 38, this useless soldier, a little under five feet tall, would literally hobble to Paris to found the Jesuits.

The first question for one under the broom tree, after one's system, one's whole structure, one's whole life has fallen apart, is "What is this tragedy asking of me, what deeper truths is it calling me toward?" It's a start.

Second truth. In our era of deadening individualism, we must reach back to grasp the ancient wisdom that we are all connected.

An example: I have a friend, Anne Spencer, from my old parish. Anne used to own a nursery, and when I first went to the parish we planted some young saplings together—now grown to huge trees. I was young, strong and healthy, but I couldn't keep up with her as she hauled those huge balled trees into the holes we dug.

I moved. She moved to the lovely seaside village of Gloucester, Massachusetts. Once vigorous and in charge, she is now 94, widowed, childless, and ailing. Many trips to the hospital, recent hip surgery, the in-charge lady is totally dependent on others. We talk on the phone occasionally. Usually upbeat, the last time we spoke I could tell that she was depressed. She felt so helpless, so useless, she said, so unable to care for herself. She is just taking up space, as she put it. She wishes God would take her.

I told her that God will call us when God is ready, but meanwhile I reminded her of our great Catholic teaching we call the Communion of Saints or the mystical Body of Christ, of how we are all connected. Therefore, we can still influence one another every bit as much as a soldier dying 3,000 miles away can make us free.

I also reminded her of our great tradition of the cloistered life based on that belief, where the monks and nuns so seemingly useless to outsiders—they're not out there producing and consuming—but whose prayers for the world are so powerful. Catholic tradition firmly believes in the poet's words, "More things are wrought by prayer than this world dreams of."

As a case in point, I reminded her that St. Teresa, the Little Flower, who died early at age twenty-four, in a seeming irony, was made patroness of the Missions because, although she never left the cloistered walls, by her prayers and sacrifices she gained more graces and conversions of others than did on-the-ground missionary St. Francis Xavier.

With that deep sense of solidarity in mind, I suggested to her that this, the cloistered life, was now her new calling, her new station in life. She had a mission. I suggested that she offer up her sufferings for others, and that each night before she retires that she go to the window and bless the world. Who knows who will benefit, what desperate soul will find a moment of relief or a fleeting sense of being loved, a slim hope that maybe all will turn out all right?

For example: It was one of the worst days of her life. Newly separated, a young woman was tired, sick, lonely, discouraged, and suffocating in the hot July heat. It was all she could do to lift her little boy into his highchair for dinner. She put his food on the tray and began to read the mail. Another bill she could not pay—it was the last straw. She leaned her head against the tray and began to cry. The little boy looked at his sobbing mother very intensely, then took the pacifier out of his mouth, and offered it to his distraught mother. She began to laugh through her tears and hugged the source of such unconditional love. Who knows, but it was a gifted moment from the cloister in Massachusetts?

Third truth: turn the cup right side up. When you're in the dumps, it's as if your cup is turned upside down and nothing enters. It's all hopeless and bleak. No refreshing rain can fill it, and so life is empty and bitter. Learn the lesson of the upturned cup, a wisdom found in the lovely poem by Grace Noel Crowell entitled "For One Who Is Tired."

It goes like this.

Dear child, God does not say
"Today, be strong."
He knows your strength is spent,
He knows how long the road has been;
How weary you have grown.
For he who walked the earthly roads alone,
Each bogging lowland and each rugged hill,
Can understand, and so he says, "Be still
And know that I am God." The hour is late
And you must rest awhile; and you must wait
Until life's empty reservoirs fill up.
As slow rains fill an empty, upturned cup.
Hold your cup, dear child, for God to fill.
He only asks today that you be still.

That's a lovely image. It's an image for those who are hurting, grieving, in sorrow or just struggling with something. The poem says maybe you need to just sit a while and rest and turn your cup right side up to God; let your dry reservoirs fill up again. Stop trying to control it.

So that's it. Three truths for those under the broom tree: first, ask. What is the weeping asking of me? With the past in ashes, can I rebuild a new, better, loving, and more meaningful life? Second, remember we are all connected. In your suffering, join the spiritual cloister and each day offer the world your prayers and blessing. Third, turn your cup right side up and let go and let God.

Under the broom tree is a painful place to be, but it may be the beginning rather than the end.

20TH SUNDAY, OT
CYCLE B
PSALM 34:2, 4-5, 6-7

46

Relics—A Matter of Taste and See

What I am about to share will sound sweetly nostalgic to all the Catholics here over age sixty, and densely unrelatable to those below sixty:

The Catholic Church of yesterday had a texture to it, a feel: the smudge of ashes on your forehead on Ash Wednesday, the cool candle against your throat on St. Blaise's Day, the wafer-like sensation on your tongue in Communion. It had a look: the oddly elegant sight of the silky vestments on the back of the priest as he went about his mysterious rites facing the sanctuary; the monstrance with its solar radial brilliance surrounding the stark white Host of the tabernacle; the indelible impression of the blue-and-white Virgin and the shocking red image of the Sacred Heart. It even had a smell, an odor: the pungent incense, the extinguished candles with their beeswax aroma floating ceilingward and filling your nostrils, the smell of olive oil and sacramental balm. It had the taste of fish on Fridays, unleavened bread, and hot cross buns. It had the sound of unearthly Gregorian chant, *flectamus genua*, and the mournful *Dies Irae*. The Church had a way of capturing all your senses, of keeping your senses and your being enthralled.

Those were the days! But by and by the cohesive and ethnic neighborhoods, who passed these traditions on, dissolved with changing demographics and industrialization. Mom and pop stores where they knew your name proved no match for Costco and Walmart, who knew your zip code, and children got educated out of the allure of mystery into the soulless demands of the marketplace.

Still, the Catholic Church, at least officially, has retained some of its Catholic imagination, its sense of sacramentality; that is, seeing the world of spirit through the lens of material things: stories and legends, statues and holy water, stained glass and votive candles, saints and religious medals, rosary beads and holy pictures, novenas and missions—and relics, the topic of our homily today.

Some of today's secular sophisticates mock relics—things that belong to the saints—while never once apologizing for their Elvis collectables, autograph albums, or their ardent bids for Judy Garland's red shoes from the *Wizard of Oz* or Bon Jovi's guitar. In a way, relic-hunting is part of our innate curiosity and our desire to get near a famous person in the hopes that some of the magic, the aura, the charism, the holiness, will rub off.

Sometimes, as we know, human nature being what it is, some rogues traffic in bogus relics—feathers from the wings of the Archangel Gabriel—and some bring holy things down to the level of magic and superstition—such as the ladies I used to witness who used miraculous medals for Bingo markers. Still, relics play a role in connecting us to the sacred.

My mention of relics, in general, has been provoked by a renewed interest in one of the most famous of them all—the Shroud of Turin. The Archdiocese of Turin in Italy, to commemorate the birth of St. John Bosco, a Turin priest who founded the Salesian Order in the 19th century to help poor young people, displayed, for the first time in five years, the famous Shroud of Turin this past June. More than a million people saw the fourteen-and-a-half-foot-long piece of linen. In fact, on June 21st Pope Francis, whose family comes from the area outside of Turin, was there to honor it and pray before it. Thus, once more, the most controversial relic in Christianity, a shroud believed to be the burial cloth of Jesus, came to the fore. The issue for some: Is it really his burial cloth, or is it a medieval forgery?

The whole controversy exploded when it was photographed in 1898 and the result revealed a negative image, front and back, of a man who was severely beaten, scourged, and crucified. Bleeding on the head suggests a crown of thorns, while wrists and feet show nail wounds, and a wound in the right side. There was no trace of pigment suggesting someone painted it. It appeared to be the burial cloth of Jesus. Or was it?

Over a hundred years later, in 1988, carbon 14 tests dismissed the Shroud as a 13th or 14th century medieval forgery. It was pronounced a fake. Later, however, scientists said wait a minute. They demonstrated that those tests were flawed because those previous scientists had unknowingly taken replaced medieval stitching from where the cloth had been rewoven and repaired. The question remains very much open.

Many scientists continue to study it, and today the Shroud of Turin Research Project simply says that, so far, any medieval forgery is difficult to prove. Even if it were a medieval forgery, even today, with all our scientific know-how, no one can figure out how anyone could have possibly done it and, so far, no one has been able to duplicate the image on the shroud or explain how it was produced. It remains an intriguing Catholic relic and riddle.

Bottom line: the shroud's message, that touching image displaying torture, crucifixion, thorns, nail marks, and wounds—whether genuine or not—the shroud's message is that the bruised and battered figure depicted on it does say something eternally true: "Greater love than this no one has than to lay down one's life for one's friends."

God's Time

It's not often that a preacher skips over the readings to preach on the Responsorial Psalm, but today's caught my eye as the perfect introduction to the theme of the need we each have for hope and trust, especially in stressful times.

The refrain, as you may recollect, is "I will walk before the Lord in the land of the living," and its first verse is:

> *I love the Lord because he has heard my voice*
> *in supplication,*
> *Because he has inclined his ear to me the day*
> *I called.*

Well, Lord knows, we call—and sometimes call and call and call and wonder if anyone's listening.

So, I thought we'd take a look at this psalm and my mind, for some reason, immediately shot back to a story that's been around a while—many of you may have heard it—but I felt that, nevertheless, it was so on target, I thought I would repeat it. It's the story of a daughter, a father, a dog—and grace. Here it is.

The daughter was beside herself. Her father was chronically ornery, disagreeable, and rude. He was always on her back criticizing her. She was at the breaking point.

The background: Her father had been a lumberjack in Oregon, a man who enjoyed being outdoors pitting his strength against nature. He entered grueling lumberjack competitions and his shelves were filled with trophies.

But, as some of us well know, the years marched on.

The first time he couldn't lift a heavy log he joked about it; but later in the day his daughter saw him through the window outside alone straining to lift it. He became irritable when anyone kidded him about his advancing age or when he couldn't do something he had done as a younger man.

Four days after his 67th birthday he had a heart attack and was whisked to the hospital. He was lucky. He survived. But the daughter noticed that something inside her Dad had died. His zest for life was gone. He obstinately refused to follow the doctor's orders. Suggestions to help were turned aside with sarcasm and insults. The number of visitors thinned and then stopped. He was soon left alone.

Her husband, Dick, and she asked her Dad to come to live with them on their small farm, hoping the fresh air and rustic atmosphere would help him adjust. Big mistake. Within a week after he moved in they regretted the invitation. Nothing was satisfactory. He criticized everything his daughter did 24/7. She became frustrated and moody, taking it out on her husband. She and her husband prayed, but it seemed God was silent. But something had to be done about that man's troubled mind, his disruptive presence. The daughter decided she had to take some steps.

So, one day she sat down with the phone book and methodically called each of the mental health clinics listed in the Yellow Pages. She explained her problem to each of the sympathetic voices who answered in vain. Just when she was giving up hope, one of the voices suddenly exclaimed, "I just read something that might help you! Let me get the article . . . ." She listened as the voice read. The article described a study done at a nursing home. All the patients were under treatment for chronic depression. Yet their attitudes had improved dramatically when they were given responsibility for a dog.

She was desperate. The very next day she drove to the animal shelter. After she filled out a questionnaire, a uniformed officer led her to the kennels. She moved down the row of pens, each contained five to seven dogs of all sizes and stripes, all jumping up trying to reach her. She studied each one, but rejected one after another for various reasons: too big, too small, or too much hair.

Now the daughter's voice:

"As I neared the last pen, a dog in the shadows of the far corner struggled to his feet, walked to the front of the rug and sat down. It was a pointer, one of the dog world's aristocrats. But this was a caricature of the breed. Years had etched his face and muzzle with shades of gray. His hipbones jutted out in lopsided triangles. But it was his eyes that caught and held my attention. Calm and clear, they beheld my eyes unwaveringly."

"I pointed to the dog. 'Can you tell me about him?'

"The officer looked, then shook his head in puzzlement. 'He's a funny one. Appeared out of nowhere and sat in front of the gate. We brought him in, figuring someone would be right down to claim him. That was two weeks ago and we've heard nothing. His time is up tomorrow.' He gestured helplessly.

As the words sank in, I turned to the man in horror. 'You mean, you're going to kill him?'"

'Ma'am', he said gently, 'that's our policy. We don't have room for every unclaimed dog.' I looked at the pointer again. The calm brown eyes awaited my decision. 'I'll take him,' I said."

The daughter drove home with the dog on the front seat beside her. When she reached the house, she honked the horn twice and was helping her surprise out of the car when her father shuffled onto the front porch.

"Ta-da!" Look what I got for you, Dad!" she said excitedly. Her father looked, then wrinkled his face in disgust and said, "If I had wanted a dog, I would have gotten one. And I would have picked out a better specimen than that bag of bones. Keep it! I don't want it!" He waved his arm scornfully and turned back toward the house. Anger rose inside her. Her temples pounded and she cried out, "You'd better get used to him, Dad. He's staying!" Her father ignored her. She screamed, "Did you hear me, Dad, he's staying!" At those words, her father whirled angrily, his hands clenched at his sides, his eyes narrowed and blazed with hate.

The daughter again: "We stood glaring at each other like two duelists . . . when suddenly the pointer pulled free from my grasp. He wobbled toward my dad and sat down in front of him. Then slowly, carefully, he raised his paw. Dad's lower jaw trembled as he stared at the uplifted paw. Confusion replaced the anger in his eyes. The pointer waited patiently. Then Dad was on his knees hugging the animal."

Well, it was the beginning of a warm and intimate friendship. Her father named the pointer Cheyenne. Together he and Cheyenne explored the community. They spent long hours walking down dusty lanes. They spent reflective moments on the banks of streams, angling for trout. They even started attending Sunday services together, her father sitting in a pew and Cheyenne lying quietly at his feet. Her father and Cheyenne were inseparable throughout the next three years. Her father's bitterness faded, and he and Cheyenne made many friends.

The daughter picks up the story again: "Then late one night I was startled to feel Cheyenne's cold nose burrowing through our bed covers. He had never before come into our bedroom at night. I woke Dick, put on my robe and ran into my father's room. Dad lay in his bed, his face serene. But his spirit had left quietly sometime during the night."

"Two days later, my shock and grief deepened when I discovered Cheyenne lying dead beside Dad's bed. I wrapped his still form in the rag rug he had slept on. As Dick and I buried him near a favorite fishing hole, I silently thanked the dog for the help he had given me in restoring Dad's peace of mind."

The morning of her father's funeral dawned overcast and dreary, reflecting just the way his daughter felt. But as she walked down the aisle to the pews reserved for the family she was surprised to see so many friends her father and Cheyenne had made filling the church.

The pastor began his eulogy. It was a tribute both to Dad and the dog, who had changed his life. And then the pastor turned to Hebrews 13:2, "Do not neglect to show hospitality to strangers, for by this some have entertained angels without knowing it."

The daughter: "When he said that, the past suddenly dropped into place for me, completing a puzzle that I had not seen before: the sympathetic voice that had read just the right article . . . Cheyenne's unexpected appearance at the animal shelter . . . . His calm acceptance and complete devotion to my father . . . and the proximity of their deaths . . . And suddenly I understood. I knew that God had answered my prayers after all."

She goes on: "Life is too short for drama and petty things, so live and love while you are alive. Forgive now those who made you cry. You might not get a second chance. "God answers our prayers in his time, not ours."

End of story and back to where we began, back to our psalm:

> *I love the Lord because he has heard my voice*
> *in supplication*
> *Because he has inclined his ear to me the day*
> *I called.*

48

The Atheists Among Us

Atheism, the belief that there is no belief, there is no Divinity, no afterlife, no ultimate purpose to life, has burst upon the modern scene and is struggling for acceptance and dominance.

Many of today's young, who have abandoned religion, are attracted to atheism. In fact, a full one-third of Americans in their 20s, 30s, and 40s describe themselves as having no religion—there are more atheists among young Americans than ever before—although surveys indicate that they really are not strictly atheists as such. They are simply the disaffected, the indifferent and, like most of us, almost totally religiously illiterate, so they have no contravening arguments and, often raised in non-practicing households, have no memory of religious ritual or celebration.

Some of the young tend to be of the "spiritual but not religious" variety, and some apt for cafeteria Catholicism. Having trouble with the Church's teaching on sexuality, authority issues, and feeling the impact of the negative publicity surrounding the clergy sexual abuse, they pick and choose. Still, I must add, other young people work to make Catholicism work for them and they frequent nifty websites like Busted Halo, StrangeNotions.com, or they participate in gatherings like Manhattan's vibrant Romero Center.

Adding to this, they, like ourselves, are the products

of an all-pervasive and dominant secular culture, a massive commercial media and a neutral school system where they learn to embrace the notion that all behavior is relative—what is sin for you is virtue for me and vice-versa; it's a who-can-really-say-that-Hitler-was-bad? sort of reasoning—and that being "judgmental" is life's worst horror. Mostly, they unthinkingly embrace, as gospel truth, atheism's foundational tenant, namely, that science is incompatible with religion.

Those very aggressive intellectuals, who have launched a full-fledged war against religion calling it spurious and redundant—writers like Christopher Hitchens, Richard Dawkins, Sam Harris, and Daniel Dennett (they call themselves the "Four Horsemen of the New Atheism") have proven popular and suggest a growing acceptance of atheism although, according to the last Pew Survey only 2.4% of Americans are declared atheists.

The atheists are struggling for a place in the sun. They are a diverse group and are far from united. There are, for example, those atheists who are aggressive, who actively seek to eradicate every vestige of religion from the public square, people who like Bill Maher mock it at every turn. These are the people who put up those insulting billboards at seasonal times like the one depicting a ten-year-old who declares that she's going to enjoy Christmas this year now that she's abandoned the old fairy tale of Christ's birth.

Then, on the other end, there are the reluctant atheists like this doctor, who wrote, "My entire life has been one long search for faith. I haven't found it. I do not believe in God. Having said that, which should lift an eyebrow or two, I want you to know that I love the idea of God. I love piety. Without it you lead your life unmoored, in a state of isolation. You are a tiny speck in a vast universe. I'm jealous, frankly. I feel as though I've missed out on the greatest thing that can happen to a person—faith in God. It must be wonderful."

One book has this famous opening sentence, "I don't believe in God anymore and I miss him."

As I said, the atheists are far from united. They know what they don't believe, but are still struggling to sort out what they *do* believe and, since they never know for sure, it is a belief system. They are sharply divided over identity, whether they should try to seek converts, or if they should offer a substitute for religion. Right now, they're increasingly seeking social acceptance and have concocted morale builders like the annual "Darwin Day" or the "Reason Rally" to gain public recognition. Some, who want to go to church but don't want God, have actually set up Atheist churches like the Sunday Assembly churches founded in Britain by two comedians who are avowed atheists. And there's some 200 of them worldwide where they can and do celebrate marriages and funerals and other rituals without the mention of God, where they "de-baptize" people who have left a particular church, and where they can satisfy the deep human urge to get together to chant, sing, recite secular prayers, explore meditation, and share their awe at the overpowering beauty and wonders of nature.

The atheists are looking for a way to blend their atheism with a sense of mystery but without God. Some of them, like Ronald Dworkin, speak of a "religious atheism" which makes room for mystery and wonderment while seeking to give some holistic pattern to life. Someone calls them "melancholy atheists, unbelievers with guilty consciences." In short, in their quest for community, their appreciation of aesthetics, their need for ceremony and ritual, and that whiff of "something else," they have reinvented religion and the parish church without God. Some famous atheists faithfully attend such churches. They can't quite get a sense of transcendence out of their system.

They should re-read Henry James's classic "The Variety of Religious Experience." There, he claimed that it is in defense of truth that religion is justified—the truth provided not by logic or science alone but by experience and reflection. Atheists are locked into limited "scientific truth," valuable and helpful but limited. For one thing, Quantum mechanics has upset the certainties of science in every single field (that's another homily). There is a will to believe that corresponds to something out there. "A man's religion is the deepest and wisest thing in his life." James wrote. Story, poetry, mystical experience, nature—all provide windows to a truth beyond measuring.

Don't be daunted by the New Atheists who, by now, are becoming tiresome. There *are* answers to them and it is fatefully dreadful that religious illiteracy is so off-the-chart high with people trying to cope with some very smart, up-to-date people with religious knowledge they learned forty or fifty years ago.

I have news for you. A lot has developed since your last CCD class, and high school or college education. There have been tremendous strides in biblical studies, the development of doctrine, and insights into church history over the past 100 years—thanks to dramatic discoveries of old texts, documents, and artifacts.

The old Baltimore Catechism was invaluable, as was the Model-T Ford back then. But a lot has happened since then. However, our ignorance of "what has happened" makes us vulnerable before the atheists. And we are the good guys. Imagine our children who don't even have that anymore, whose sole source of information is a secular, skeptical media.

But there we are, a thumbnail peek at the New Atheism. There are, as I said, answers to it, but, as experience shows, none is better than a life boldly lived in faith.

28TH SUNDAY, OT
CYCLE B
MARK 10:17-27

49

"But Wait!"

Our lives revolve around stories. Ever since we came to be on the planet, it has been our stories that give substance and identity to our lives. From the beginning, the old mythologies supplied the stories that tried to answer the big questions: Why are we here? Why do we have to die? Why do good people suffer? What is the meaning of life? Is there a God?

However fanciful or colorful, foundational stories bind people together, give them identity, and build community. We all have our national myths, our super heroes, our core events that tell us who we are. Greeks have Homer, the Norse Beowulf, the French Roland, the English Arthur. We have Johnny Appleseed, Paul Bunyan, and Betsy Ross. The Hebrews have Moses and the Christians have Jesus, the man who had nowhere to lay his head.

In a word, we live by stories and the images and ideals they provide. We *are* our stories. They shape our lives. In the past, our stories came down to us from wisdom figures, national or family lore, or from agreed upon assumptions about fair play, the golden rule, justice, retribution, kindness, greed, jealousy, and so on.

In our time, however, there has been a radical change. The stories that occupy us and influence us most have been taken over by the marketplace. They are *commercial* stories. They come almost entirely through the totally saturating media: movies, television, the internet, and smart phones via YouTube, Facebook, Twitter, Instagram, and websites.

Like tireless evangelizers, in and out of season they purvey the stories of our culture, the stories that tell us who we are and what we are to value. They tell us what we may say and what we may not say. They are the catechisms of our times, and they all have one thing in common. *They are brought to us by people who are trying to sell us things*. They are narrated by the high priests of our culture, well-paid celebrities, and their message is literally everywhere. Every conceivable global space, however vast, however tiny, is advertising's ubiquitous around-the-clock billboard.

The underlying storyline that unites them all is that possessions and carefully crafted bought images tell everyone who we are. They are our deepest identity. Life, as the old saying goes, means that the one who dies with the most toys wins or, as the new saying goes, "The one who dies with the most Facebook "likes" wins." And so, the perfect human being is the one who conspicuously consumes, and the more often the better.

I recently saw a full-page ad showing a young woman sitting in a canoe on a beautiful lake with shimmering water, lovely trees, and a blue sky. She is not caught up in the beauty of the idyllic scene. The gorgeous solitude is saying nothing to her. That's because, oblivious to the nature around her, she is looking at her smart phone. The caption beneath in small letters says, "When the market calls"—and then in very large letters—ANSWER IT."

Yes, 24/7, the corporations are there to make it all happen. As a recent article put it: "Amazon is quietly changing how it entices people to buy . . . Amazon is in the middle of an ambitious multiyear shift from a store selling one product at a time to a full-fledged ecosystem. Amazon wants to be so deeply embedded in a customer's life that buying happens as naturally as breathing and nearly as often."

The rise and brandishing of brand names certifies our arrival as a to-be-noticed consumer. Who am I? I'm a Calvin Klein, Armani, Lamborghini, Rolex, Remy Martin, Jimmy Fallon kind of guy. I'm a Jimmy Choo, Harry Winston, Neiman Marcus, Gucci, Beyoncé kind of gal.

Talking about a carefully crafted image, recently Parisians howled when they found out that its president paid his hairdresser more than $10,000 a month to cut his hair.

It's not that he's necessarily a vain, wicked man. What *is* profoundly sad, however, is that there are many desperately poor people in France, and the annual sum of $132,000 spent on cutting the presidential hair could feed many of them—that thought is not even on his mental or moral radar. He has to foster his image. He must look good to his constituencies.

It has been noted how men today are now catching up with women in tonsorial costs and that it is now not uncommon for top salons to charge $300 to $800 on up for a man's haircut. Every reflective Christian who looks at a starving refugee child should cringe, but we don't because we too have been brainwashed, and the *last* thing the advertising world wants us to do is reflect, hence the constant ads, business, entertainments and distractions of our rapid-fire lives. "But wait! Buy two and we'll throw in the state of Vermont!" Yes, when the market calls, answer it.

Let's go elsewhere. Think of sports and its identifying multimillion-dollar logos that, like the ashes we wear on Ash Wednesday, visibly signal a new religion. Think of its multimillion-dollar salaried players as the new lavished-upon royalty. Recently, Von Miller signed a blockbuster, ground breaking $114.5 million-dollar contract with the Denver Broncos. He got $23 million just for signing on and was promised $61 million over the next nine months. As part of a $6 billion-dollar sports industry, the corporation called the Denver Broncos expects to get that back and more from its fans, promotions, and merchandising and television rights. That $114 million dollars paid to one human being to play ball could raise the poverty standards of most of the world's third world countries for many years.

So, we're up against it. Sunday soccer replaces Sunday service. Stores are open Thanksgiving, Christmas, and Easter. Online shopping is around the clock. Funerals are "happenings," weddings, the average running from eighty-five to a hundred thousand dollars, are destination extravagances. Sex, sin, and scandal are books, movies, mini-series, and franchises.

How about this? Parents are going crazy about their children and smart phones, and how to exercise parental control. The job is made much harder if the parents themselves are out of control. Still, the question remains: How soon *should* children have them? You kids are going to hate me for this, but let's start with the recent survey that says that ten-year-old children, and even those as young as six or seven are clamoring to own them; the survey finds that many do, and *also* finding that on the average, sexting (sending nude photos of oneself) begins in the fifth grade, pornography consumption at age 8 and pornography addiction around age 11. In another survey, Common Sense Media found that 50 percent of children admitted that they were addicted to smart phones. It also found 66% of their parents felt that their kids overdid it.

My point: since biologically that part of the brain which controls impulse does not mature until the twenties, kids with smart phones lack impulse control. Advertisers know this and competition, celebrity-obsession, and lifelong loyal associations with brand names are forged here, as well as consumer habits. Additionally, unless otherwise grounded, it forms the lifelong, never-ending search for the products and the images that will earn the most likes and, if truly fortunate, fame.

To be sure, smart phones give many blessings. Let us acknowledge and praise this fact. They can lay open the wonderful magic of the world, the universe, connections, and friendships. They can also effectively become addictive and expose children to a way of materialistic living that is not the way of Jesus. They can and do sap time better spent elsewhere, in face-to-face relationships.

I know all this sounds like doom-and-gloom, sourpussing our national motto, "shop till you drop," but it's really a call to recalculate our values and shift our allegiances a bit. We sorely need to do this because our culture has become materially full yet morally empty. Look at the polls. They tell us that we as a nation sense that the center is not holding, that something more than 'bread alone' is needed.

As David Brooks summed it up in one of his columns, "We need to be more communal in an age that is overly individualistic; we need to be more morally minded in an age that is overly utilitarian; we need to be more spiritually literate in an age that is overly materialistic; we need to be more emotionally intelligent in an age that is overly cognitive . . . . we need to be infused with the sense that we have souls not just bodies, vocations and not just careers, that sex is not just a physical act but a fusion of loving souls, that marriage is a covenant."

All this means that somewhere along the line we have to stop and ask: Can having a Justin Beiber T-shirt *really* hold the weight of human life? Are there better songs that, like the old Negro spirituals, we can sing in austerity and that hold us together in times of terrorism, racism, corporate greed, political paralysis, broken families, and the terrible growing scourge of our drug epidemic? Can our media stories, that ask us only to consume and not to sacrifice or stretch and live for something higher and deeper, really carry us?

We say there is: stories of good Samaritans, prodigal sons, mountaintop beatitudes, golden rules, stories of people of sacrifice, decency, and faithfulness. But in order to hear them, we've got to turn down the noise, lay down the smart phone, give away some of the "stuff" that is suffocating our spirit, and spend some time in quiet reflection, communal prayer, spiritual reading.

We need to join forces with anyone who makes rough ways smooth, fills valleys of despair with hope, restores faith and lifts our sights to something and someone greater than ourselves. We Christians need to be reacquainted with the one who said that there is no greater love than to give one's life for one's friends—which we do by giving our time, unmediated presence, forgiveness, compassion, food, drink and where, distraction free, we dry one tear at a time.

28TH SUNDAY, OT
CYCLE B
MARK 10:17-27

50

The Cry of the Poor, Home-style

Mark Twain's Huckleberry Finn says it well: "It ain't the parts of the Bible I *don't* understand that bother me; it's the parts I *do* understand."

Today's gospel is one of those Bible parts we *do* understand but, in a way, resent. The gospel is basically talking about money and we don't want to hear it. Not only in the sense that "they" (preachers) are always talking about money (not true) but because money is such a personal matter. It's nobody's business how much I make or don't make, or how I spend my money.

But, think about it because money does matter, because a vast, very large portion of our lives is working hard to get it—most of our waking hours—because we perhaps never have enough, because it causes most arguments in marriage, because it is so determining in our lives, because getting, managing and spending it fills our days. It's foolish to think that such a large segment of our lives would not be a critical element, not only in our material lives, but in our spiritual lives as well.

So, let's talk a bit about money. First obvious truth: its distribution is economically and socially lopsided. Some people have enormous amounts of it. Let's see: a few years ago, Hedge Fund Managers like Steven Cohen of SAC Capital Advisors made $24 million dollars, Kenneth Griffin of Citadel $185 million dollars, Daniel Loeb of Third Point, $700 million dollars, and Nelson Peltz of Och-Ziff Capital Management, $385 million dollars to name just a few. I can't even fit these figures into my mind. They sound so surreal.

On the other hand, concerning money, some people have very little or none of it. Last week, for example, PBS news showed hundreds and hundreds of homeless people sleeping on the streets in sight of the luxurious high-rises of Los Angeles, one of the richest cities in America. The homeless there and throughout America, the richest nation on earth, are growing in alarming numbers.

In between the hedge funders and the homeless are most of us ranging from doing somewhat well to struggling. And within our range, extracting our money, is the non-stop goal, the 24/7 drive of advertising that generates not only endless seductions to translate desires into needs but constructs a world in which we are effectively protected from, cut off from seeing the needs of others. Intellectually we know the needy are there. Emotionally, practically, imaginatively, spiritually the poor are invisible.

The perimeters of our daily lives are like Atlantic City's dazzling casinos that have no windows so you can't see the abject poverty and addictions a dozen blocks away. So, we spend and spend. The spending controls our lives as we are urged to upgrade our software and Apple watches, and fill our closets and shelves with merchandising products from the latest Disney movie or celebrity clothing. After all, who dares go to school with last year's backpack or to work with last year's clothing style? Who wants a smart phone that is a year old? What is new, what is hot, what is in—I must have it! I have, as they say in a culture where image is everything, a statement to make and brand names brand me as the ultimate consumer. The conditioning is complete.

And, all right, let's not play the Grinch. Some of the spending is fun and good for the economy. That's not the point. The point is there is no proportionate vision of the poor in our Christian hearts, no fundamental consciousness, no background spiritual awareness, that some of our money belongs to them. Our entertaining, energizing distractions, our noisy "Shop until you drop" anthems drown out the cry of the poor.

We are good people and, when asked, are wonderfully generous. But awareness of the poor, so essential to biblical spirituality, is largely absent from our lives. This unawareness is the money challenge, no matter what we make. A good part of our spirituality is what we do with our money.

Picture yourself, then, in this gospel. You are the one—the rich young man or woman—whom Jesus looks at with love. You hear him asking you, "Sell what you have, give to the poor and come follow me,"—not literally, but you get the point: follow Jesus in concern for the needy. Be holy. The one who has two coats gives one to the poor, Jesus said on another occasion. There it is, plain and simple—and hard.

So, anyway, with that said, it's time to offer some practical considerations. You've heard of the movie, "The Dirty Dozen"? Well, this is the Clean Half Dozen list. Listen:

First, ask the proper questions. Do take time to ask yourself how your money and its use defines your Christian life. What do you use for yourself? Ask, proportionately, what do you give to others? Review your life. A typical example—a question of proportion - and I use it not because I'm a priest but because I'm an American. If on vacation, I and my two priest friends have dinner on Saturday night at, say, a restaurant equivalent to Shipwreck or the Breakers or Daniel's Bistro, and we know that with drinks and a tip we're going to drop at least sixty or seventy bucks apiece. At Mass the next day, I drop in five bucks in the collection basket and feel good about it. Somehow that doesn't sit right, doesn't seem, as I said, proportionate. Let's reflect a bit on how we proportion our money between fun and obligation, luxury and need.

Second, tithe as a family. Give ten percent of your income to a charity that you have all discussed and agreed upon. Research a worthy one. And, as an aside, use common sense. You have no moral obligation to give to every appeal that comes your way no matter how many photos of pitiable children, animals, coins, stamps, or personalized address labels they contain. You didn't ask for them. You have no obligation to honor them or respond to them.

Just take what you want and toss the rest and don't feel guilty. Otherwise you'll soon wind up in one of the photos among the poorest of the poor. Better to get one or a few accredited charities where most of the money goes to its goal than dozens that get scattered and whose operating expenses exceed your charity. In any case, tithe as a family.

Third, duplicate. That is, when you and the kids go shopping duplicate one extra item (the "Jesus item," you might dub it)—say, for example, if buying a can of tuna, buy one more or a sweater at a sale, duplicate and buy another; when you come home, drop them into your family charity bin or basket. When the basket is full, bring it to a food pantry. And when you drop it off, be sure to have the children or grandchildren with you.

Fourth, from the start, teach your children the power of the Hi-Five. Programmed consumers that they are, from the first moment you plop them in front of the TV and able as they are to recognize brand names within eight months of their little lives, train them in the art of the Hi-Five.

That is, they must learn as a personal act of piety that, of every fifth purchase they make, that fifth one belongs to Jesus. Don't buy the fifth—the fifth doll, CD, dungarees, shoes, magazine or whatever, but give its price to charity. Only the kids and the Lord need to know where it goes. Teach them early. When they Hi-Five each other, it can remind them of the challenge to be aware of others.

Fifth, get up close and personal. Every few months, maybe every holiday time, you and the family, perhaps along with others (maybe a neighborhood project?), visit the poor. Get a taste and feel for people who don't have what we take for granted. There's the Sisters of Mercy in Asbury Park, the Catholic Worker or Covenant House in Manhattan, and so on. See what poverty looks like. Take a look at Jesus in the food line.

Sixth, have the "Loose Change Coffee Can" on your table. Label it boldly, "For the Poor." Before every dinner, empty the pocket and purse of loose change and drop it into the can—and that means *everybody*, from guests to elementary school kids. It's a custom, tell your guests. It tells us who we are. It can even be fun.

So, our clean half dozen that will sensitize us to the cry

of the poor. To summarize: first, reflect on the proportionate use of money between *our* luxuries and *others'* needs. Second, tithe as a family. Third, when shopping, duplicate for Jesus. Have a household Charity Bin for that extra item you buy for the poor when you're shopping. Fourth, teach your children the personal holiness and devotion of the Hi-Five: every fifth would-be purchase belongs to Jesus. Fifth, get up close and personal by occasionally visiting centers that serve the needy. Sixth, adopt the custom of the loose change coffee can.

These little things are designed to keep us alert to others less fortunate. They help us confront the gospel question, "Master, what must I do to inherit eternal life?" and they help us find its answer, ''Go, sell what you have and give to the poor."

A very important postscript: I ask you to notice that all these suggestions are within the family—that seed bed of the faith, the first hand that rocks the religious cradle, the domestic church which precedes in time and importance and anything that comes later. The family comes before any pope, bishop, priest, or nun. Religion, like charity, begins at home. It's there that children learn to recognize, identify, and respond to the cry of the poor. Just a reminder.

28TH SUNDAY, OT
CYCLE C
LUKE 17:11-19

51

Cured on the Way

This is a beloved and familiar gospel, this oft-told story of the ten lepers. But I want to invite you to see it in a new light. I want to suggest to you this morning that this timely gospel has something profound to say to us especially at this moment in our history. And it does so in three ways, for basically it's a gospel that speaks of loss, of time, and of gratitude. Let's examine each of them.

First, concerning loss. I don't know how these lepers contracted it, but leprosy was common enough in those days. Whatever the cause, the disease represented a terrible loss in their lives. Loss of health, mobility, livelihood and perhaps, worst of all, the loss of community. For, with society fearing contamination, they were now cut off, isolated, and segregated from the rest of society. Shunned like pariahs living on the fringes of villages. What could be worse than being forever segregated, isolated from the mainstream of life?

These lepers of our story, then, represent people with loss in their lives—and that would mean most of us: loss of loved ones, loss of health, loss of employment, loss of a marriage, loss of trust, loss of dignity, loss of self-esteem, loss of faith in our government, church, our institutions, loss of security, and of feeling safe. Yes, like the lepers, some time or another, we all know loss. Hold this in mind.

Secondly, this gospel speaks of time. This is most intriguing, most significant. Recall the gospel text: "Jesus, Master, have pity on us!" And when Jesus saw them, he said, "Go show yourselves to the priests. "And *as they were going* they were cleansed." Did you notice it? *As they were going* they were cleansed. They weren't healed instantly on the spot, right then and there as happened on other occasions. *They were healed later, on the way*, maybe much later. This is important to remember.

I try to picture it. I wonder when they first began to notice the healing? How far had they gotten? How long was it?—a day, weeks, months, years? Did they simply, at one point, notice that the skin had cleared up, the spots had disappeared? Was it sudden or was it gradual? I don't know. All I do know is that they were cured, not right away, but *on* the way, that is, on their life journey. And I think that this, *in fact, is how it happens for most of us*.

Oh yes, I've heard stories of some people with the leprosy of depression or sadness, the loss of their loved ones, the drying up of faith, the slavery of addiction to drugs or alcohol or sex, the at-their-wits-end over a sick or wayward or difficult child—some, I say, cried out like the lepers, "Jesus, Master, have pity on us!" And he does! Right away. They find immediate healing. *Some* do. Some do, but very few.

No, it's not that way for most of us, isn't that so? Most of us, I am afraid, like those lepers, continue to plod on with our lives, treading our life's journey, deeply wounded and crying out again and again, "Jesus, Master, have pity on us!" till we're tired of it, till we wonder if anyone is listening, till we wonder if we'll *ever* find peace and healing. But, emboldened by this gospel, I want to offer this hope, the promise that it holds out to you and me: that, almost subconsciously, quite imperceptibly, on the way, on our journey, however long, just like these lepers, healing does happen, *will* happen, in strange and different and surprising ways.

I think of Michael Hingson. He is blind and was born that way. Yet he and his dog somehow escaped the collapsing Twin Towers on September 11th. Naturally, he made the press. He says he has never taken his handicap as an excuse to do nothing. He says, "I grew up in a family where my parents insisted that I had the same responsibilities as everybody else. I understood that my life was what I was going to make of it. So, I worked." He earned a master's degree in physics, got married, and became a regional manager at his firm. More importantly, he devotes himself to the Guide Dog Association where he encourages independence for blind children.

He was born handicapped. Like the lepers he was isolated by his blindness. He prayed for a miracle. His prayer was granted, but not in the way he thought. It was only on the way, as his life unfolded, that grace abounded for. It is because of him, despite his blindness, his handicap, his loss, that many children learn to cope.

Bryan and Renee Cloyd lost their daughter Austin at the terrible tragedy at Virginia Technical Institute back in 2007 where a crazed gunman mowed down 33 people. They could not bring their daughter back to life, but on the long journey of their grief, they took the many donations sent them and, in their daughter's name, gave them all to a program that repairs dilapidated houses in the poorest parts of Appalachia. A death gave way to hope for many poor people.

Then there are those parents who have lost children to drunk drivers. What a terrible tragedy! But some mothers have gotten together, as you know, and formed MADD, "Mothers Against Drunk Driving," to work hard so that other mothers do not suffer their same loss.

Will they or any of the others ever forget their children, or their loss? No. But—and this is the point—in time, that grief will no longer be central. Serving others as a means to saving other lives now is a path to their journey of healing. That's what I mean. It will take time. Healing will happen "on the way" to bring us to another, deeper stage of our lives as personal grief moves to communal love and service. These stories tell us that over time, "on the way," healing can take place. The scars will always remain. There will always be bad moments when we break down and cry over our losses, but the difference is that they will no longer be the center of our lives. That's the key, the miracle: our losses and grief are never forgotten, and will no longer define us. Helping others will, however. That's when we will know we are healed on the way. Our losses will have rendered us wounded healers, full of empathy for those in the same situation, bent on the good that we can do and which arose from our tragedies.

Finally, this gospel presents us with gratitude. The lepers came back—at least one did—to give thanks. My message is that if all goes well on the spiritual journey, if we can overcome bitterness, we will learn to give thanks from the ashes of our losses: thanks for the acceptance, the forgiveness, the patience, the growth we have experienced.

About twenty or so years ago, there was a great movie starring Dustin Hoffman called *Little Big Man*. Towards the end of that movie, there is a very touching scene in which a Native American named Old Lodge Skins has lost his physical health and is going blind; he knows he is dying and he begins to pray to God. This is what he prays,

"O Lord God, I thank you for having made me a human being, I thank you for giving me life and for giving me eyes to see and enjoy your world. But most of all, Lord, I thank you for my sickness and my blindness because I have learned more from these than from my health and from my sight."

And *that*, also, I think, would be the ultimate reason why, like Old Lodge Skins, we would show gratitude for our losses. They can contain hidden blessings.

An ancient prayer puts it this way, and let me end with it:

> I asked God for strength, that I might achieve.
> I was made weak that I might learn humbly to obey.
>
> I asked for health that I might do greater things.
> I was given infirmity that I might do better things.
>
> I asked for riches that I might be happy.
> I was given poverty that I might be wise.
>
> I asked for power that I might have the praise of all.
> I was given weakness that I might feel the need for God.
>
> I asked for all things that I might enjoy life.
> I was given life that I might enjoy all things.

I got nothing that I asked for
But everything I had hoped for.

Almost in spite of myself, my unspoken
prayers were answered
I am, among all people, most richly blessed.

Amen.

31ST SUNDAY, OT
CYCLE A
1 THESS., 2:7-9, 13

52

The Mortara Affair, A Heads Up

"While we were among you, we were as gentle as any nursing mother fondling her little ones."

If only St. Paul's opening words were heeded, a scandal would have been avoided. Let me explain.

More than 150 years ago, it was a heart-wrenching story that made the worldwide press, a story that bitterly divided Catholics and Jews in Italy and provoked an international scandal. Here's what happened.

Edgardo Mortara, a Jewish boy from Bologna, a papal state under the control of the Vatican, was secretly baptized by a maid when he fell ill. On June 23, 1858, when he was six years old, the boy was forcibly removed—kidnapped—by the papal police from his family and raised as a Catholic—all with the blessing of Pope Pius IX. Despite the anguished pleas of his parents and international indignation, the boy was never returned.

To us hearing this story today, it's an outrage. But let's look deeper. What's operating here is the weight of the scriptural admonition in John's gospel where Jesus explicitly says, "Unless a man is born again of water and the Holy Spirit, he cannot enter the kingdom of God." Later, St. Paul would add that there is no other name under heaven whereby people can be saved except that of Jesus. All this was literally interpreted as no baptism, no salvation. So, what that compassionate maid did back in 1858 was what some people did in my lifetime, for example, some zealous nurses who secretly baptized babies in the hospital.

It was surely a kindness as they saw it. The stakes were high. There was that scripture we cited and early Church Fathers, like 3rd century St. Cyprian and the 13th century Pope Boniface VIII, all who forthrightly proclaimed that there is "No salvation outside the Church." The babies had to be rescued by baptism. Without Church membership, without baptism, the babies would not go to heaven. Over time, some theologians felt something was awry. Although mindful of that scripture and believing that unbaptized babies could not enter the kingdom of heaven, they also knew that the babies did nothing deserving of hell, so they came up with what they thought was a compassionate middle ground solution: they invented limbo. Not the first prize, but a small comfort. Still, a heart-breaking side effect remained. Adding to the grief of some mothers whose babies died before baptism, was the thought that they would never be in heaven.

Still, that no-baptism-no-heaven urgency prevailed. The old Baltimore Catechism that I grew up with had explicit directions on how to baptize in case of an emergency. I remember we practiced on baby dolls. Also, by that time, showing a new global awareness that, in fact, the majority of the world was *not* Christian nor baptized and, therefore, would wind up in hell—which appeared to be excessive to say the least—the theologians came up with two other symbolic baptisms that they claimed would fill the bill: baptism of blood, and baptism of desire. Baptism of blood referred to those martyred for the faith before they had a chance to be baptized in water, and the Baptism of desire referred to all those people, innocently ignorant of Jesus, the Church, and baptism yet who lived decent and good lives as best they knew how and had an "implicit" desire for baptism. *If* they knew about its necessity then they surely would have desired it, but they didn't know better. They passed muster and would get to heaven. But the point remained: baptism or hell, or at least limbo.

Anyway, all this was well in play in the 19th century. The baby, Edgardo Mortara, although a Jew, however innocently, was baptized. The mindset was that it automatically made him a member of the Church and, therefore, subject to higher Church law in a land that the pope ruled over. It was unthinkable that he would not be raised Catholic. The Church had prior rights. With that mentality operating and perhaps an added touch of anti-Semitism, Pope Pius IX felt justified in sending his troops to claim his ward.

It was another blow to the Jews. Ironically, Bologna had at one time a thriving Jewish community with strong links to the city's university, the oldest in the world. Bologna once boasted eleven synagogues and was also known for its Talmudic academies, but under a papal decree issued some 300 years before the Mortara affair, the Jews were forced to live in a ghetto as they did elsewhere in Italy. In the decades that followed, hundreds were expelled from Bologna, an expulsion that lasted 200 years.

Most people have long forgotten about this incident or, like yourselves, never knew about it, that is, until three years ago when a man named David L. Kertzer published *The Kidnapping of Edgardo Mortara*. Even then the story would have remained of limited interest. But now no more, and I give you a heads up. Now Academy Award-winning director Steven Spielberg is making a film about the ill-fated battle by Mortara's parents for the return of their son. The film, likely to be well-done and well-acted and hopefully free of stereotypes, is certain to cast fresh light on this controversial real-life drama and raise old hatreds when it is released.

There is already speculation about how the movie will impact relations between the Vatican and the Jewish community after there has been so much gain and harmony, when Catholic-Jewish relations have never been better than they are today. Yes, pause over that statement. Official relations between Jews and the Church have been totally and completely reversed with Vatican II's documents on ecumenism and the nature of the Church, documents which explicitly state that the gifts and the call of God to the Jews "are irrevocable" and, furthermore, that salvation is granted to *all* people of good will regardless of baptism or Catholic Church membership, that God's love is broader than the confines of the Church—which indeed does contain the fullness of revelation but which also recognizes God's presence in other religions. As a Vatican II document states, "Those who, through no fault of their own, do not know the Gospel of Christ or his Church, but who nevertheless seek God with a sincere heart and, moved by grace, try in their actions to do his will as they know it through the dictates of their conscience—those too may achieve eternal salvation."

Specifically, as to the Jews, popes like John Paul II and Benedict XVI have long ago forged cordial connections with them by removing all anti-Semitic references in the liturgies and remaining in cordial dialogue. The result: there is great harmony today. Likewise, dialogue with the Jews and other faiths, has been a priority for the current pope, Pope Francis, since his election four years ago. Recall that Francis invited then-Israeli President Shimon Peres and Palestinian President Mahmoud Abbas to pray for peace with him at a historic Vatican meeting in 2014, and called for Jews and Catholics to work together for peace during an emotional visit to the Rome synagogue in January of last year. This year, [2017] the pope received a group of rabbis at the Vatican, including his longtime friend from Argentina, Rabbi Abraham Skorka, who presented him with a new edition of the Torah. Also, earlier in the week, the Vatican Museums and the Jewish Museum of Rome announced their first-ever joint exhibition on the history of the menorah, the Jewish symbol, which has also inspired Christian artworks and sculptures.

Interestingly, at the museums' exhibition lunch, the Mortara case was brought up. Cardinal Kurt Koch, the Swiss cardinal in charge of the Vatican body responsible for promoting Christian unity, said it had little relevance to relations between Jews and Catholics today. "That's an historic event," he told the Religious News Service. "It has nothing to do with relations today." He's right. We've come a long way and you must be aware of that.

Still, it's a sensitive issue that will now receive new attention once the film is out. Seated in his office above Bologna's main synagogue, the city's chief rabbi, Alberto Sermoneta, said Mortara's story *is* worth remembering. He said, "It is a symbol of the forced conversion that was done at the time. The spiritual leaders of that era breached human rights and the laws of nature by removing that child from his family. When I was a child at Jewish school, we all studied the Mortara case. It is shocking." Adds Lucio Pardo, former president of Bologna's Jewish community, "It showed the Church could not continue to operate on the basis of medieval laws, and it was a violation of human rights and our concept of the family. It stole Mortara's adolescence, his father died of a broken heart and the family was destroyed."

For us, it's a sad bit of history like the Crusades or the Inquisition. When the film comes out, our enemies, of course, will have an "I-told-you-so" field day in underscoring the Church's innate intolerance. More moderate people, however, will admit our sins with regret but rejoice that we have come such a long way, that what has been is not any longer, that last century's enmity is this year's embrace, and that we *are* capable of repentance, bridge building, and moral progress. The truth is we Catholics have an historical sense that "the-Church-always-in-need-of- reformation" and has been in our ecclesiastical genes ever since Peter denied, Judas betrayed, Thomas doubted, Paul persecuted, James fled with John and the rest—but they all gave their lives for Christ and started something unstoppable.

In its own way, the Steven Spielberg movie can be a testimony: to the Church-haters, it will be a testimony to evil, narrow-mindedness and prejudice and that has some merit; but to the open-hearted, it will also be a testimony to grace, to not only to what has shamefully been but to what can gloriously be. It will be a validation of all those Church prophets who all along boldly said to their church that "a disagreement is one thing, persecution for another's beliefs is another," that your concept of God is too small; those prophets who made us re-read the gospel as if for the first time, "Love your enemies, pray for those who persecute you," "Father, forgive them, for they know not what they do," "forgive seventy times seven"—prophets who, like Jesus, were often distained and rejected by their own people, but who would remain insistent and win the day.

So, to some the Mortara Affair is the story of intractable hatred, prejudice and persecution. To others, it is also the story of the journey from the gospel forgotten to the gospel remembered. This is why Vatican II said forthrightly and honestly, "The Church embracing sinners in her bosom, is at the same time holy and yet always in need of being purified, and incessantly pursues the path of penance and renewal."

A postscript: Edgardo Mortara eventually became a priest and fled Rome rather than return to his family. He remained a priest, and loved his priesthood. He died in an abbey in Belgium in 1940.

32ND SUNDAY, OT
CYCLE C
LUKE 20:27-38

53

Purgatory

A true story.

After more than fifteen years of battling cancer, the Lord called a lovely lady home. The young celebrant and his deacon were both wearing purple Roman vestments. In his homily, the priest told the congregation that the purple vestments were to remind us that her soul is not in heaven yet but rather currently in Purgatory. That's why he couldn't wear white.

He went on to explain that Purgatory was inevitable because all are imperfect. In the long run, however, it's a good place to be since it meant that she was someday destined to enter heaven but that right now, at this moment, she is suffering in Purgatory receiving her final cleansing, and since she is no longer able to advance her own cause, we who remain must pray for her soul.

My reaction: This 65-year-old lady who loved to garden, loved her family and friends, and loved her God was in fiery Purgatory for sure?

Let's review Purgatory. While the noble practice of praying for those who have died predates Jesus, the naming of Purgatory as a place of being cleansed by fire took a thousand years to come into focus, dating to around the late 12th century. The concept was later formalized in the mid-15th century Council of Florence and then in the 16th century Council of Trent. The theologians of the time, in seeking to justify Purgatory as a place of temporary cleansing by fire, looked back to 6th century Pope Gregory the Great who wrote, "As for certain lesser faults, we must believe that, before the Final Judgment, there is a purifying fire."

There are three paragraphs in our contemporary *Catechism of the Catholic Church* that outline the tradition of the Church as it relates to Purgatory. Nowhere, however, in these paragraphs does it state where, when, who, or how long anyone goes to Purgatory. In this regard, one cannot help remembering that, based on what Jesus said on the cross to the criminal next to him, "I tell you truly, *this* day you will be with me in paradise" (Lk 23:43)—that at least *he* was not going to spend much time, if any, stopping off in Purgatory for his sins.

In the 13th century, the great Franciscan, John Duns Scotus, took the position that any final cleansing took place instantaneously upon death, his premise being that one should count on the immeasurable and unconditional love of God. Rome, however, not fully wanting to relinquish control over grace given so freely and unconditionally, did not embrace his opinion. Rather, in the Middle Ages it adopted the theology of time spent in Purgatory and invented the industry of selling indulgences to shorten that time.

But let's go back to Gregory's metaphor of a "purifying fire." It was an ancient metaphor long before Gregory. For example, Jesus, in his parables, spoke of being cast into the eternal fire. But this was never meant to be taken as an actual physical fact. Rather, the notion of fire, then and to this day, as we know, is a powerful and popular figure of speech. It seldom means, as I said, actual physical fire. Rather, we use it all the time to denote emotional fire, emotional heat, and passion.

A long time ago—you really have to be old to remember this—there was a popular song titled, "I don't want to set the world on fire; I just want to start a flame in your heart." Nobody thought it was a song about arson. The movie, "In the Heat of the Night" did not refer to a town's burning down. Or there's "His desire was enflamed by her dancing," or, in current lingo, "He had the 'hots' for her." The Sacred Heart of Jesus logo has his exposed heart in flames, indicating his passionate love for us. All are metaphors that make good poetry and striking imagery. They don't describe a literal burning fire in an actual physical place.

It was Pope Saint John Paul II who taught that Heaven, Hell, and Purgatory are not actual places but rather states of being, and it's good to think of them this way:

> Heaven is being in the utterly blissful state
> of love fulfilled.
> Hell is being in the awful state of love forever
> frustrated.
> Purgatory is being in the temporary state of
> love-so-near-yet-so-far.

That is to say, it is a state of the heat of anguished yearning, laced with hope that someday it will be consummated. In this respect, we might helpfully describe Purgatory as the Church's expression of St. Augustine's famous words, "Our hearts were made for thee, O God, and they are restless until they rest in Thee." Purgatory is a restless place. That is its suffering. Yes, it is an uncomfortable state of restlessness, a state of painful frustration, like two separated lovers straining to reach each other and living in the hope that someday the embrace will somehow happen.

Purgatory, therefore, is not necessarily a place of physical fire. It is a state of emotional, spiritual fire, an aching longing—and by our prayers and sacrifices, we, the Communion of Saints, can soothe that longing and shorten the distance to consummation, and we must keep them up. We must continue to pray for what we call the Poor Souls—or more accurately, the yearning Souls—in Purgatory. Our prayers are an encouragement to them.

Our Mass cards, too, are a precious public way of inviting the community into our faith that all will be well; into our beloved's hope that all will be soon completed; and into the Good Shepherd's love that makes all things new again. We add that we also pray for the dead because the truth is many of us need to heal our relationship with them that at times was less than perfect. There is usually some unfinished business between us. Our prayer helps wash clean what is painful between us.

Finally, we pray to remain in communication in the same way as we would hold someone's hand. So that's why, with all that background I have a hard time with that priest narrowly preaching to the family that their wife and mother and grandmother will someday get to heaven, but *meanwhile,* right now, she hasn't made it there yet but is writhing in the terrible physical torture of burning fire for a while. How does he know she's there? How does he know for how long? How does he know it's physical fire? It seems to me that what he's saying is, 'Yes, Mom's gonna make it to heaven someday, but right now let's pray that her current terrible ongoing burning torture is shortened.' These are words of comfort? I don't think so.

As for those purple vestments, leave them in the closet for Lent. Put on the white vestments of the Resurrection.

While we're on the subject, a postscript about hell. These days hell has fallen out of favor. Our hells, we say, are here on earth. The Holocaust, ISIS beheadings, the torture and killing of children, and so on—are our hells. And if we have trouble with the age-old question of how a good God could allow such earthly horrors, then we wonder how he could possibly allow eternal ones such as hell. So, we do away with hell in the effort to make God, well, more humane.

But to do away with hell is also to do away with human choice. If there is no possibility of saying no to God, then none of our yes's count either. Our no's have no meaning and human salvation turns out to be totally predetermined. Our choices are fake. If there is no hell then no matter what we do, what choices we make, there's only one result: heaven. We can't escape it. God has forced it upon us. So, we're not really free. But the existence of hell assumes that our choices are real and that we are free. Hell, like heaven, is a way of asserting that things have meaning and our actions have consequences, and that the use of our free will can mean life or death, salvation or damnation, and heaven or hell.

We don't know its nature. Are hell's fires real or, as we said, is hell that most painful of all realities: desire, longing and love forever frustrated, forever incomplete?

Heaven, hell, and purgatory are realities of faith. They beckon and they motivate. They bring to mind St. Paul's powerful words, "No eye has seen nor ear has heard nor has it entered into the human imagination what God has prepared for those who love him." (1 Cor. 2:9)

CYCLES A, B, C
JOHN 3:1-10

54

Born Again?

Sometimes when I used to travel a lot, I would wear my Roman collar, and other times not. On short trips I would use it, but not on the longer ones. The reason is that on every trip the sight of a Roman collar brings out all kinds of responses and reactions, and a long trip leaves you too vulnerable for too long. Better to go undercover.

The seatmates usually fall into recognizable categories. There are hostile ones who, when sighting me at a distance, ask for a transfer—or, in extreme cases, a parachute! There are the hostile, snarky ones who ask how I can possibly stay in such a corrupt church. There are increasing numbers of ex-Catholics who are anxious to justify their defections. There are the sincere searchers who can't quite hack the Church but want to ask questions. But the most interesting category by far is the born again Christian.

Anxious for my soul, they breathlessly ask, "Are you born again?"—with the runner-ups, "Do you accept Jesus Christ as your personal Savior?" and "Are you saved?" These questions clearly suggest that, for the genuine Christian, there must be some dramatic experience in one's life that suddenly transforms it, a vision maybe, a voice, an unexpected, unexplained happening that turns your life around. In short, the pointed challenge to the question "Are you born again?" is asking if you have had a definable spiritual experience? For some people, I repeat, you're not a Christian, not a real one anyway, unless you have experienced some kind of dramatic conversion, if you're not "born again."

And, since you didn't and aren't, you feel kind of let down; you feel like a second level Christian, a pale lukewarm specimen compared to the enthusiasm of your accuser. You realize you're no match for the exuberance of your questioner who is waving the Bible at you. Perhaps you even envy his or her convictions and sincerity and evangelical spirit because, truth to tell, there is a real and powerful religious experience that has energized their faith, a reawakening most Catholics dearly need. How many of us profess to know God personally? How alive to God's holy presence are we, who find Mass boring and awareness of the sacred almost non-existent? In any case, given our own limited sense of the divine, encounters with the enthusiastic Born Again is a little unsettling and makes us wonder if we really love God.

The whole scene is reminiscent of the young man who has fallen deeply in love, full of lightness, excitement, whimsy, song, and poetry. He visits his grandparents who have been married 45 years. As he's sitting with his grandfather at the breakfast table, the young lover asks. "Don't you just get all tingly inside every time Grandma walks into the room?"

His grandfather looks over his shoulder at his wife, who is frying bacon. "Well," he hems and haws, not wanting to disappoint the boy. "I guess. I mean, I think I know what you mean."

"Don't you get light-headed thinking about her?"

The grandfather pauses, "Light-headed? Well, not exactly."

The grandson is disappointed. He can't even imagine that feeling less than madly, crazily, and ecstatically in love is not the norm. At this point, he can't see that other, different experiences of love can be valid, that there are many signs of devotion and that the enthusiasm he feels is only one of them—and a minor and fleeting one at that. The truth about love that lies deeper escapes him or her right now, but this next story reveals what it is.

In the novel *Captain Corelli's Mandolin*, that takes place in occupied Greece during World War II, Dr. Lanni, a physician, offers some timely advice to his daughter. She has fallen in love with Captain Corelli, a dashing officer from the Italian army unit that's occupying the village. In the village, the doctor's words offer a lifetime of experience. He says:

"When you fall in love, it is a temporary madness. It erupts like an earthquake, and then it subsides. And when it subsides, you have to make a decision. You have to work out whether your roots are to become so entwined together that it is inconceivable that you should ever part. Because this is what love is. Love is not breathlessness. It is not excitement. It is not the desire to mate every second of the day. It is not lying awake at night imagining that he is kissing every part of your body. No—don't blush. I am telling you some truths. For that is just being in love, which any of us can convince ourselves we are. Love itself is what is left over, when being in love has burned away. Doesn't sound very exciting, does it? But it is!"

The same revelation is put more popularly in the *Fiddler on the Roof.* You may recall, this duet where Tevye, asks Golda, "Do you love me?"

> Do I what?
> Do you love me?
> Do I love you? With our daughters getting married and this trouble in the town, you're upset. You're worn out. Go inside. Go lie down.
> Maybe it's indigestion.
> Golda, I'm now asking you a question. Do you love me?
> You're a fool.
> I know. But do you love me?
> Do I love you? Twenty-five years I've washed your clothes, cooked your meals, cleaned your house, given you children, milked the cows. After 25 years, why talk about love right now?
> Golda, the first time I met you was on our wedding day.
> I was scared.
> I was shy.

I was nervous.
So was I.
But my father and mother said we'd learn to love each other. So, I'm now asking, Golda, do you love me?
I'm your wife!
I know. But do you love me?
Do I love him? For 25 years I've lived with him, fought with him, starved with him. Twenty-five years my bed is his. If that's not love, what is?
Then you *do* love me?
I suppose I do.
And I suppose I love you, too.

My point is that the love of Jesus is also shown by constancy, not just by thrills and high blood pressure. It seems to me that sometimes the "born again" Christian fails to appreciate the everyday slow shifting growth of true love, the varied expressions of love for those who haven't had a dramatic conversion. This is the love that allows for many honest ups and downs on one's life journey—perhaps maybe even those ups and downs that are required for growth, necessary for growth—which brings to mind the wonderful writer, 45-years-married Madeline L'Engles' wise words:

"Our love has been anything but perfect and anything but static. Inevitably there have been times when one of us has outrun the other, and has had to wait patiently for the other to catch up. There have been times when we have misunderstood each other, demanded too much of each other, been insensitive to the other's needs. I do not believe there is any marriage in which this does not happen. The growth of love is not a straight line, but a series of hills and valleys. I suspect that in every good marriage there are times when love seems to be over. Sometime those desert lines are simply the only way to the next oasis, which is far more lush and beautiful after the desert crossing than it could possibly have been without."

So, there are ways to love Jesus and yet live through doubtful and dark times when life isn't either/or, when one is still processing his or her relationship with God.

In fact, I think searchers with doubts and misgivings are special people on the faith journey.

Are you born again? No—at least not in the sense that *I've* ever in my life had a vision, an encounter like, for example, Moses at the Burning Bush or Bernadette at Lourdes. I've never heard voices or seen the sun stand still or had a dramatic experience that turned my life around. I envy those who do and did. I'm still plodding along the hills and valleys of the faith journey.

"Are you born again? "Yes, I'm born again" is an ok and wonderful answer and good for those who can declare it. But so is "no" or "maybe" or "I'm working at it." Or, best of all, the proof of my faith, like the proof of my love, is in the constancy of my journey even when I sometimes wander off the path, even when I am sometimes disappointed in my guides.

In the end, real love is like Peter's answer to Jesus' question, "Will you also go away?" The answer being:

"Lord, to whom shall we go? You have the words of eternal life"—and *this* from someone whose faith would tank out around a courtyard fire, but who gradually got back on track older, wiser, and a truer lover.

Lectio Divina

(Proclaim this slightly edited version of this gospel to enhance the homily)

A Reading of the Holy Gospel According to John (20:11-18)

Mary Magdalene was standing outside the tomb where the dead body of Jesus had been buried. She was weeping. She happened to turn around and saw Jesus standing there, but she did not know it was Jesus. He said to her, "Why are you weeping? Whom are you looking for?"

Supposing him to be the gardener, she said to him, "Sir, if you have carried him away, tell me where you have put him and I will take him away." Jesus said to her, "Mary!"

She turned to him and said, "Rabbouni!' Jesus replied, "Do not hold on to me because I have not yet ascended to the Father. But go to my brothers and say to them. "I am ascending to my Father and your Father, to my God and your God."

Mary Magdalene immediately went and announced the good news to the disciples,

"I have seen the Lord!" and she told them
that he had said these things to her.

The Gospel of the Lord

Most people are familiar with the Latin term, *Lectio Divina* or, roughly in English, "A divine reading." It means reading the Bible meditatively, slowly, pausing over sentences or words, and entering into the story or event, even identifying with the characters. In short, it's an unhurried, prayerful immersion into this or that passage picking up catch words or incidents that speak to one, invite one to enter deeply into the mystery.

The gospel we just heard provides a good example of how its elements might speak to different people. Let me pick out five possible hooks that might catch some. No need to pay attention to all five or even any of them. They're just mentioned to provide an example of *lectio divina*.

The first words that might make us pause, "Why are you weeping?"

"I'm weeping," Mary responds, "because they have hurt and killed my master, a decent man, one with the face of God. I'm weeping because I miss him, because I can't even find his body."

We respond: I'm weeping because I have lost my husband. I'm weeping because I lost my daughter to drugs, or my wife to Alzheimer's, my sweet love who doesn't even know my name anymore. Because my health is waning. Because of the depression that never lets up. Because the world is mad with slaughter and washes up three-year-old refugees on the shore.

I have a lot to weep about. With Magdalene, I could go on and on with my own litany. But someone has asked me why *I'm* weeping. Someone wants to know. Someone is interested. Someone is there to listen. Pour out your heart.

• • •

Mary thought Jesus was a gardener. Strange. Intriguing. Remember where she is. She is at the place where they buried a dead man. She is at a tomb, a graveyard, a place of death. What's a gardener, one whose task is to sow life, green shoots and bright flowers—what's a gardener doing in a place of death? He's planting hope. That's a nice touch I might pause to pray over. In my place of weeping, of loss, of empty soul tombs, I sense a gardener. Dare I believe? Is there a life-giver, a defier of death, hovering nearby? Did the gospel writer intend to put death and garden, stench and sweetness, darkness and brightness together to give me hope?

• • •

"Mary!" Not "woman" or "hey, you" or "Ma'am," but the gardener called her by name. Let that sink in. She is not just one among countless millions, not just a face in the crowd, not an anonymous statistic but "I know mine and mine know me." "I no longer call you servants but friends." What a lift of joy when someone knows us and calls us by name. It's a one-to-one in that gospel, and in my life. Jesus, the life-giving gardener, calls me by name. He knows me. Music to my ears. He cares.

• • •

"But go to my brothers and say to them . . . . 'Brothers? Stop right there!'" He's got to be kidding. Some "brothers!" One, the leader, the "rock"—nice irony—shamelessly denied even knowing him. Another betrayed him. James and John wanted to be at his left and right in his kingdom yet when he did enter it they were nowhere to be found. Jesus had to be content with two thieves at this right and left. The others fled, weren't even around when he needed them most. They slept in his agony and the Roman soldiers couldn't even locate one of them to help Jesus with his cross. They had to commandeer a stranger. Jesus had every right to say, 'Go to those deadbeats, those weaklings, those fair- weather friends' . . . but he doesn't. Instead he calls these sad specimens of humanity "brothers." How sweet the sound. How compassionate the heart. How forgiving the soul. How comforting the message. I am not beyond the pale. Whatever I have done—whatever—I am brother. I am sister. Jesus is Mercy. I must linger on this one.

• • •

Finally, Mary Magdalene is told to go to the foundational apostles and announce the good news, the gospel, to them. Mary thereby becomes an apostle to the apostles. She goes to these dejected has-beens and gives them the good news, He is risen! She has herself become a gardener, planting life where there was despair, and it reminds me that this is also my role: to plant seeds of hope in dark places, and words of comfort in dead places. The note, the phone call, the visit, the ministration, the feeding the hungry and clothing the refugee, the sharing of the burden, and making things grow.

Thus, *lectio divina*. I have picked out five places where one can enter into this gospel. You need only one or two, or wherever the Spirit leads you. These were just suggestions, possibilities of reading the Bible with both mind and heart, of letting the sacred scripture speak to you. In short, this method is not just a reading, but a *divine* reading.

JANUARY 1, SOLEMNITY OF MARY
CYCLE A, B, C
LUKE 2:16-21

56

Mary, Untier of Knots

In the year 1645, England's House of Commons passed the following decree: "That all such pictures as have the representation of the Virgin Mary upon them shall be forthwith burned."

And so, after the Reformation, not a single significant statue of Mary remained in the churches of England, even in the famous Lincoln Cathedral despite the fact that the building was dedicated to her. But jump to the year 2014. After a gap of 400 years, a seven-foot limestone sculpture of the Blessed Virgin Mary was unveiled in that same cathedral. The cathedral's dean said that this would remedy the fact that there has been little acknowledgement of Mary for much of its life. Yes, even the reformed churches have finally come to realize that Christianity can never be complete without Mary.

Pope Francis knows this. When he was a student in Germany, Pope Francis became familiar with a famous 18th century painting titled "Mary, Untier of Knots." It was based on the idea that, while Eve tied humanity in knots thorough her disobedience, Mary untied them by her obedience to God's word. In one of his New Year's addresses, the pope said, "Jesus cannot be understood without his mother," and invited the crowd to chant with him three times, "Mary, Mother of God." And so they did, loudly.

Pope Francis then added, "No other creature has ever seen God's face shine upon it as did Mary. She gave a human face to the eternal Word, so that all of us can contemplate him. She, the Mother of God, is also Mother of the Church and through the Church, the mother of all men and women and of every people."

Giving God a human face is the point of this simple poem:

I know that God is infinite,
But like Him not that way a bit;
I love Him, yes, but like him less.
God is too big for me, I guess.

But not too little, no siree!
In Mary's arm, on Mary's knee.
For then I like Him even more
Than I had loved Him heretofore.

God through Mary with a human face. Because of such words, such a tradition, I didn't want the Advent-Christmas-Epiphany stories to go by without saying something about one of its central figures, Mary. I want to talk about her and why she persists, why Mary won't go away, and why Christians embrace her so through the ages.

I want to bypass all the heightened official titles we know her by: Immaculate Conception, Lady of Lourdes, Immaculate Heart of Mary, Our Lady of Mt. Carmel, the Assumption, Queenship of Mary, and the unofficial ones such as "Untier of Knots" and all the rest. As I said, I want to know *why* she persists. I want to see her before all the titles, before the accolades, before all the brocaded gowns, halos, and Renaissance landscapes. I want us to see Mary as scripture saw her. Come with me.

The first introduction we get from Scripture about Mary, especially from St. Luke's gospel, is that Mary is the first disciple of Jesus—and the most faithful. Luke makes that point by telling us that when the angel Gabriel comes and asks—not demands—her to become the mother of the Messiah, Mary says "yes" and then remains faithful to that yes even in the most difficult times.

Mary was thus the first follower, the first believer, the first disciple and remained so all her life. She is present at the birth of Jesus. That we know. What we don't always appreciate is that later, over some 30 years later, after decades of a hidden life, she reappears in the Upper Room when the Pentecostal Spirit fell upon the first disciples and, thus, she is also present at the birth of the Church. So, Mary is the mother of Jesus and also the Mother of the Church. She bookends the great mystery of our redemption. That's why she persists.

And that brings us to a second incident in the gospel. It happened when her son grew up, now in the full bloom of his ministry. The gospel story tells us that one day, while he was preaching to a receptive crowd, Mary and her relatives appeared on the fringe of the scene and sent word that they wanted to see Jesus. Word was passed up the line till someone near Jesus said, "Jesus, your mother and relatives are out there and they want to see you." Jesus, looking around at the crowd and stretching out his hands in a wide gesture, and looking over the heads of the people to his mother, said, "But who is my mother, my brother, my sister? It is the one who does the will of my heavenly Father."

To others it may have sounded like a put-down, but Mary smiled and knew better and accepted the compliment. Her son was saying that her claim to greatness was not that she was his biological mother, but that she kept the word of God. The early Church took note of that.

But, to go back to those beginnings. When Gabriel told Mary she was to be the mother of God, what did she say? She asked a question, "How can this be?" And there we are. There *we* are. There's the human question. There's our question. How many times have we asked, "How can this be?" How can I tackle this challenge? How can I survive the loss of marriage, my spouse, my child, my health, my mind, or my job? How can I carry on? Mary—wife, mother, widow—persists because she was the first among us Christians to ask that very human question. We can relate to her and she to us. We are not alone.

Next, we move to her "meanwhile" life. Meanwhile, the reality is that Mary of Nazareth *is* of Nazareth. That is to say, we must remember that she is living in occupied territory, not a medieval Italian countryside. She, therefore, experienced what every occupied people experience today: second-class citizenship and discrimination.

Worst of all, worst of all, she had to submit to that enforced silence that all oppressed people endure. For example, early on, she had to keep her mouth shut while her heart broke at the slaughter of the holy innocents. Later, she was forced to stand on the fringe while she saw her son publicly humiliated as a public criminal, unable to get to him to give him some comfort. A few hours later, holding her dead son in her lap on Calvary she was permitted the only thing allowed her—a sobbing cry, a primal scream, and endless tears. The woman whom we of a later day call the all-powerful mother was, in her day, powerless, reduced to submission and silence.

Mary persists because we know what she knew. So many today know her physically and morally forced silence and powerlessness. It can be as hidden and subtle, say, as those parents who are grieving over their adult children's divorces or lifestyles and have to bite their tongues to keep silent; they know they can say only so much if they want to see their grandchildren.

The enforced silence and powerlessness can be as hidden as someone enduring a demeaning job or an immoral workplace because they need employment. Or it can be as out in the open as the politically correct tyranny that silences any criticism of unchristian values, the vulgarism of so much of the media, the easy pornography, the glamorization of violence, and the celebration of the shallow.

Mary's been there: mouth shut and heartbroken, she persists at our side.

Next, Mary is the keeper of memories. Remember what Luke said? Mary didn't understand what was going on but she treasured all these things in her heart. Thank heaven she did. When times got tough, she remembered. She remembered times of grace, times of joy. She remembered the heavenly visitor, the strange Magi from the East bearing gifts. She remembered God's kindness to cousin Elizabeth. She remembered singing that God had done great things for her and holy is his name.

Those memories came in handy. She needed those memories when swords began to pierce her heart. She recalled them for Jesus' early followers when they were suffering persecution. She retold them when the apostles were dejected and languishing in the dark empty time between death and resurrection. She recounted them at the Upper Room while nervous disciples awaited Pentecost. Mary persists because in our own times of despair, of greed, war, beheadings, broken homes, and of a church in turmoil, her memories and song reassure us.

Finally, Mary persists because, in a sense, she has to do so. Remember on Calvary, as Jesus is dying, he looks at his mother and then he looks at his disciple John, who represents the Christian family, and says, "Son, behold thy mother!" And he gives away his last and most precious possession; and to his mother, "Mother, behold your son!"

So we, Mary's children, are united by an unbreakable bond. Mary is the mother of the God made flesh, the mother of the Church, our mother, the mother of all those who sing, suffer, and search. Neglect, decrees, and persecution cannot dim her loving presence or power. In every age, she continues to reveal the face of God. In every age, she unties knots.

57

The Opie Complex

Did you know that, among all the female figures depicted in art, Mary Magdalene is second only to the Blessed Mother in popularity?

Why not? Throughout the gospels, history, legend, and lore she runs the gamut from saint to sinner, from the apostle with the soul of faith to the reformed prostitute with a heart of gold, and from weeping disciple to steamy harlot. She is often identified with the woman who broke into Simon the Pharisee's house during dinner hour and washed Jesus' feet with her tears and then dried them with her hair. Hence, her signature art prop of the ointment jar. You can't get more dramatic than that. Later, she was conflated with Mary, the contemplative sister of the overly busy Martha, both siblings of the expired Lazarus.

Over time, further colorful embellishments have her as a beautiful young noble woman corrupted by luxury and then repenting—dramatically, of course. She also became identified with St. Mary of Egypt, a repentant prostitute. Legend has her migrating to southern France where she became a preacher, miracle-worker, and contemplative before retiring to Provence as a hermit. All and all, she can't be missed as a subject for both serious and pop art, pulp fiction, biblical movies, celebrity gossip and, of course, Jesus' wife, or the "Holy Grail" in Dan Brown's fantasies. In popular culture, she's become an ongoing cash flow brand name.

Let's set the record straight. The records show—that

is, the gospels—that Mary Magdalene is named some 14 times, more than anyone else outside the apostles. She is one of the seven Mary's mentioned in the New Testament: Mary, mother of Jesus; Mary, wife of Clopas; Mary of Bethany; Mary, John Mark's mother; Mary, an unknown worker; and Mary, the mother of James and Joses. The surname Magdalen is likely taken from the village of Magdala, where she was a Jewish woman of Jesus' time.

The Jewish Talmud informs us that Magdala was a town of loose morals—mention which may have contributed to Mary Magdalene's reputation. The gospels of Mark and Luke reveal that Jesus cast out seven demons from her, whatever that means, probably being healed of some mental or physical illness. We also note that the gospel of Mark lists a group of women three times, and each time Mary's name appears first indicating her importance among the companions of Jesus. She travelled with Jesus as one of his followers and, with other women, probably supported Jesus on his mission. Significantly, she was present at the Crucifixion and is mentioned by name as being there. Further, Mark and John specifically tell us that later she went with other woman to anoint Jesus' body and was the first person to see Jesus after his resurrection.

At the tomb, the women saw that the stone had been rolled away and they were dumbfounded. It was Mary who had the wit to run back to Jerusalem to tell Peter, the leader of the apostolic band. On hearing Mary's news, Peter and John, as you may recall, ran all the way to the tomb but found nothing and so they left.

But Mary stayed on to grieve, her tears, as Pope Francis expressed it, reminding us that "sometimes in our lives, tears are the lenses we need to see Jesus." Unwilling to abandon her Lord, it was then, through her tears, that she saw a man she thought was a gardener. She beseeches, "Tell me where his body is and I will take it away. I will care for him and give him decent burial." It was then that she heard the most important one-word revelation of her life, "Mary!" She is then told to go and relate to the apostles what she saw, namely, that Jesus was indeed risen and was going ahead of them into Galilee. From this mandate came her greatest title and basic fame as "the Apostle to the Apostles." Mary Magdalene: steadfast, loyal, apostolic to the end.

No wonder the poet wrote of her:

> Not she with traitorous kiss her Master stung,
> Nor she denied him with unfaithful tongue,
> She, when Apostles fled, could dangers brave,
> Last at the cross, and earliest at the grave.

So much for the record. Later, as we noted earlier, things began to get out of focus. Put off by similar names in the gospels, rumor and speculation began to run wild. By the fourth century, Mary Magdalene got confused with the woman who washed Jesus' feet, and no less an advocate than Pope Gregory the Great around 591 mistakenly identified Mary not only as that anonymous foot washer but also as the Mary of the Martha-Mary team. The seven demons Jesus expelled from her, according to Gregory, morphed into the seven capital sins with the emphasis on lust. It went downhill from there as Mary's reputation as a fallen woman caught hold.

For most of us, that is the Western Church projection that we have inherited. It must be said that the Eastern Orthodox churches never accepted this hyped version of Mary Magdalene. They kept to the scriptures and saw her as a disciple, even, at times, suggesting she was a virgin. Later, the Protestant Reformers pretty much accepted the repentant sinner model.

Finally, however, in 1969 the Catholic Church rejected the sinful woman washing Jesus' feet and the sister of Martha association and went back to the gospels, focusing on Mary as faithful disciple and the one to whom the Risen Jesus appeared and who spread the good news of the Resurrection. The Church has officially and formerly listed her as an Apostle, the "Apostle to the Apostles," reviving an old epithet going back to the 10th century and Pope Francis raised her memorial to a full blown liturgical feast. She has been restored.

So, there it is. Which is not to say that the repentant sinner or hot-breathing hussy images are gone. The movies, knowing well that sex sells, can't resist presenting Mary Magdalene as the harlot. Think of Martin Scorsese's

The Last Temptation of Christ, or Andrew Lloyd Weber's *Jesus Christ Superstar* where the fallen Mary sang, "I don't know how to love him," or Mel Gibson's *The Passion of Christ*. Centuries before in 1324, the Church unwittingly fostered the slander by establishing the first Magdalene House for unwed mothers.

I sometimes wonder how the real Mary Magdalene feels about all this. She must be frustrated. In fact, every time I think of her, I think of Ron Howard, formerly Ronny Howard, now in his sixties and, as you know, a noted movie director, saying dismally in an interview, "When people meet me they still call me Opie." With all the TV reruns of the Andy Griffith shows, he can't shake being Opie Taylor. Mary Magdalene understands.

But, anyway, now you know. Despite the speculations ranging from the noble to the notorious, start thinking of Mary Magdalene as the groundbreaking and unusual woman she is: active in the first church, mentioned in scripture, close disciple of Jesus, loyal to the end, faithful to the core, among the first to witness the Risen Christ, evangelizer, endowed with the unique title of "Apostle to the Apostles," and unofficial patron saint of the misunderstood. Quite a résumé.

58

Feast of Our Lady of Guadalupe

People are fascinated with relics, artifacts, and old writings, especially any associated with Jesus and his times. There are the sensational and the phony, like the blockbuster *The DaVinci Code,* and there was the media frenzy over a so-called gospel fragment that Jesus had a wife—the "hottie," Mary Magdalene of course—or a few years ago a book that made Judas the hero, or the revelation of the finding of a bone box with "the brother of Jesus" written on top, and so on.

There's a whole black market of relic trading and, a huge industry of fake stuff out there, though the fraudulent never deters books and TV series whose vision is confined to pop and profit.

I mention this because a nice and balanced counterpoint is a CNN series that is worth seeing. It is called "Finding Jesus: Faith, Fact, Forgery." It takes on very sensibly such things as the Gospel of Judas, the Gospel of Mary Magdalene, the Bones of John the Baptist, the True Cross, the Shroud of Turin" and others. I hope you get a chance to see it. This series doesn't cover it but its mention does provoke me to talk about one such related phenomenon, one especially dear to the Hispanic community but interesting to all. That is the feast we celebrated a few weeks ago on December 12th, the feast of Our Lady of Guadalupe. Most vaguely remember the story, but let me review it.

In the 16th century, in 1531 to be exact, according to early accounts the Blessed Mother appeared to a 57-year old peasant named Juan Diego. He happened to be walking along Tepeyac Hill near what is now called Mexico City when he came upon an apparition, a woman, a maiden, whom he came to recognize as Mary. It was a momentous and awesome experience. Later in trying to convince the archbishop of what he had seen, he was eventually asked for some sign to prove what he said.

Upon returning to Mary he told her of the archbishop's demand and Mary told him to climb to the top of a hill to gather flowers to bring back to the archbishop as a sign. He climbed the hill and there he found Castilian roses which were out of season and not native to the area. The Blessed Mother herself carefully arranged the flowers in Juan's *tilma* or rough burlap-type cloak, telling him to open it only in the presence of the archbishop.

When Juan Diego arrived back at the bishop's residence and opened his cloak, the flowers fell on the floor but, amazingly, what was left on the cloak itself, on the surface of the *tilma*, was the image we now know as Our Lady of Guadalupe. And it was a revelation in every sense of the word: in the image Mary appeared to be wearing the colorful native dress of an Aztec princess.

Well, to make a long story short, word soon spread around like wildfire. There were mass conversions and eventually a shrine was built on the spot where Mary appeared. It remains one of the most popular pilgrim sites in the world.

In time, as always happens, skeptics became curious about that image on the rough cloak and proclaimed that it was a forgery. Yet, in spite of centuries of investigation, some amazing and unexplainable qualities have been discovered about this *tilma* and I want to share four of them.

First, the *tilma* image has qualities humanly impossible to duplicate. It's made of cactus fibers, is of poor quality, and has a rough surface making it difficult to wear much less paint a lasting image on it. Scientists say careful investigation showed that no technique was used to treat the surface yet the image is like silk to touch while the rest of the cloth remains coarse. Infrared photography reveals no brush strokes Experts say that it's still impossible to recreate the texture and coloration that has no animal or mineral elements. Besides, synthetic coloring didn't exist in 1531.

Second, if it is just a painting on coarse cloth, it has outlived all attempts to reproduce it. The replicas all fade in time in the Mexican climate but in 116 years, without any kind of protection, exposed to humid and salty air and tens of thousands of candles full of infrared and ultraviolet radiation from the candles near it, the *tilma* remains vibrant.

Third, the *tilma* strangely seems akin to the human body. That is, it maintains a temperature of 98.6 degrees Fahrenheit, the same as that of a living person. A gynecologist concluded that the dimensions of Our Lady's body in the image were that of an expectant mother.

Finally, the *tilma* seems to be indestructible. In 1785, a worker accidentally spilled nitric acid on the image. Over the next 30 days the image reportedly restored itself. In 1921 an anti-clerical activist hid a bomb with 29 sticks of dynamite in a pot of roses and placed it before the image inside the Basilica. When the bomb exploded, a brass crucifix was bent and the marble altar rail and window that were 150 feet away shattered. But the *tilma* remained fully intact.

There's the story. It fits into the general category of interesting stories about Jesus and Mary and Christianity in general. For skeptics all this probably doesn't prove much but to those whose minds and hearts are open to a sense of the divine, a breath of Presence, who are aware that there are many things not easy to explain in our world, such things affirm that we are not alone, that now and then a love breaks through and that Mary, the mother of God, is our mother too.

59

On My Sixtieth Anniversary

When the sixtieth anniversary of my ordination came around on June 4th, someone suggested that I might revisit all my old parishes. I thought it was a good idea—but, of course, not *all* my old parishes. After all, my first parish was at St. Mary's, New Monmouth, but that was 60 years ago. I figure that by this time all those folks have either died, or have physically or mentally relocated. So, I skipped that—and St. Joe's in Keyport, and Our Lady of Perpetual Help in Maple Shade as well for the same reason. So, I started with St. Benedict's in Holmdel and worked my way to today.

So . . . 60 years, 34 books and a dozen parishes later, let me briefly tell you something about myself. Briefly, indeed, as I will tantalize you by letting the details go for another time and other circumstances, where a Manhattan and a good dinner will unseal my lips.

One of six children, I was born in Jamesburg, went to Sacred Heart School in New Brunswick, two years of high school at St. Peter's in New Brunswick, then to the minor seminary, St. Charles, in the boondocks of Catonsville, Maryland where, after a week, I was expelled for not knowing Latin—despite my two years of Latin in high school. Here I was, a high school junior with no place to go. My poor parents scrambled and finally got me into Seton Hall Prep in South Orange.

Then, as an incoming senior, I reapplied to the seminary and went back fully expecting to be accepted as such, but instead I was put on trial and ignominiously made to go back and repeat the 9th grade with all those little sniveling freshmen.

If that weren't bad enough, I was consigned the following year to a small special remedial class for slow students and pushed through with the result that I never went to fourth year high, never graduated high school and I have no high school diploma or any degrees.

Those are the bare facts, and maybe I should stop there, but I'll go on with a few more items plus an early story and an embarrassment. I was ordained a priest in 1955 and the bishop sent me to, at that time, a very little rural place in the boondocks called New Monmouth, which is part of Middletown, with a wonderful pastor, Father Bob Bulman. Out in the sticks, no paved roads or sidewalks, it was a great place to start the priesthood. There was just one little incident when I first arrived. Hence, the following story which I've told before, though where, I can't remember.

The first week there I had to drive into the little village, if you can call it that, called "Campbell's Junction"—consisting of a general store, a barber shop, and a small liquor store—to get some things, and I couldn't find a parking place. The only one left was in front of the liquor store. So, I parked there and went about my business. Well, it seems there were two elderly sisters who lived nearby and who were the self-appointed watchdogs of the town. Before long, word had got around the parish that the new young priest had a "drinking problem." Me, who has a glass of wine now and then and a very occasional Manhattan!

Well, eventually I was able to trace the rumor to its source. So, about two weeks later—

Father Bulman, warned me not to do this but I did it anyway since I saw his heart was not in the warning—I drove to the junction and parked my car in front of the sisters' house, locked it, walked home and left it there overnight. I never heard any more rumors from them again.

After wonderful years there, I was sent to St. Joe's in Keyport, one of my more colorful assignments. Now the embarrassing story. While there, a young couple, Maria and Alberto, came to see me. Effervescent and excitable, Maria was distraught because she could not have a baby and came to cry and weep, and asked for my earnest prayers—which I just as earnestly promised.

About six months later, the town was having its annual Memorial Day parade and I, as the young curate, was invited to be on the platform with the local dignitaries to offer a final prayer. As one of the ladies' groups came marching by, who should be marching among them but Maria and, not only Maria, but a very *pregnant* Maria. Looking up, she saw me on the platform and, excitedly pointing to her very extended womb, in a voice that could be heard all over Monmouth county, she shouted, "Thanks to you, Father Bausch!"

But at Keyport, I had one of those life-changing experiences. Back then—we're talking early 60s—there was a new lay movement for married couples called the CFA, Christian Family Action [CFM, Christian Family Movement in most dioceses]. Participants met monthly and used a guidebook to study the gospel following the three movements of Observe, Judge, and Act.

It was, as I said, an early lay movement. I was invited to be their young chaplain and, because it was a lay movement, I was not allowed to speak until the meeting was all over. I remember that they made me sit on my hands because if I can't use my hands then I can't talk [last three words are mouthed].

I was never so humiliated and humbled in my life. Not because I had to sit on my hands but because, forced to be silent for two hours, I had to listen, really listen, to their stories of how, day after day, they struggled to be good Christians. Month after month I listened to them struggling inwardly with shady practices at the company at which they worked, the politics of the workplace, the compromises they were forced to make, the fear of losing their jobs, difficulties with children—school, rebellion, drugs—trying to make ends meet, hardly ever getting a vacation, trying not to lose faith in hard times, struggles with prayer, not feeling God's presence, and doubts.

And slowly, I began to realize what a privileged, innocent life I led. Gradually, I began to realize with some guilt that I would always have a job no matter how poorly I performed. I had no accountability to the people. I could go home that night and get a full night's sleep with no colicky baby or sick child to attend all night. I would take my scheduled vacations and not have to pinch pennies. In short, I began to realize that *these* people were the saints on the frontline. I began to feel I was not worthy of them. I knew in my sinking heart that I was incapable of their heroism.

By the time it was over, I knew I had found my priesthood's core: that they, the laity, would teach me, not only the other way around. I gained a profound sense of reverence and respect for their lives and gifts, and when I became pastor I made it clear to the people from day one that I was there to promote and call forth the gifts and charisms they already had, to teach them who they were as a People of God, to support and learn from them, and to make them aware that this was their parish. I was temporary and would leave some day, but they were permanent; in every sense, they were the local Church. I was sent there to serve, to remind them who they were. I never failed to consult them. The Keyport experience had defined my priesthood.

After Keyport came Maple Shade, the very last parish in the diocese near Camden: being sent there was a punishment for something I had written in a magazine that the people in the chancery found offensive. They originally had wanted to throw me out of the diocese entirely, but finally decided on exile. It turned out to be a good place and there I had, if not another "life-changing experience, a significant one that changed my life.

I had taken three or four seminarians down to a small bungalow at Point Pleasant Beach for a week of relaxation. It turned out that it rained heavily all week. The young adults went bar hopping and found other amusements, but I was stuck in the bungalow for six days of wet confinement. It so happened, however, that I had brought my typewriter—older folks here can explain what that is to the younger ones—and some notes so I figured, since I'm stuck, I might as well type out some of my written notes for some conferences I had given.

At the end of the week, I had a small typed booklet and

decided, on a lark, to send it to a publisher out west. To my total surprise, they accepted it—and asked for more. Since I had given many conferences already, I typed them out too and so began, totally unsought, something never in my mind or intent, a writing career, and from that beginning one book has, over the years, grown into 34, some of them prize-winning. Talk about surprises of the Spirit! It was at Maple Shade, by the way, that I acquired, for the rest of my parish life, my beloved German Shepherd—at first one, then two—who spread in equal amounts companionship, joy, and dog hair over my life.

Then, on to St. Benedict's in Holmdel with the delightful Father Bill Anderson, where we lived in two old farm houses. His house eventually burned down and my 102-year-old house, after three years of living there, was condemned by the township as unfit for human habitation.

And, finally, to Colts Neck where I spent 22 very happy and creative years as pastor, sprinkled with annual summonses to the chancery carpet. During that time, as the parish grew in fame, my book topics expanded to cover parish life and were so well received that I started to get invitations to speak all over the country. I must have lectured in about half the dioceses here, and also abroad in Ireland and England, and gave workshops in several dozen colleges, universities, and conference centers.

There, that's enough to tease you with! Then, all of a sudden, I realized I was old enough to retire! And I said to myself, "Where did the years go?" They went by just as fast as I spoke those words, and I knew they went by fast because, when I would go to a class reunion, all my classmates had gotten so old they didn't recognize me!

Well, if that saying is true—and I can vouch that it is—that "Inside of every old man is a young man asking what happened," I tell you this: Through my store-bought glasses, looking past my liver-marked hands, gray hair and failing body, ignoring for the moment the eight decades plus of life and pondering 60 years of priesthood, the answer is clear: grace happened.

How else to explain God's writing straight with the crooked lines of my life? I look at these hands with its arthritic crooked fingers—a symbol of all my imperfections, shortcomings, and sins—and marvel as I think of all the children over whom they poured the baptismal waters. I think of over 60 years of signing the cross over repentant sinners, pressing the healing oils on the foreheads of the sick, offering the Sacred Host to nourish the yearnings of pilgrims, joining other hands in matrimony, holding the hands of those in excruciating pain or grief or despair and, not the least of which, gesticulating to urge on the homiletic word, the point in the classroom, the lecture, the conferences—thousands and thousands of them—or to tap the keys that eventually morphed into books.

It all becomes a symbol of an undeservedly graced priesthood. And this is despite, at times, a singularly un-graced leadership and shameful scandals that have sullied our Church. But in this regard, I readily recall the words of another octogenarian, the late Jesuit, Father Walter Burghardt:

"In the course of a half century," he wrote, "I have seen more Church corruption than you have read of. I have tasted it. I have been reasonably corrupt, myself. And yet, I love the Church, this living, pulsing, sinning people of God with a crucifying passion. Why? For all the Christian hate, I experience here a community of love. For all the institutional idiocy, I find here a tradition of reason. For all the individual repression, I breathe here an air of freedom. In an age so inhuman, I touch here tears of compassion. In a world so grim and humorless, I share her rich joy and earthy laughter. In the midst of death, I hear an incomparable stress on life. For all the apparent absence of God, I sense here the real presence of Christ."

I say "amen" to that.

Enough: let me end with a dialogue that I read years ago—when and where I can't remember - but it says it all:

> And the Lord said GO
> And I said, who me?
> And God said, Yes, you.
>
> And I said,
> But I'm not ready yet,
> And there is company coming
> And I can't leave my family.

You know that there is no one to take my place.
And God said, You're stalling.
And the Lord said GO.

I said
But I don't want to
And God said
I didn't ask if you wanted to.

And I said,
Listen, I'm not that kind of person
To get involved in arguments.
Besides, my family won't like it.
And what will the neighbors think?
And God said, Baloney.

And yet a third time the Lord said GO
And I said, Do I have to?
And God said, Do you love me?

And I said, Look, I'm sacred.
People are going to hate me
And cut me to pieces.
And I can't take it all by myself.
And God said,
Where do you think I'll be?
And the Lord said GO

And I sighed,
Here I am . . . send me.

Sixty years ago, God sent
and sixty years ago, I went
and here I am bent
but not yet spent
—with the help of a lot of friends.

Thank you.

Funeral Homilies

JOB 2:11 - 3:1 & JOHN 15 & 16

60

A Premature Death: Why?

Ever since people have been on Earth, they have struggled with life's basic questions: Why are we here? Is there a God? Why must we die? Why do people suffer? What is life all about? All ancient writings around the world tackled these questions, especially the why-do-we-suffer question or, more to the point, why do innocent people suffer or, as the title of a modern book stated, "When bad things happen to good people." Why?

The Hebrews tried their hand at the problem. They came up with the Book of Job—and found no more satisfactory answers than the others did, but it had its own point of view. This Hebrew version of the old question is a now familiar tale: bargaining with God, an Earth patroller called Satan (not yet the demon of later times) says to God, no wonder Job is faithful to you: he's got it made. Would he love you as much if you stripped him of everything from top to bottom? Give it a try. God does. Dazed and decent Job is severely downsized in every way, as we might put it, financially, physically, emotionally, and morally.

As you heard in the first reading, three friends come to console him in his misery and, as the text says, before they spoke they sat with Job in silence for seven days and seven nights. (Unfortunately, when they did speak it was in platitudes. They should have kept their mouths shut!)

Note that, as was the custom, they did not speak for seven days and nights. The enormity of Job's plight was so profound, so pitiable, so deep, so searing that there were no words capable of speaking of it. Modern people, addicted to action, have trouble with this. They often say to me in times of loss, I don't know what to say. They feel they must say *something,* no matter how inadequate or even sometimes inane. I always tell them, forget the words. Say nothing. Just be present. Just be there.

That's why I feel useless and frustrated trying to utter words that cannot carry the weight of the loss. The question, "Why do bad things happen to good people?" is especially burdensome when it comes to Patti Madzin. I've seldom met a sweeter, kinder, gentler person. From the time I met her when I was privileged thirty-nine years ago to witness her marriage to Drew—himself a very special person—to seeing her at church years later when I was serving at St. Catherine's in Farmingdale, I was, like so many others, captivated by her gift of being just who she is, a person who made people want to be nice, who made them feel good, who charmed and touched people in a special way, a beautifier of the home and the world.

So why? Why did she die out of season? Why was the accident helplessly witnessed by her husband? Why the involvement of a dear neighbor and friend? So, I join others in the grief, the anger, the burden of the "whys?"

In search of some solace, I move to the Bible's later pages, to a bittersweet scene in an upper room in Jerusalem where a Master and twelve disciples are happily gathered for a meal only to have the mood subverted by the Master, Jesus, who, as you heard in the gospel, suddenly turned the talk to parting and leaving and the pressures the little group will soon feel. "Do not let your hearts be troubled. Believe in God, believe in me," he said. Yes, he was telling them that he was "going away" and he realized the sorrow they would experience.

Well, whatever they felt on hearing these words, the disciples never dreamed that "going away" would be so sudden, so brutal, or so horrendous. And this would happen to one of the sweetest, kindest, gentlest persons they knew. Only later—later, much later, after their shameful and disgraceful abandonment, denial, and betrayal of their beloved friend—would they recall his words, "You will have pain now *but* I will see you again and your hearts will rejoice." They were still waiting for that "but." So far, nothing but pain.

They happened to be doing the waiting in the Upper Room. After their miserable performance, after their flight back home trying to duck the Roman soldiers, little by little, one by one, they reconsidered, they rethought, and, though still confused and uncertain, for some reason they found themselves heading back to Jerusalem and to that same Upper Room. Why not? There at least were memories of *him*, of fragrant bread broken and sweet wine shared.

So, one by one these wretched and mourning men came back, surprised to find others. Each sat behind the locked door mired in his own thoughts, his own loss, his own guilt, and his own "whys." And just when the dark mood was most oppressive and heaviest, Jesus comes through the locked door, stands in their midst with all of the glaring wounds that life had dealt him and breathes "Shalom!" into their sagging spirits. Not judgment, not blame, not hate, but "Shalom"—"peace," and all was made new again.

That "Shalom-in-the-midst-of-terrible-mystery" is what we cling to, that makes us believe that the bad thing, the very bad thing, that happened to good Patti is not the last word.

• • •

Meanwhile? Meanwhile, like Job's friends we must remain present to one another in our silence, in our perplexity, our hurt—*and* in our persistent second-guessing of God and where he was when all this happened. The Book of Job, as I said, tries to tackle the unanswerable question of where was God in all the tragedy and it doesn't quite succeed, but it steadfastly believes that there is an answer somewhere. It reminds me of the story of a group of rabbis who put God on trial after the horrors of Auschwitz had been exposed. God in the Dock, so to speak. They found God guilty and then, when their deliberations were finished, turned to evening prayer.

As our loss settles inward, our grief abates, our anger relaxes, and our burden adjusts then let us slowly return to evening prayer where we are not alone. It is a place where we are present to one another as a faith community who will pray when we cannot, sing when we choke on the words, and rejoice together when we are in tears.

For Drew, Andrew, Fil, and the family, I suggest that as best you can, struggle to keep life's cup turned up and not down; when you're in the dumps nothing can enter your upside-down cup. No refreshing rain can fill it, and so life is empty and bitter. To counter this, I leave you with lines from Grace Noel Crowell's poem:

> Dear child, God does not say
> "Today be strong."
> He knows your strength is spent,
> He knows how long the road has been
> How weary you have grown.
> For he who walked the earthly roads alone,
> Each bogging lowland and each rugged hill,
> Can understand and so he says, "Be still
> And know that I am God." The hour is late
> And you must rest awhile; and you must wait
> Until life's empty reservoirs fill up.
> As slow rain fills an empty, upturned cup,
> Hold your cup, dear child, for God to fill.
> He only asks that you be still.

Loss is hard to live with and "why" is harder, but remember, we do have promise. We have Shalom. Let this comforting truth slowly fill your cup.

LUKE 10:38-42

61

Helen Kozabo, Rest in Peace

You may wonder why I choose this gospel about Martha and Mary. I confess that I usually avoid it because, try as I might, I can never disassociate it from an old illustration of this gospel I saw years ago that still sticks with me and distracts me. It was a cartoon showing Mary sitting attentively at the feet of Jesus while, from the kitchen door, a frying pan aimed at Mary's head is sailing across room. You know: "How about setting the table?"

But I choose it anyway because I have always thought of Helen as the perfect combination, both Martha and Mary, the activist who contemplated and the contemplative who acted. Not that she ever thought that. She would disavow it.

But she was. She was a nurse at Riverview until retirement. She was active in the community and the parish, a behind-the-scenes person: Colts Neck Fire Co. #1, the Martha-Mary Guild, and Holy Spirits here at St. Mary's, the Colts Neck senior citizens.

She was gentle and kind—everybody said that—a Christmas celebrant, and the matriarch who gathered the clan at her house full of decorations, cheer, and plenty of good food.

And at 89, she was an old-timer. Helen goes way back. Most outsiders don't know that Helen was born in Colts Neck,—the old Scobeyville area where Tease and

Steve Colando lived—one of the rare natives. So was her mother. When St. Mary's was doing its anniversary book, the parish turned to Helen as the oldest parishioner who was baptized in the original St. Mary's when it was on Heyers Mill Road.

Her passing is more than the passing of a life. She's the passing of an era—like the passing of Dick and Bill Flock and Charlie Crine, Irene Smith, Mrs. Sadelecki, Frank and Fances Cahair, Alice Remney, her husband Bill who died six years ago, and a host of others who laid the foundation for this town.

One thing about Helen is that in all the years I knew her, I never saw her angry or in "poor-me" mode. To me, she always seemed to have a sense of peace, a deeper core that she tapped, and a faith that was unassailable.

I always liked Helen from the first day I met her in 1972. In fact, as time went on, I saw her and Bill often as I took care of her sister Margaret Buckalew till she died. She was so cooperative. From day one, she and Bill were some of my most ardent supporters, flowing with the changes in civic and church life, embracing the programs. And she never, ever forgot my birthday or anniversary even when I left St. Mary's. Over the years, I could always count on two cards from Muhlinbrink Road: Helen and Bill Kozabo and Nancy Runge, our faithful non-Catholic who sang in our choir.

In the years since I left St. Mary's, I saw Helen regularly every now and then and in these latter years of her illness and, finally, for the past two years when she was bedridden. Her niece, Terry, as it turned out, is a member of Holy Innocents parish where, for the past year, I have been celebrating weekend Masses. Terry would appraise me of Helen's condition and lately told me that Helen was getting worse. So, I visited her about three or four weeks ago. As usual, Helen would always smile and chuckle a bit.

And then, as usual, we would reminisce a bit. It was fun. For her 89 years on Earth, she was remarkably alert and had an incredible memory—and then, as always, there was evidence of that sense of peace again, the feeling that, even as she lay bed-bound and her kidneys were failing, something was going on deep down inside her and it was good. It was, of course, her rooted faith. As Terry said, "She was a woman of great faith and prayed every day." Truly a gentle Martha-Mary.

I'd like to end with a story that reminds me of Helen. It's from a rabbi, but it has Helen written all over it. He writes:

Two years ago, I was invited to address a conference that took place in the synagogue in Harrisburg, Pennsylvania, where I grew up. I had been back twice before. Each time it seemed that I was stepping into the past. My family had moved from Harrisburg when I was ten years old. Now I drove through the streets not as an adult, but as a child. With the eyes of a child, I saw the homes where my friends used to live, the river my brothers and I walked along, the modest four-lane street we thought was the greatest thoroughfare in the world.

The overnight flight landed early in the morning, and so I arrived at the synagogue an hour before my talk was scheduled. At the invitation of the organizers, I wandered the building, looking for a quiet spot to review my notes and collect my memories. I found myself in the small chapel, alone. Although I had previously returned to the synagogue, I had not been in that chapel for almost thirty years. It looked the same. When I sat down, I remembered Mr. Weiss.

Mr. Weiss led the children's services. Each week as the parents went to the main service, they would drop off all the kids at the chapel for prayers with Mr. Weiss. He was an old man, a Holocaust survivor, with an Eastern European accent and a gentle face. Mr. Weiss had no charisma, but he was kind. The children loved him. I loved him. Week after week, Mr. Weiss would assign us parts in the service, encourage us, and guide us through. When someone did a particularly nice job, Mr. Weiss always had a reward handy. He would sneak a Luden's cherry cough drop into our hands.

I treasured those cough drops. They were small red jewels, a sign that I had done well, and that Mr. Weiss approved. Now, as I sat in that same chapel, Mr. Weiss came back to me. Though I had not thought about him in years, he was newly vivid in my imagination, his hand on my back, helping me through the prayers. Why had Mr. Weiss been so important to me? When Mr. Weiss was pleased, I believed God was pleased as well. We were children at prayer, looking for favor. Mr. Weiss was God's representative. . . . Mr. Weiss knew God, and we knew Mr. Weiss. Through him, each of us prayed as we were supposed to, and believed what we were taught."

Well, we knew Helen and she knew God. It's as simple as that. That's why every time before I left her and blessed her I fought to get up the courage to ask her to bless me. I would have felt better, but she would have been embarrassed so I never got around to it.

Anyway, for many people Helen was their Mr. Weiss. Now she's God's. Rest in peace, dear friend.

JOHN 14:1-6

62

Lillian Riley, Waiting for Death

I begin with a story as I shall end with one.

A professional storyteller by the name of Dan Yashinsky was telling stories at a downtown arts center when a restless group of kids stomped in. They were ten-year-olds from a Catholic school in a new housing development. In they came, munching potato chips and blowing bubble gum, clearly not in a listening mood. Since it was close to Halloween, Yashinsky wisely lit a candle, turned off the lights, and started telling ghost stories; it wasn't long before they were hooked.

He wound up telling them one of those summer camp scary stories where, you know, the narrator's voice gets quieter and quieter until the moment when the ghost grabs the poor victim, and then he raises his voice loudly and says something like "I gotcha!" and the kids scream and jump into one another's laps. That's exactly what happened.

Well, when the lights came on, the children lined up to leave, talking excitedly about their shocking experience. Yashinsky noticed one girl standing quietly, holding something around her neck. He asked her if she liked the stories and she said, "Oh, yes, but when you told the last one I didn't jump."

"I noticed," he said, "How come?"

"Because when I knew it was going to be scary, I held the Blessed Virgin Mary."

She showed me the medal she was still holding. "You should get one, too."

"I'm not sure I should," he answered. "I'm Jewish."

"That's okay," she said sagely, "Get a Jewish one."

Then he makes this telling comment: "Writing my book about storytelling as an art and way of life, I have often remembered the girl's good counsel. When you know something scary is coming, you must find and hold onto your own source of reassurance and wisdom. You must have a steady beacon to guide you through perilous waters."

That story tells us everything we need to know about Lillian Riley because the one thing, the one summary truth, we can say about her is that her life was unerringly guided by three steady beacons that defined and supported her, those three enduring "F's" of a successful life: family, friends, and faith.

Family. This South Jersey, Camden-Catholic High school girl met the love of her life, Carl, in college and they were married in 1955. She and Carl lived simply, traveled extensively. It was a truly good, really dedicated, and loving sixty-year-old marriage. People noticed the deep love between them. They had three children, seven grandchildren, and two great-grandchildren. They were always there for them. When their daughter Lillian became seriously ill, they traveled out West and stayed with her until she died. Family meant everything to her.

Friends. She had so many of them, so many lifelong ones. I have to guess that it was her many considerable gifts that brought her into constant contact with friends because she excelled at so many things: bowling and bocce—she won several tournaments—she was an avid reader and charter member of the Book Club at Four Seasons, a formidable bridge player, a writer for their monthly Newsletter. Along with Carl, she ran the Friday Night movies at the Clubhouse there, was a member of St. Mary's women's, group and, on top of all that, a knowledgeable bird watcher. She cherished her friends and vice-versa.

Faith. It was as strong as her values and opinions. She and Carl lived their faith. It wasn't a Sunday affair. They were long and contributing members at St. Mary's, where I first met them. For more years than I can remember I know she belonged to a faith-sharing group until the day she died—and even when some of them crossed the Delaware and moved to Pennsylvania, they continued to meet. For some seventeen years, I know, she went with the Rugarber's, Imholte's, and Grassi's to the Weston Priory monastery in Vermont on retreat.

In times of trouble—she had her share—like the girl in our story, Lillian held onto her faith to steady and guide her.

It was only natural then that, when she found out the startling news of her terminal cancer, she would ask to see me. I remember she was comfortable, alert, and even looked good. Before I anointed her, we chatted. I remember asking her if she was old enough to recall the old, old days when at the Easter Vigil Mass on late Holy Saturday Night the choir chanted the Litany of the Saints in Latin and the congregation responded. I remember it well because for years as an altar boy I struggled with my peers to stay awake—not always successfully.

The choir would sing in Latin, names like *Sancta Theresa, Sanctus Michael, Sanctus Johannis* and so on, and we would all reply, "*Ora pro nobis*," "Pray for us." "*Sanctus Petrus, Sanctus Thomas, Sancta Agatha, Ora pro Nobis*." It went on forever. Then, when the list of saints—and ourselves—were exhausted, the Litany switched gears and went on with many heartfelt petitions like: "from fire, storm and flood" and we would all sing in reply, "*Libera nos, O Domine*." "Deliver us, O Lord," "From pestilence, disease and war," *Libera nos O Domine*, Deliver us O Lord. But for some reason, out of all of them, I always remembered this one: "From a sudden and unprovided death, *Libera nos, O Domine*, Deliver us, O Lord." That petition,—"from a sudden and unprovided death," I think, was heard in Lillian's case.

It's a mixed bag. Dying suddenly relieves the mind and the agony of a long vigil and knowing one is slowly dying does concentrate one's fears. Knowing, however, also provides the blessings of time: the poignant goodbyes, the reconciling words, the reminders, signals and silent gestures of deep affection, the golden memories, the shared tears, the ministrations of neighbors and hospice, the pilgrimage of relatives near and distant, like the ones who came from Montana, Colorado, and Japan, the bequeathing of gifts: jewelry, mementoes and so on, or the planning of the liturgy. I think Lillian appreciated the gift of time and made the most of it.

I also like to think that in her silent moments, perhaps moments of apprehension and fears, with eyes closed, Lillian fell into the role of the person of my second story, a brief one. It's a story about a long-ago celebrity of his time, a well-known playboy, wit and editor of the famous British publication *Punch*. His name is Malcolm Muddgridge and one day this now quite old man, this skeptic "got religion." Because he was so famous, the elite, the sophisticates, who felt betrayed by him, couldn't ignore him. They allowed him his fifteen minutes of fame and then dropped him. He had committed the unpardonable sin. Not only did he get religion, he got the worse possible kind. He became a Catholic. He did so because he was inspired by the presence and work of Mother Teresa. Anyway, elderly when he converted, he wrote many lovely things. Among them are these words which could have been, might have been, Lillian's, words that I can hear her saying:

"As I approach my end, I find Jesus' outrageous claim ever more captivating and meaningful. Quite often, waking up in the night as the old do, I feel myself to be half out of my body, hovering between life and death, with eternity rising in the distance. I see my ancient carcass, prone between the sheets, stained and worn like a scrap of paper dropped in the gutter, and, hovering over it, myself, like a butterfly released from its chrysalis stage and ready to fly away.

Are caterpillars told of their impending resurrection? How in dying they will be transformed from poor earth crawlers into creatures of the air with exquisitely painted wings? If told, do they believe it? I imagine the wise old caterpillars shaking their heads—no, it can't be; it's a fantasy.

Yet in the limbo between living and dying, as the night clocks tick remorselessly on, and the black sky implacably shows not one single scratch of gray, I hear those words: "I am the resurrection," and then I feel myself to be carried along on a great tide of joy and peace."

I firmly believe that so it is, was, with her. With her peaceful death and Easter chrysalis stage now completed, we can say this of Lillian Riley: with her steady, rock bottom beacons of family, friends and faith, she

made a life,
made a marriage,
made a family,
made a community,
made a church
—made a difference.
Thank you. May you rest in peace.

O Tempora! O Mores!

63

Deaths of Despair

"What profit would there be to gain the whole world and forfeit one's life?"

Full disclosure: I *know* this is Labor Day weekend and I should preach accordingly, but two things have absolutely compelled me down a different path. The first is that gospel question of Jesus: *What profit to be brainy and rich but lose your soul, your destiny?* The second is, what better time to wrestle with that question than at the opening of school when education, along with our culture, purports to give an answer.

So, with sincere apologies to anyone here still hurting from any personal experience of the suicide of a loved one, what I *am* going to speak about specifically is adolescent suicide, not the uncommon suicide you know prompted by mental, physical or emotional causes, but the now frighteningly common ones prompted by our culture itself. Listen.

In California on November 4, 2014, a sixteen-year-old boy named Cameron, a straight A student, leapt in front of a commuter train. Just three weeks prior three other students committed suicide, one jumped to his death from the family home. All were from very wealthy neighborhoods although adolescent suicide is equally spread among the very wealthy and the very poor.

The largest school district in California, in fact, recorded more than 5,000 incidents of suicidal behavior. Nationwide, the statistics tell us, since 1999 there has been an alarming national increase of deaths from drugs, alcohol abuse, and suicide, especially among white Americans. Social scientists have been particularly baffled by the fact that the suicide rate among girls ages ten to fourteen has tripled and that suicide is now the second leading cause of death among adolescents and young adults, and the tenth leading cause of death overall in the U.S.

Unfortunately, there's more. Depression, a source of suicide, is now the most common serious medical or mental health disorder in the U.S. and, according to data from the Department of Health and Human Services, more than 3 million adolescents reported at least one major depressive episode in the last year. It seems that most people who die by suicide are suffering from some form of depression and loneliness.

What has happened? Robert Putnam of Harvard has an answer. He has documented a dramatic decline in what is called "social capital." He has exposed the obvious, what you and I know: the fabric of support and connections to family, friends, neighbors, the old "thick" neighborhoods, hang outs, parish churches, local organizations have disappeared. Blue collar jobs have declined, women's roles have changed.

Then there's isolated suburban living, the dominance of television, the ubiquitous Internet and the virtual world of smart phones. Surveys show us that today's teens spend from 6 to 8 hours a day on them (on the average, *everyone* checks his or her phone 43 times a day) Today's iGen, as the social scientists call them, the generation born after 1995, is the first to spend their entire adolescence with smartphones in their hands so they spend more time with screens and less time interacting with each other.

All this plus the homogenization of worldwide brand name identities have bleached local particulars into a common flat secular consumerist living as the inner life has been transformed into outer look-at-me "lifestyles."

Indeed we see social fragmentation everywhere in our country. Family ties are clearly much weaker and mutual obligations less binding than in the past. Divorce rates remain high and more Americans are simply opting out of marriage entirely. Corporate loyalty no longer exists. High mobility prevents roots. Individualism has destroyed community.

On top of this the social fabric has further frayed as the world has been stripped of universally binding truths.

In short, there is no coherent narrative anymore to bind us together. Yesterday the comedian Mort Stal used to quip, "Ask a Californian who he is and he points to his car." Today in answer to "Who are you?" we get, "I am a Calvin Klein, Armani, Lamborghini, Rolex, Jimmy Fallon kind of a guy." "I am a Jimmy Choo, Harry Winston, Neiman Marcus, Gucci, Beyoncé kind of a gal." I am, in short, a collection of brands, nothing deeper. Lose my brands, I lose myself. I am nothing and that is intolerable.

So a vacuum has been created, and, for many, alienation and depression fill the void. Let me quickly add that depression and suicide are complex phenomena. Biological, genetic factors, and out-of-kilter chemical imbalances are surely part of the mix but *they are not the whole picture*, not for those seniors, for example, who eat their dinners alone in front of the television, or for the kid whose family meals are non-existent but a solitary frozen dinner at the computer, or the young adult who lives in a virtual world.

There's another major factor contributing to alienation, depression, and suicide: the sharp decline of religious practice. Too many families have dropped out of organized religion. Too bad for there is a sizable body of medical research which suggests that prayer, religious faith, participation in a religious community, and practices like gratitude and forgiveness can reduce the rise of depression, diminish drug abuse, and aid in recovery.

An example is the Harvard study of suicides among women and the connection to religious participation. Let me quote an assessment of the report:

"Between 1996 and 2010, those who attended any religious service once a week or more were five times less likely to commit suicide. Those who identified as either Catholic or Protestant had a suicide rate about half that of U.S. women in general. Of the 6,999 Catholic women who said they attended Mass more than once a week, none committed suicide. . . . self-identified Catholics who did not attend Mass had suicide rates comparable to those of other women who were not active worshippers."

Well, it's easy to spot the reasons: church attendance is by its very nature a social activity that prevents isolation. Judaism and Christianity have strong moral prohibitions against suicide. Moreover, religious faith instills a sense of purpose, meaning and, most of all, connection and presence. As one lady said, "I don't know what I'd do without church." In short, a community of faith provides meaning and an identity beyond appearances and an inner worth beyond the external number of Facebook "likes."

The reality is that today we are too-willing victims of the all-embracing social media networks, which teach us that our value lies in our usefulness and achievements, in what we do rather than who we are. Sadly, we pass these cultural convictions on to our kids who, whether from rich or poor precincts, are pressured in a thousand ways to perform, to up their résumés, to get into the right schools, to do *well*—not necessarily to do *good*—and that is lamentable.

Lamentable *is* the right word. It evokes that powerful passage from Chaim Potak's *The Chosen*. It's the pitiable scene where a distressed father is wailing to his friend Reuben about his brilliant son, Daniel. Wailing? Today's parents would be proud to have such a brilliant overachiever with a mile-long résumé to show off like a trophy and have him graduate with honors from Princeton or Harvard and acquire high status and higher salary.

But this wise father sees it differently, sees his son's one-sided brilliance as a curse not a blessing.

He cries out, "Reuben, the Master of the Universe blessed me with a brilliant son. And he cursed me with all the problems of raising him. Ah! what it is to have a brilliant son. Not a smart son, Reuben, but a brilliant son, Daniel, a boy with a mind like a jewel. Ah, what a curse it is to have a Daniel whose mind is like a pearl, like a sun.

"Reuben, when my Daniel was four years old, I saw him reading a story. He swallowed it as one swallows food or water. There was no soul in my four-year-old Daniel; there was only his mind. He was a mind in a body without a soul.

"It was the story in Yiddish about a poor Jew and his

struggle to get to Israel before he died. Ah, how that man suffered! And my Daniel enjoyed the story, he enjoyed the last terrible page because when he finished it, he realized for the first time what a memory he had. He looked at me proudly and told me back the story from memory and I cried inside my heart.

"I went away and cried to the Master of the Universe, 'What have you done to me?' A mind like this I need for a son? A *heart* I need for a son, a *soul* I need for a son, *compassion* I want from my son, righteousness, mercy, strength to suffer and carry pain: *that* I want from my son, not a mind without a soul!"

With all the personal, parental, and institutional emphasis on our children doing well rather than doing good, we are mass-producing brilliant minds without souls, people who cannot carry pain. The daily news is full of them. Why not? What is useful has replaced what is good. Efficiency has become the highest human value. The mastery of Big Data, not the mastery of life, is now the stated goal of education as universities increasingly drop the humanities and philosophy courses.

Above all, personal freedom is the apex, offered as the highest good, only the word "freedom" today means being totally unchallenged and uninhibited in doing what you want. Freedom in this sense is the enthronement of the "Sovereign Me" and overrules all other considerations. If art is whatever the artist says it is, so too are morals. If *I* think it's all right, then it's all right. Anybody else's comment is "judgmental." And not only do I have *my* truth, and you have *your* truth but if your truth offends me I shut you out or rush to a "safe house" where I do not have to talk to you. So walls remain, bridges are not built, and we settle in as the divided nation we are today.

In short, the embracing of such "freedom" produces a culture of anything goes and when anything goes, nothing counts and, when nothing really counts, life is ultimately meaningless and for some, in extreme cases, suicide is the only logical answer to meaninglessness. "Deaths of Despair," as the psychiatrists call them, are inevitable.

Let me end with an interesting current tidbit: even Communist China is experiencing our emptiness and reacting against it. Recently, *The New York Times* carried the story about, of all things, religious revivals in Communist China, officially a thoroughly secular state.

"Hundreds of millions of people"—yes hundreds of millions—"hundreds of millions in China in recent years have turned to religions like Taoism, Buddhism, Christianity and Islam, seeking a sense of purpose and an escape from China's consumerist culture . . . People are asking, 'How do you make sense of your life?' An awful lot are looking for something bigger than themselves . . ."

Unknowingly they have pondered Jesus' question.

So, yes, by all means, we need to plumb the scientific and chemical factors that bring on depression and suicide, but:

> until we carry a sense of the Holy Spirit within us,
> until we offer something or Some*one* bigger,
> until we embrace a love that cherishes us as we are,
> until we prize "we" over "I,"
> until we learn to do good with as much fervor as we are told to do well
> suicide statistics—"deaths of despair"—will continue to rise.

Bottom line: school opening provides an opportunity to take a closer look at our and our children's lives.

64

Charlottesville, Virginia

Last weekend our gospel was about two people who couldn't stand each other: Jesus, male and Jewish, and a feisty and annoying petitioner, a female Canaanite. Long centuries of distain and hate had made them that way, and nasty words were exchanged. Jesus even resorted to the usual macho insult by calling her a dog.

But a conversation was begun, as sharp as it was, and a connection was made. A face-to-face encounter was forged and suddenly a wall crumbled; a bridge of compassion and healing was built and both travelled it.

"Who do you say that I am?" asks today's gospel. Answer: Jesus, you are obviously a reconciler and a peacemaker. We know this because this is not the first time you have crossed borders, nor the first time you have dealt with outsiders who hate you.

Let us count the ways. Once, on a journey, as the gospels report, Jesus and his Jewish disciples were about to go through Samaritan territory because it was the shortest route to get to Jerusalem. But the threatening and snarling Samaritans, with their banners and rallies and slogans, would not let them pass. The disciples were infuriated and two of them, the hotheads James and John—"Sons of Thunder" the gospel calls them—show their hate by asking Jesus to let them hurl down fire on them and fry those bigots. Jesus simply rolls his eyes and says, "Let's take the long way around."

If that weren't bad enough, later he goes on to tell the parable of a *good* Samaritan, a Jewish oxymoron if there ever was one! And then there are those other incidents. Jesus crosses borders and touches the *untouchable* lepers, thereby making himself unclean. He heals the servant of a hated military Roman occupier of his land—that took hutzpah. Again, Jewish and male, he sits at a well with a woman and a Samaritan where, once more, under the blazing sun, sharp and nasty dialogue melts into revelation and love.

Then there's his tough and unapologetic talk about loving one's enemies, praying for the wretched people who are persecuting you, giving your coat if your vest is asked of you, going two miles when only one was requested, and forgiving seventy times seventy.

In an Upper Room, he, "Lord and Master" as he calls himself, performs the slave ritual of washing the feet of his denier, his betrayer, his doubter and fair-weather friends—all turned moral enemies. In the Garden of Gethsemane, he tells his misguided followers, who seem not to have learned anything by being with him, to put down the sword. "For those," he said, "who take it up will perish by it." Jesus accepts the help of a foreigner to carry his cross, dies among miserable thieves promising them paradise, and prays for those who are putting him to a terrible death.

"Who do you say that I am?" One answer is that clearly Jesus is one who crosses borders, who, at great cost to himself, transcends history and hate, deception and distrust, and who will not return evil for evil.

Well, maybe we shouldn't be surprised. It seems that his acceptance of those not his own, his border-crossings, are in his genes. If you recall, at Jesus' birth Matthew starts off his gospel with Jesus' genealogy. Among all Jesus' Hebrew ancestors, Matthew includes foreigners and outsiders—and not very noble ones at that. There's the Canaanite prostitute Rahab, the Moabite, Ruth and the Hittite adulteress, Bathsheba, not to mention that he and his parents, Mary and Joseph, were for a time themselves immigrants and outsiders in a country not their own.

Anyway, when played out in reality, Jesus' example and teaching are awesome to behold. I think, for example, of Corrie ten Boom from Holland, praying for and forgiving the Nazi soldiers who eventually beat her to death in a concentration camp, leaving a note behind which read, "Tell them—the outside world—that there is no pit so deep that Jesus is not deeper still."

Perhaps, for us, we might remember the movies. Let's start off with *Driving Miss Daisy*. You recall the plot: two protagonists: Miss Daisy Werthan, an elderly haughty Jewish woman, and Hoke Colburn, an African-American chauffer. They represent two people as opposite as you can get: two races, two religions, two genders, and two people from different sides of the track who, by an act of fate, are thrown together.

We watch grace unfold as the slow grinding process of the years lead this white and haughty matron, now elderly and sick in a nursing home, to grasp the hand of her self-effacing chauffer and declare, "Hoke, you're my best friend." A complete turnaround. A conversion. A lesson. The "Who Am I Jesus" still here.

In *The Defiant Ones*, Noah Cullen, a black man, and Joker Jackson, a white bigot are handcuffed together by a sheriff with a warped sense of humor. They escape a Southern prison. Despite their mutual loathing, the prisoners must endure each other's company and we watch, as in time and through terrible episodes, mutual regard begins to replace the loathing.

The movie's closing scene has the two men, one wounded and the other too exhausted to run anymore, waiting for the posse. The sheriff eventually finds them laying on the ground, the black man singing defiantly and cradling the wounded white man in his arms. Hate had turned into love. Two people at a well.

Then there's *In the Heat of the Night*—most of you recall it—an African-American lawyer from Philadelphia, Virgil Tibbs, finds himself in a Southern town where he comes into conflict with a redneck police chief, Bill Gillespie. We all watched as their mutual hostility eventually turns into mutual respect, leading at the end of the movie to a scene in which the police chief, with a smile, says to Tibbs as he boards the train home: "Virgil, you take care now."

Yes, take care: take care to be like Jesus.

Now take a breath and think. You know where this is going, don't you? It's going to Charlottesville and Barcelona and all the other places just like them where enemies dwell. Only the names have changed. Yet the conclusion is the same. No one can be a neo-Nazi or a white supremacist and at the same time be a Christian. They are incompatible. They cancel one another out. You *cannot* join hate with holiness.

65

Black Pioneer: Augustus Tolton

The gospel of a hated outsider [Canaanite woman and sick daughter] prompts me this Sunday to share some timely facts that educated Catholics should know. There are 2.9 million black Catholics in the United States or about 3.8% of the total Catholic population. There are almost 800 predominately black parishes out of some 21,000 US parishes and six U.S. dioceses are headed by black bishops. Statistics show that black Catholics attend Mass more that white Catholics: forty-eight percent of them in contrast to only thirty percent whites. Some tewnty-seven percent of black Catholics wish more of their friends attended church, in contrast to only seven percent of white Catholics who do.

Black Catholics have had a slow start in the United States, and black Catholic clergy even more so. Today, let's go back and take a look at one of them, a priest named Augustus Tolton who has the distinction of being the first recognized black priest in the United States. Here is how he got that honor.

He was born on April 1, 1854 in Missouri, one of four children. Augustus was named after the African bishop, the great St. Augustine. Of course, being that time and place, he and his siblings were all automatically born into slavery.

The family they served was the Elliots, who were Catholic and who had all their slaves baptized into the faith.

(There are still Elliotts living in the area.) When the Civil War broke out in 1861, Augustus' father, Peter, joined the Union Army, where he lost his life from dysentery.

When he was seven, Augustus' mother, Martha, fled to freedom by rushing to Hannibal, Missouri, and then crossed the Mississippi River. The trip was dangerous and included a ride in a rowboat where they had to duck gunshots. They got to Quincy, Illinois, which was free territory and where former slaves gave them safety and access to the Underground Railroad.

There with his brother Charley, aged ten, Augustus, aged nine, went to work in a tobacco factory making cigars. Imagine that—a couple of young children working in a factory. (Charley would die young of pneumonia). Later, Augustus worked in a saddlery shop. Meanwhile, fortunately, the Tolton family was embraced by a local pastor, an American-Irish immigrant, Father Peter McGirr, who himself had come to America at the young age of fifteen during the Irish potato famine.

He helped them hold onto their Catholic faith. Augustus first went to a segregated school and then to the all-white St. Boniface's Parochial school, but the parents there were outraged.

They sent the pastor and religious Sisters threatening letters. A rock was hurled through the rectory window. The kids tormented Augustus, calling him a bastard because he had no father. Despite of the support of the Sisters, Gus (Augustus) continued to encounter such deep prejudice there that he lasted only three months.

It was Father McGirr who again came to the rescue. He took all the Tolton children into his school of St. Peter's, where many of *his* parishioners also protested the presence of a black student. But Fr. McKirr held fast. He preached fiery sermons on the expansiveness of Christianity to remind people what the gospel meant.

The opposition eventually died down. Meanwhile, Augustus, an intelligent and pious lad, felt the desire to become a priest. But there was a problem: he was black, and the American Catholic seminaries were closed to him. His parish priests had larger (and more Christian) hearts, and so they decided to tutor the young man privately.

In 1878, he was admitted to the Franciscan College in Quincy, Illinois as a special student but his parish priests, never giving up, finally managed to have him enrolled in the international Propaganda Seminary in Rome where he learned fluent Italian as well as the ability to read Latin and Greek. When he finished, Augustus naturally thought he would be sent to Africa as a missionary but an enlightened Cardinal at the College, knowing full well the resistance the new priest might receive, nevertheless felt that America needed a black priest and, being a democratic nation, as he'd heard, felt this would give them a chance to prove it.

So, Augustus was ordained on April 24, 1886 in St. John Lateran's in Rome and returned to America. He came into New York and offered his first Mass on American soil at St. Benedict the Moor, a black parish church on Bleeker Street in New York City, and was the first black priest in the United States to offer Mass in their church. The next day, he celebrated Mass for the Sisters in Hoboken. He was then off to Quincy, IL where Father McGirr had arranged a royal welcome.

He was an associate for two years at St. Joseph's parish in Quincy, Illinois, where he quickly gained a reputation as a fine preacher—even to the point of drawing many of the German and Irish Catholics to the Mass meant for blacks. He soon became "Good Father Gus." His instruction classes became popular and he labored hard to make converts, but was discouraged by the poor response. He worked hard, was gracious to both backs and whites. A local newspaper described him in glowing terms and his church was often filled with standing room only.

It wasn't long before he was asked to speak at public gatherings. Nor, sad to say, was it long before racism and jealousy raised their ugly heads from both Catholic priests and even from envious black Protestant clergy. Especially hurtful was the strident prejudice of the new pastor at St. Boniface in Quincy, a priest named Father Michael Weiss, who began to refer to him openly as the "nigger priest."

Father Weiss had come to financially rescue the parish and was jealous of the money going to the negro parish. He was losing parishioners to Father Gus. Gradually, he forced Father Gus to only minister to blacks and declare that any white donations belonged to white parishes. Not content with that, Father Weiss outright told Father Gus to go elsewhere. He wound up in the Archdiocese of Chicago, whose Archbishop was anxious to have him.

There he served as pastor of St. Joseph's and, when that closed, he took up his duties in a black church called St. Augustine's Association which met in the basement of a half-finished church named St. Mary's. It eventually became Chicago's first Negro parish, and Father Tolton was Chicago's first black pastor as well as this country's first black priest. This parish would become the center of black Catholic life for more than 30 years.

Father Tolton lived in a house behind the church and his mother served as housekeeper. He hoped the church would be completed, but his people were very poor. Still, he tirelessly ministered to them by making the rounds to visit the sick and needy and generally wore himself out.

All along there were bright spots. Not all were so prejudiced as those Catholic parents who did not want him, or those Catholic kids who were following their parent's example by tormenting him, or the Catholic clergy who shamefully distained a brother priest because of his race. We have already seen the kindness of Father McGirr. Then there were the Franciscan Friars, the School Sisters of Notre Dame, the Josephite Fathers, and Sister Katherine Drexel of Philadelphia who all extended welcome and support to Father Tolton.

In 1897, after returning from a diocesan retreat on an extremely hot day while walking home from the train station, he had a heat stoke. He was rushed to Mercy hospital, but he did not survive. He died that night at the age of 43. His body was brought back to Quincy, where he was buried in St. Peter's cemetery. He had a large funeral, according to the newspapers, "four blocks long plus streetcars . . ."

But, would you believe, even in death he apparently faced prejudice even though it was remarkable that, back in 1897, he was allowed burial in a white cemetery at all. He was placed so deep in the ground there that another white priest could be buried above him and Tolton's inscription wound up on the backside of the large cross that marks the other priest's grave.

Fast forward a century or so later. The year of 2009 had been dubbed "The Year of the Priest," and so Chicago was looking for a local priest as a model, an icon, an example to hold up to the people. Many immediately thought of Fr. Augustus Tolton. Times had changed and the Cardinal of Chicago lost no time in setting in motion the process of his canonization, which is still in progress.

A long journey but, by the grace of God, the slave boy had come a long way. So, by this time, thankfully, had the Church.

66

One of Us

The woman named Mary, whom we honor today and about whom we know so little, has intrigued us for twenty centuries. We don't know when she was born or when she died, but we can place her in history. We know where she lived and who were some of her friends and family. But that's all. So why does she persist throughout the ages? What is her appeal? The answer is to be found by stripping away all those images which the centuries of art have left us and going back to the basic gospels. Let's concentrate on them to discover who Mary really was, in reality.

When we first meet her, Mary is the object of an ugly rumor: she is pregnant and without a husband. Her fiancé, Joseph, is of the mindset to officially deny her and anything about the pregnancy by quietly putting her at a distance. That she was innocent, invaded by the Spirit, was not believed.

So right away, people down the ages who have suffered from false rumors, who have had their reputations soiled, who have been misunderstood and maligned, unwed mothers, have identified with her.

Then, too, there is her very human anxiety and fear. What is this all about—this Mother of God business? "How can this be," she asked the angel incredulously. "What does God want? What about Joseph? How can this happen? How can I do this?"

Confused and scared and full of questions, Mary is all those throughout the ages who have cried out, "How can

I tackle this challenge? How can I survive? What does God want of me?" What's it all about, Alfie?

When her son was born, shepherds and angels rejoiced while the power-brokers seethed and conspired to kill her baby. They wanted his life, and his spirit. And, right away, parents today and down the ages who are often faced with so many soul assassins have identified with Mary. They know well enough that there are people out there waiting to kill their children. The people who are waiting to sell their children drugs, or the media who glamorizes uncommitted sex, and the hawkers with cash registers for hearts who teach them that we *do* live by bread alone, the soul-snatchers of false values—all are after their children to kill their spirits. Parents know what Mary knew and fear what she feared.

Mary had to flee with her husband and child and become a refugee in a foreign land. In doing so, she immediately joins the countless displaced persons, the homeless huddling in the world's doorways and sleeping on the nation's grates and the 60 million refugees walking the earth today—these lowly who need to be lifted up. They are cousins under the skin, and they can identify with Mary.

When he is an adolescent, Mary loses her child. She becomes every parent, every teacher, every mentor in history who can't communicate with a teenager, who loses them to gangs or drugs; whose kids have joined the small army of runaways roaming the streets, exploited by the sex trade, abused and beaten. Many can identify with Mary here.

At some point—we don't know when—this wife and mother became a widow. She buried her husband, and everyone who has ever lost a spouse has cried Mary's tears, and felt the gnawing void in their belly while returning to an empty bed. They can identify with her.

When her son is old enough, he leaves home to begin his mission and he leaves a widowed mother behind—and suddenly every mother and father who see their children grow up and leave them behind—especially those in nursing homes—knows what she is feeling in her heart.

When she walks the streets now that she is alone, she has to give way to the rough Roman soldiers and leering men passing by. She has to move quickly and duck into the shadows. As a minority woman in an occupied territory, as a widow with no man around, she is always subject to sexual and physical exploitation and discrimination. Every person with no rights, every minority figure who has to swallow their pride, or everyone ever called *nigger* or *wop* or *spic* or *fag* can identify with Mary.

When she hears rumors that her son is preaching nearby, she goes with some relatives to see him but can't get to him because of the crowd. She has to be content with sending word that she's out there on the fringe. The message arrives to Jesus that his mother and his relatives want to see him and he, gesturing to the crowd, asks, "Who are my mother and brothers and sisters? Everyone who does the will of God is my mother and brother and sister."

It sounded like a put down, a message to tell his mother to go home, but she saw it for what it was, what she always had known: her glory was not primarily that she was his biological mother but that she was closer to him than anyone else because she loved God and, even when she didn't understand it, did God's will. And every little person on the sideline, off-center, on the fringe who doesn't understand what's going on, but simply clings fast to God's will, can identify with Mary.

And then that Son is caught—betrayed by one she has had over for dinner many a time—brought to a mock trial, beaten and humiliated and hung on a public cross. She arrives in time to see him hanging there, every inch of her mind and body straining to go to him, but she is forced by the soldiers to keep her distance.

And suddenly, every parent who has seen their child on a cross, every parent who wants more than anything else in the world to help their grown children dealing with alcoholism, living in sin, raising children with nothing or not even having them baptized, or while going through a divorce—every parent who witnesses such "crucifixions" yet who must keep their distance, who are *told* to keep their distance, can identify with Mary and pray and suffer in silence.

And finally, she cradles the broken dead body of her only son in her arms and sobs uncontrollably and there she is, once more: every parent who has lost a child, any friend who has lost a friend, any classmate who has lost a classmate through an overdose or gunshot wound, can identify with Mary of the Pieta.

This is the woman—this pilgrim who savored the ups and downs of life. *This* is the ageless woman who has been given to us as a legacy: "Son, behold thy mother." And here we are today beholding her. But it is good to remember that we're beholding her now that it's all over. In this feast of the Assumption, the Church has, frankly, romanticized her.

It clothes her with the sun, puts the moon beneath her feet, halos her head with stars, dresses her in medieval robes, paints in winged cherubs to do her bidding, places her against a background of Italian villas and has her whisked up to heaven to the sound of Handel's *Messiah*.

But we should understand that's all metaphor, figures of speech, and storytelling. What it means to say—all this heavenly glamour—is that Mary who is Everywoman, Everyman, is blessed now because, unblessed in many ways in life, she remained faithful.

In all of the unfairness of life she clung to God. In virginity, in motherhood, in widowhood, at home, as a wanderer in a foreign land, with a living child, and with a dead child, she clung to God. So she becomes a woman for all ages and that is the secret of her enduring popularity and her appeal. She is us.

And the Church elevates her, not because she started out as great and traveled a privileged path, but because she was a handmaid, a slave of the Lord and traveled a lowly path. But then God who is mighty, has done great things for her. God has lifted her up when down, fed her when hungry and because she responded to God's loving invitation wherever it would lead her, saw to it that all generations would call her blessed.

That's what we're doing right now: calling this woman of our flesh and blood, our experience. Blessed. Yet this is not honoring someone far away and high above us. No, we're calling blessed someone who is near and right with us at every human step. The message of this feast is a sign of hope for us. It is meant to be a preview of coming attractions for all who cling to God in perplexity and adversity. Mary, the Church says in this feast, is what we shall be.

She is promise fulfilled, humanity completed, and faithfulness rewarded. Simply put, she is us at the end of the journey we are traveling. That is why Mary is so compelling. She is indeed a *Woman for All Times and All Seasons*.

67

The Barque is Sinking

This gospel is both rich and timely. It relates to us in so many ways today as it did back in the time it was written, a terrible time when the Romans had just burned down the Temple, slaughtered and deported the people, and murdered Peter and Paul. No wonder the early Church, feeling itself sinking, preserved this gospel, or that today's Church resonates with it.

"*Meanwhile the boat was being tossed about by the waves . . .*" and, today, like Peter, we are frightened.

Globally, think of how planet Earth is being tossed about as never before. Whatever the reasons, our climate is changing: average temperatures have risen drastically and recent decades have been the warmest in 1,500 years. Glaciers are melting, seas are rising, and animals are becoming extinct.

Politically, the threats of North Korea are truly alarming, the non-stop wars and butchery abroad continue, the displacement of millions goes on and on, and at home our murder statistics daily expand to new records. We have homeless people in the land of plenty and the widest skyrocketing financial inequality in the past half century.

Socially and morally, we have lost our moorings. All the surveys show discontent. The old moral culture of accepted norms that once united us has broken into competing ideologies. A pervasive secular progressivism and the glorification of the individual have emptied our souls, dismantled our neighborhoods, and fractured our relationships. Consumerism has replaced concern, outer image has replaced inner character, and celebrities have replaced saints.

And then there's us, Catholic Christians. From early times, the boat, or the "Barque of Peter," was a metaphor for the Church. As then, so now, it also is being violently tossed about. It's being overwhelmed by the waves of sin, loss, and persecution such as never before.

There's the stain of the sexual abuse scandal, the official dismissal of religion from the public square, and decline of church attendance—an overall collapse. An article in this week's *Times* (8/8/17) is about eighteen parishes in the Archdiocese of New York on the block for sale—emblematic of what's happening.

Closer to home, Bishop O'Connell recently released some Trenton Diocesan statistics that are troubling: today we only have 107 parishes. That's down some twenty percent from the past ten years, and more parishes will close or merge. There are about 850,000 baptized Catholics in our diocese.

Of those, he notes, only thirty percent attend Mass on the weekends. There's a critical shortage of priests. The young have disappeared. Catholic schools are closing at record numbers.

And on a personal level, there are things that frighten us. Parents are frightened because they can't control the institutional secularism that pervades our society: schools without God, soccer games on Sunday, or stores open on Thanksgiving and Christmas Day. Easter sales start on the first Sunday of Lent, soft and hard pornography everywhere, and a terrible drug scourge that currently is swallowing up the country.

Seniors are frightened of disability, of the coming day when family takes away their car keys. Mid-lifers are frightened of losing their jobs, or having a mid-life crisis.

Teenagers are frightened of being counted out by the "in" crowd, of getting too few "likes" on Facebook. Children are frightened of the dark, their parents' quarrels and divorce, being picked on, and being different.

For Peter in the sinking boat, it was a combination of the destructive wind, the massive waves and the terror of drowning that frightened him, but these are some of the things that frighten us.

So now, by this time, if you came here today anxious to hear the good news, then you're winding up depressed. Sorry about that—but, unfortunately, it's all true.

But, remember, that's only half of the gospel. It's time to move to the other half and, as Christians, take grasp of the underlying hope in which it gives. That hope is found in the gospel's two final lines.

The first line is, "*Take courage. It is I. Do not be afraid.*" The second line is, "*Immediately Jesus stretched out his hand and caught Peter.*"

Yes, from our fears and concerns, the image we need to clasp to our souls in these times is Jesus amid the waves, saying, "It is I. Do not be afraid," and stretching out his hand to us.

Remember, when corruption was about to drown both Church and state he raised up the poor man from Assisi. When the French Revolution profaned the Cathedral of Notre Dame in Paris, the aftermath saw a great flowering of spirituality.

The world has always been seeded with people who grasped the hand of Jesus and made a difference. On our Catholic calendar of this August alone we find people like Saints Alphonsus who founded the Redemptorists, Dominic who founded the Dominicans, Francis who founded the Franciscans, Ignatius who founded the Jesuits, Maximillian Kolbe who took the place of an about-to-be-executed prisoner in a Nazi concentration camp, and Catholic journalist James Foley who decided to stand with the suffering and was beheaded by ISIS. September brings us Saint Peter Claver, who ministered to the slaves, and Michael Judge of September 11th memory.

Then there's people like Louis Braille, Mother Teresa, Dorothy Day, Madame Curie, Florence Nightingale, Mahalia Jackson, Bill Wilson, Catholic convert Rose Hawthorne who comforted those with cancer, Barnard Lichtenberg who boldly denounced the Nazism that sent him to Dachau concentration camp to die, Queen Emma of

Hawaii who built hospitals to care for her people ravaged by diseases introduced by the Europeans, and Quaker Tom Fox who went on a mission to Iraq to work for peace and assist the families of imprisoned Iraqis. In 2005 he was kidnapped by Al Qaeda and killed. His body was found on a garbage heap. There's also Josephine Bakhita of Sudan, a slave and Catholic convert, who lived and died serving others. Finally, if the Church in the West is sinking, the Church in Africa is flourishing.

I could go on and on with my list, but you get the idea. So much is wrong, so much *is* frightening, so much is sinking but too so much good is being done every day by people who have made a difference, who have reached out to the Someone who comforted them with his words, "Do not be afraid" and, hand in hand, inspired their deeds.

The good news is that there are millions today who still reach out to grasp the outstretched hand of Jesus, and one day, God will raise up one of them as God has always done in the past.

I'd like to think that person might be among us here today. Don't sell yourselves short. There's a hand reaching to you. Like Peter, catch it and save us.

68

September 11, 2001—15 Years Later

September 11, 2011. This is the date when the World Trade Center in New York was destroyed by terrorists, the Pentagon was partially leveled, the fields of Pennsylvania exploded and nearly 3,000 innocent people, mostly young, lost their lives—a date that became a turning point in American history.

Prior to that, for decades we had seen in the movies and watched on television the horrors of war. We winced as whole villages were burned to the ground; the billowy smoke the only indication that men, women, and children once lived there. We looked aghast at the continuous black fumes from the Nazi gas chambers. We sat in horror to watch the footage of the bombings of Britain, Poland, France, Germany, the Netherlands—cities towns, hamlets, castles, cathedrals all went up in flames. We watched in fascination the death-dealing mushroom clouds over Japan. In *Life* magazine we checked out the photographs of the massive mounds of human skulls in the Cambodian killing fields.

Eventually we all began to watch those horrors with a certain detachment, even those who lost loved ones in the wars, as Hollywood turned carnage into entertainment and killings into box office, mass exterminations into discussion panels and unspeakable horrors into back page notices. So we flipped the pages of *Life* magazine to see what Madonna was doing.

And, in a way, it's no surprise. All those things, those terrible unmentionable things, were "over there" in Europe and Africa and Asia and South America. *We* were never bombed. *We* were never invaded. *Our* skies never saw war smoke or explosions. *Our* cities were never wiped out. So we tightened our belts, used our ration stamps, bought our bonds, and mourned our dead soldiers who died "over there." But in our land, we were free of the personal, gut horrors of war and could never quite resonate with the metaphors and desperate prose of our allies who walked stone-eyed and ash-dusted amidst the half-houses and half-bodies of their neighbors.

That is, until September 11, 2001. The unbelievable had happened. Invincible America had been violated. America had been terrorized. In the very blue skies of a beautiful day there was sudden black smoke; and where there were two massive towers housing thousands of people—nothing.

The halls of Congress were evacuated, leaders were led to bunkers, airlines shut down, and a continent of dismay and an ocean of tears flooded the land as people simply couldn't believe what they were seeing on TV. The country was brought to a standstill. I remember it well. Many of you remember it well.

Yes, those among us who witnessed all this will never forget those images of the jets crashing into the towers, the fireballs of flame, the towers themselves collapsing before our very eyes, the ash-covered streets, the people jumping to their deaths from high windows, the herds of people walking zombie-like across the bridges taking them away from suffocating smoke. We remember the staggering preliminary reports of brave people killed by falling concrete: 350 firefighters, 200 Port Authority employees, 40 police officers, 700 workers each from various financial companies, 266 people on the airplanes, nearly 200 at the Pentagon.

These "preliminary figures" were, of course, people: our parents, spouses, children, lovers, relatives, friends, all with names, faces and histories. I remember people holding up photographs pleading, "Have you seen my husband? Have you seen my daughter? Have you seen my father? Have you seen my niece? Have you seen my friend?" I remember those heartrending cell phone calls from the doomed airplanes, all ending with a soulful "I love you." For the survivors on the ground, there were the painful realizations that these people died before we had a chance to tell them how much they meant to us. No doubt about it, there was a sudden new awareness of the fragility of life, an awareness emphasizing that we all have a limited time to love out loud, an awareness that reminded us poignantly that indeed we must turn to love those nearest us and realign our priorities.

Yes, all of a sudden, seeing all of our old reliable identities of image, wealth, and celebrity revealed for what they are, we were forced to look deeper, forced to turn elsewhere for answers. And many did. Many united in tragedy, and grew closer to family, country, and God.

But—within the past 16 years, without us meaning it or wanting it—it just happened. Slowly the everyday practical memory of 9/11 began to fade as a host of new sophisticated technological marvels began to claim our attention, not for just a little bit, but 24/7: the around-the-clock advertising and consumption, the television, the internet, the smart phones. Before we knew it, ever so slowly gadgets trumped people, celebrities replaced saints, malls upended churches, greed undermined sharing and the Sovereign "I"—propagated by the media and the universities—replaced the nation's "we" as in "*We* the people."

The result is that today, sixteen years later, nations are at war, 65 million refugees swamp resources, North Korea threatens, politicians are at odds, drugs ravage our communities, identity politics spawn hate and division, religion has faded, and financial and social inequality is greater than ever.

Following 9/11, 2001, America united in the embrace of family, friends, and faith. Today, in 2017, with a different mindset, having lost faith in its government, leaders and institutions, America is now more divided and less hopeful than ever.

But here I must in conscience pause and add that on the other hand there *is* an other hand. We have restored the Pentagon and rebuilt the World Trade Center. On the other hand, we recognize that we are really good people. Witness then as now, the outpouring of help, the long lines of blood donors, the army of volunteers, and the everyday heroes beyond counting. Look at our outpouring of aid to Texas.

In emergencies, we are magnificently kind, generous, and compassionate—often to the point of heroism—so we know that we *can* do better and *be* better. But still, on the everyday level, the dominance of the media forever trying to sell us something, the alluring marketplace of profit alone, success equating with growth, efficiency, production, consumption and celebrity have taken over and distract us and, with Christmas sales already appearing in September, push noble thoughts and action out of mind, out of fashion.

But we are here today in this sanctuary we call church, determined to shake these things off, if only for a moment. We are asked to remember, not only 9/11, but who we are and what we must do. We know that we owe it to the 9/11 victims of yesterday and today to seek a restoration that includes the interior life, the moral life. We know that both as individuals and a country we need a spiritual renewal. We need leaders who look beyond the bottom line, who don't see us as consumers but as people capable of reversing the "I" back to we.

We, Christ's people, know we need to see to it that our own individual lives will look beyond the walls of hate, that we need to build bridges and elect decent people to office. Above all, we know that we, each one of us, no matter how unimportant in the world's eyes, can and must make a difference.

Ponder two simple stories that underscore this truth.

You may not know this but a few days before 9/11 the universal Church celebrates the memory of a man named Frederic Ozanam. Frederic Ozanam lived in the aftermath of 19th century France, reeling from the horrors of the Revolution and class warfare with its reign of terror, blood a foot deep in the streets, the deaths of thousands and a Church on the wrong side of the argument.

Frederic hated his country's divisions and was especially appalled at the divisions between the rich and the poor, and aghast at squalor within the urban areas. Convinced that Christianity was about deeds of love, he did something. He formed a group of ordinary everyday Christian people who would immerse themselves in the world of the poor and marginalized. The point: his unknown, unimportant little group of ordinary people eventually became the Vincent de Paul society and there is no parish in the world, no corner of the earth that has not been touched by it, by one man's vision and action.

My second story is whimsical but no less striking. It's one of the morality fairy tales we all knew when I was a kid, the story of Chicken Little. The story is that word—and panic—had gotten around that the sky was falling.

One day the proud and haughty rooster was walking home and saw Chicken Little lying on his back with this tiny spindly legs sticking upwards.

"What in the world are you doing?" asked the rooster?

"The sky is falling," replied Chicken Little, "and I am holding it up."

The rooster sneered, "What? You think a little twerp like you can hold back the sky? Ha!"

Chicken Little replied with those immortal words, "One does what one can."

Yes, today 9/11 plus the subsequent terrorists acts at Fort Hood, Garland, Boston, Orlando, San Bernardino, Little Rock, Queens, Moore, Chattanooga, Columbus and St. Cloud weigh heavy on us but they also challenge us, *as they must*, for mere remembrance without action is sentimentality.

So act. Pray. Build bridges. Embrace as your personal motto, "One does what one can." Say a kind word, do a good deed. Nobody sees, nobody knows but love is released, a momentary goodness, and it joins with the love and creativity and energy released by all the others that day and gathers force and Jesus is here.

Yes, each year let us continue to gather together as we are today, not only to remember 9/11 but also once more to remember who we are: one nation under God.

69

The Ten Commandments of Forgiveness

"*... unless each of you forgives your brother from your heart.*"

That forgiveness is such a frequent gospel theme is not surprising since it figures so much in Jesus' ministry—for which we are grateful since we are all in much need of forgiveness, both in receiving it and giving it. We all have done some stupid and immoral things, from sniveling lies to large betrayals—and worse. None of us wants the burdens of shame and guilt as we live. We want forgiveness. None of us wants justice when we die. We want mercy.

But meanwhile, we are reminded that forgiveness to us depends on our forgiveness of others; we are forgiven to the degree that we forgive others. A sobering thought.

So let me share with you what I call the Ten Commandments of Forgiveness. You will not, and need not, remember them all—don't even attempt it—maybe, perhaps, just the ones that strike a chord with you. So, let's begin: the Ten Commandments of forgiveness.

The First Commandment is: Forgiveness is not easy. There is no cheap grace. There is no quick fix. A mother says to her child, "Tell him you're sorry." "I'm sorry," the kid mumbles grudgingly. Doesn't mean a thing. If it's quick and easy, forgiveness is not real, especially for deep betrayals and hurts. It often takes time to work up to true forgiveness. Be patient. Keep on trying.

And along the way, ask God for help. Adopt St. Paul's wonderful phrase, "The Spirit groans prayers we dare not utter." So we could pray, "God, I just can't forgive now. I just can't! I've been too deeply wounded. So Holy Spirit, groan those prayers of forgiveness I cannot pray right now until your effort thaws my heart and wears down my hurt and resistance, and one day I can find myself saying Jesus' words on the cross. "Father, forgive them. They know not what they do."

So, First Commandment: Forgiveness is not easy.

The Second Commandment: Forgiveness is not forgetting. We say, "Forgive and forget." I don't think so. Forgiveness is about a change of heart, not a bad memory or having a senior moment. The wounds are too fresh or too deep. While forgiveness may not include harboring festering hurts neither is it about forgetting. In fact, it may be helpful to remember the point from which you have moved on, the occasion that began your journey to full forgiveness.

The Third Commandment: Forgiveness does not overlook evil. Forgiving someone doesn't mean that we accept injustice or naively make believe that all is well when it isn't. It doesn't mean denial. It doesn't mean, "Let's pretend it never existed." The terrible deed, the hurt, the fallout was real. There was evil. So number three is: Forgiveness does not overlook evil.

The Fourth Commandment is similar: Forgiveness is not indifference. What that means is where things are harmful and wrong, it doesn't just go back to "business as usual. Let the hurt and damage go on." Forgiveness is not indifference and you should do what you can to make sure the evil won't happen again.

And the Fifth Commandment is: Forgiveness is not approval. We can be forgiving and, at the same time, express our disagreement, express our disapproval of harmful behavior. It shouldn't have happened. It was wrong what I did or another did. My forgiveness in no way means that it was alright. It wasn't.

O.K. That's the first five. I'm going faster than Moses did.

Forgiveness is not easy.
Forgiveness is not forgetting.
Forgiveness does not overlook evil.
Forgiveness is not indifference, and
Forgiveness is not approval.

Here are my next five commandments. They are more positive and deeper.

The sixth Commandment is: Forgiveness is based on recognizing and admitting that people are always bigger than their faults. People are always larger than, and they are more than, their mistakes or their wrongdoings. In other words, I don't define somebody by something they said to me or the way they hurt me. They are bigger than that. Forgiveness is based on recognizing and admitting that people are always bigger and more than their faults and their mistakes.

You and I don't want to be forever defined by *our* mistakes, forever branded as worthless. St. Peter went beyond his terrible denial, Thomas beyond his doubt, Paul beyond his persecution. John Newton was glad that he has been remembered for his hymn, "Amazing Grace," and not for his slave-trading.

The seventh Commandment is like the sixth: Forgiveness is willing to allow a person who has offended us to start over again. You know, the more common thing is saying, "Never again! No way! I will never let that happen. I will never have anything to do with him again. No way!" Forgiveness means letting go of that. Forgiveness means allowing a person to start all over again.

The eighth Commandment is: Forgiveness recognizes the humanity of the person who has wronged us and also recognizes our own humanity, shortcomings, and contributions to what went wrong.

The ninth Commandment is: Forgiveness surrenders the right to get even. It's not Liza Doolittle's, "Just you wait, Henry 'iggins, just you wait!" "Boy! I'm going to get you back!" "Payback time!" "Revenge!" "Someday you'll be sorry," so dear to the media. It means letting go of that and embracing the Christian truth that forgiveness surrenders the right to get even.

And, finally, the tenth Commandment is: Forgiveness

means we wish well to the person or group who hurt us. In fact, we wish them the best. This is not necessarily the case emotionally because we may still have feelings of hate and revenge against them, but in the fullest sense that, beyond our claims to justice, like Jesus, we offer them the Father's love. We let God be the final judge.

So here are my Ten Commandments of forgiveness:

1. Forgiveness is not easy
2. Forgiveness is not forgetting
3. Forgiveness does not overlook evil
4. Forgiveness is not indifference
5. Forgiveness is not approval
6. Forgiveness recognizes that people are always bigger than their faults
7. Forgiveness allows a person to start all over again
8. Forgiveness recognizes the humanity of the wrongdoer
9. Forgiveness surrenders the right to get even and
10. Forgiveness wishes well to the offender

The gospel story begins with the longing for God's forgiveness at Advent and ends with bestowing it at Pentecost. "Whose sins you shall forgive, shall be forgiven them." In between lies our Ten Commandments of Forgiveness and the lesson is, you can't have the bookends without the middle.

70

From No to Yes

The gospel: one son said no but, for one reason or another, sooner or later—how much later we do not know—gave a yes.

And that is my entre into observing that history is full of indifferent, weak, hostile and wicked people who, regarding goodness, conversion, love, God, like the son in today's gospel—sooner or later—went from no to yes.

For starters, there were the no's to the yes's of Peter who denied, Thomas who doubted, and Paul who persecuted, but, nearer to our times, I want to share four no to yes stories.

Let's start with the mocker.

The bishop of Notre Dame Cathedral in Paris during the early part of the last century was a great evangelizer. He tried to reach out to unbelievers, scoffers and cynics. One of the stories he liked to tell was that of a young man who would stand outside the cathedral and shout derogatory slogans at the people entering to worship. He would call them fools, brainwashed, stupid, and all kinds of names. The people tried to ignore him, but it was difficult.

One day the parish priest went outside to confront the young man, much to the apprehension of the parishioners. The young man ranted and raved against everything the priest told him. Finally the priest addressed the young scoffer by saying, "Look, let's get this over with once and for all. I'm going to have you do something and I bet you can't do it." And, of course, the young man shot back, "I can do anything you propose, you black-robed wimp!"

"Fine," said the priest. "All is ask you to do is to come into the sanctuary with me. I want you to stare at the figure of Christ on the cross and I want you to scream at the very top of your lungs as loudly as you can, 'Christ died on the cross for me and I don't give a damn!'"

So the young man went defiantly into the cathedral, approached the sanctuary and, looking at the face of Jesus, screamed as loud as he could, "Christ died on the cross for me and I don't give a damn!" The priest said, "Very good. Now do it again." And again the young man, looking at the face on the cross, this time with a shadow of hesitancy, shouted, "Christ died on the cross for me and I don't give damn!" "You're almost done now," said the priest. "One more time." The young man raised his fist, kept looking at the face of the cross . . . but the words wouldn't come. He could not look at that face and say that any more.

The real punch line came when, after he had told the story, the bishop said, "*I* was that young man. That defiant young man was me. I thought I didn't need God, but found out that I did."

From no to yes.

Tom Phillips was the CEO of a large company. He had everything: a Mercedes, a beautiful home, a lovely family. He was a man of influence and moved in high circles. But Tom was not happy, In fact, he was downright unhappy. Something was missing from his life, but he didn't know what it was. But one night he had a religious experience that changed him forever. Later he said, "I saw what was missing from my life. It was Jesus Christ."

I'm not interested in him but in an acquaintance of his who at the time was the second most powerful man in the United States. Go back to the Nixon years. Nixon's Number Two man was Charles Colson who used to brag that he would run over his grandmother to get Nixon elected, and that he had an office next to the President of the United States, a six-figure income, a yacht, a limousine, and a chauffer. But secretly he, too, was an unhappy man with a growing hollowness within him. Something was missing in his life too but he didn't know what it was.

Well, as fate would have it, one August night in 1973, Phillips had Colson over for dinner and in the course of the evening told him about his conversion. The more Colson listened, the more he became convinced that Phillips had put his finger on what was causing that hollowness deep inside him.

When Colson left the Phillips home that night, he hadn't driven 100 yards from the house when he pulled up alongside the road and began to cry so loudly that he was afraid the Phillips family might hear him. Describing what happened next, Colson said, "I prayed my first real prayer. It went like this, "God, I don't know how to find you, but I'm going to try! I'm not much the way I am, but somehow I want to give myself to you." Then he added, "I didn't know how to say more, so I repeated over and over the words, "Find me, find me, find me!"

And the Lord did and he responded. A long no to yes.

Then there's Eddie, an older student and a friend of mine. We were in the seminary together. After we got to know each other well, he told me some of his story. When he was six years old, Eddie said, his mother, a very confused young woman, left him at an orphanage. Standing on the steps of the building he watched his tearful mother wave goodbye through the back window of a taxi. He was stricken by rejection and anger. Suddenly, he wrestled free from the woman gripping his arm and ran after the cab, shouting at the top of his lungs, "Mommy, I hate you! I hate you and I'll never forgive you!" He never forgot the image of his mother riding off in that taxi.

He wasn't to see his mother again for years. Yet, despite such a start, despite the lack of close family ties, Eddie never adopted a defeatist attitude. He was one of those remarkable human beings who just went on. He became a professional ice skater at an early age. Later he became a competent public accountant, ultimately owning his own firm. After several highly productive years, however, he became aware of a need within himself to serve others in a different capacity. This eventually led him to the seminary, and that's where I met him.

Shortly before his ordination, Eddie did something that left all of us astounded. He picked up the phone one afternoon, called his mother, and said, "Mom, I love you and I forgive you." After a long sobbing telephone conversation, the longest chase in years ended. For thirty-five years, Eddie said he had been chasing that taxi in his mind. Now it was over. His no had turned into yes.

Finally, Sister Mary Rose McGready, former head of Covenant House, tells a similar story. Here are her words.

Kate came to our front door Tuesday morning, ragged with dirty clothes on her back—and a little aluminum paint can in her arms. From the second she stepped inside, she made it clear to us that she and that paint can were "a package deal." Whatever she did or wherever she went, the little paint can never left her hands.

When Kathy sat in the crisis shelter, the can sat in her arms. She took the can with her to the cafeteria that first morning and to bed with her that first night. When she stepped into the shower, the can was only a few feet away. When she dressed, the can rested alongside her feet. "I'm sorry, this is mine," she told our counselors whenever we asked about it.

"This can belongs to me."

"Do you want to tell me what's in it, Kathy?" I asked.

"Umm. Not today," she'd say, and then quietly walk off.

When Kathy was sad or angry or hurt—which happened a lot—she took her paint can to a quiet dorm room on the third floor. Many times I'd pass by her room and watch her rock gently back and forth, the can in her arms. Sometimes she'd talk to the paint can in low whispers.

Early one morning I decided to "accidently" run into Kathy. "Would you like to join me for breakfast?" I asked. "That would be great," she said. We sat in a corner talking quietly over the din of 150 hungry homeless kids. Then I took a deep breath and plunged into it.

"Kathy, that's really a nice can. What's in it?"

For a long time, Kathy didn't answer. She rocked back and forth, her black hair swaying across her shoulders. Then she looked at me, tears in her eyes. "It's my mother," she said. "Oh," I said, "What do you mean, it's your mother?"

"It's my mother's ashes," she said, "I went and got them from the funeral home. See, I even asked them to put a label right here on the side. It has her name on it."

Kathy held the can up before my eyes. A little label

on the side chronicled all that remained of her mother: date of birth, date of death, name. That was it. Then Kathy pulled the can close and hugged it.

"I never knew my mother, Sister," Kathy told me. "I mean, she threw me in the garbage two days after I was born. I ended up living in lots of foster homes, mad at my mother. But then I decided I was going to try to find her. I got lucky—someone knew where she was living. She wasn't there, Sister. My mother was in the hospital. She had AIDS. I went to the hospital and I got to meet her the day before she died. My mother told me that she loved me, Sister," Kathy said crying. "That's why I went to get her ashes."

I reached out and hugged Kathy, and she cried in my arms for a long time. It was tough getting my arms around her because she just wouldn't put the paint can down. But no one minded.

Two no's moved to yes. A mother who said 'no' to a two-day-old daughter. A daughter who said 'no' to a mother who had abandoned her. But on a deathbed, a 'yes' emerged from both mother and daughter.

I think we want to meditate on these stories and how they deeply and profoundly tell us the gospel message.

The message is that the past can be reversed. The mocker could say yes to Jesus hanging on the cross for him; a politician could cry out "Find me! Find me!" after a life of lies and deceit; Eddie could stop chasing taxis, and Kathy could hear those words she so ardently desired.

From no to yes. However long it takes, the everlasting mercy of Jesus is always there.

71

Drugs

With sympathy towards those who are addicted or who have lost loved ones through an overdose, let's talk about drugs in two parts. Let's start with some dire images.

In a small town in Ohio, a four-year-old boy sat in the back seat while his parents were slumped over the front seat. They had overdosed on heroin. A three-year-old in pink pajamas is trying desperately to wake her overdosed mother in the aisle of a Family Dollar store in Lawrence, Massachusetts. A seven-year-old girl in McKeesport, Pennsylvania told the bus driver she was unable to wake her parents who were dead from an overdose, leaving her siblings ages five, three, and nine months alone in the house. In several states, infants have died from the hands of unthinking parents who gave them their drugs to relieve pain, or by toddlers thinking they were eating candy; pills are everywhere. Babies of addicts are born addicted.

In 2010, there were 3,100 people who died from heroin overdose, which is an increase of 56% from ten years ago. The year 2015 saw a dangerous spike in powerful painkillers added to heroin, making it almost fifty times stronger. By 2016, the total deaths exceeded 59,000.

On a national level today, 142 people die each day from overdosing on prescription opioid painkillers, while heroin and drug overdose is now the leading cause of death among Americans under the age of fifty. Do the math: 142 overdoses a day times 365 days. Then there is Fentanyl, a drug so toxic that just a few grains can kill.

Young adults between ages 25 and 34 are the hardest hit. Many more are brought back from the brink of death by the anti-drug Narcan. In March of 2016, *The New York Times*, in a front-page article, reported that, as the drug epidemic grows, addicts are more commonly shooting up in public places: trains, subways, buses, airplanes, restaurants, and restrooms. Therefore many funeral directors, usually inured to dealing with the dead, are visibly shaken at burying so many young people. It should be noted that these young people are not the seedy losers often portrayed in the media, but are instead good people who have gotten caught in the culture's dysfunctions.

Worse news: Women of all social and economic levels, recent surveys show, are now using heroin in greater numbers than ever. The Centers for Disease Control and Prevention, in a July 2015 study, alarmingly showed that heroin use has doubled among women between the decades 2002 and 2013, and general overdose death has nearly quadrupled. The fact is that all users, overall, are dying more frequently. Users are also typically younger and from affluent families.

Many addictions start in the medicine cabinets of people's homes, where drugs like Percocet and Oxycodone are found. In fact, the abuse of prescription drugs kills more people in the U.S. than cocaine and heroin combined. Marijuana use in high schools has increased, especially since being legalized in some states. According to federal figures, more than twelve percent of eighth graders and thirty-six percent of seniors at public and private schools said they had smoked marijuana in the past year. Here, too, users are younger and white. Since marijuana is a multibillion dollar market, states are racing to legalize it not just for medicinal purposes but also for recreational use. So far, seven states have legalized recreational marijuana, with more states hastening to follow because of the astronomical money to be made. Footnote from *The New York Times*, January 2, 2018 concerning Colorado, the first state to legalize it: "Traffic deaths involving drivers who tested for marijuana more than doubled from 2013 to 2016 according to a study published by a federal government agency in October." Just chalk it up as collateral damage to making money.

Drugs hurt the economy too, not just because of the huge cost of care and absenteeism but also for the reason that, ironically, companies in desperate need of workers can't hire them because so many applicants fail the drug test. One company in Ohio, for example, forgoes some $200,000 worth of orders because of the workforce shortage. "Our main competitor in Germany," says one executive, "can get things done more quickly because they have a better labor pool. We are always looking for people and have standard ads all the time, but at least 25 percent fail the drug tests."

You think you've heard it all? Listen to this one more fact: todays' health officials are now also alarmed in discovering that those drug and alcohol taking counterculture Baby Boomers of the 60s and 70s, who kicked the habit later as they went on to executive positions, now, in middle age, have fallen back into addiction! They are the growing segment of today's older druggies who are once again abusing drugs. As one older abuser sadly expressed, "Your mind never forgets."

Finally, hand-in-glove with growing drug abuse, hepatitis C and HIV outbreaks have spiked in the U.S. as many turn to sex to pay for their drugs.

All the way around, in width and in depth, drug abuse is apocalyptic, a diabolical scourge, an epidemic. No wonder PBS has run a powerful series entitled "America Addicted," and the White House declared the epidemic "a national public health emergency," a phrase usually applied to natural disasters. We are in a huge social and spiritual crisis.

There are many causes for the addictions. Until the recent crackdown, many doctors were over-prescribing opioids. For example, the number of prescriptions for opioids jumped from 76 million in 1991 to 219 million two decades later. Then, too, we indisputably live in a heavy drug environment and a counter culture atmosphere. There's a famous photo of a rock & roll star with a tattoo on his naked torso: "sex, drugs, and rock & roll." We live in a culture fueled by an incalculably rich illegal drug trade and the legal relentless multi-billion-dollar advertising of the pharmaceutical companies who push a drug for every ache, pain, and itch- the sooner and younger, the better.

There's social isolation and mental illness, the loss of the support and cohesion of family and neighborhood, the loss of a common set of beliefs and values, huge financial inequality, as well as a fragmented and permissive society. The social, psychological, and physiological roots of addiction are varied. Today, efforts are being made, such as doctors issuing short-term prescriptions for opioids so that the drugs will last till only a recovering patient can visit a physician. There are more needle drop-off programs. Police and physicians are more frequently treating opioid abuse as a health issue rather than a criminal problem, seeing affected people as needing medical help. More churches are reaching out on the neighborhood level. Catholic Charities has been on the front lines of the opioid crisis, offering a range of services. But the crisis will be with us a long time and the battle is far from won as overdose deaths keep rising each year and grief fills the hearts of survivors, perhaps some of you here. As a twenty-four-year-old addict lamented, "It was fun, but by the time it stopped being fun, it was too late." Yes, too late.

With this young woman in mind, let me now focus away from the victims to those who are not caught in addiction (for now anyway) but who just are seeking a high, a buzz, because, you know, sometimes life is routine or dull or boring or unexciting and in our special effects, celebrity driven, viral happenings society that's not good enough to draw "likes" on Facebook. So, you gotta jump start life. To counter this attitude, I want to call to mind an old forgotten churchy tradition called, archaically, "The Mystical Body of Christ" or "The Communion of Saints," or we can use the simpler ordinary term: solidarity.

Solidarity, as its name implies, is the enemy of our society's celebrated pathological individualism where the sovereign "I" lives, rules, judges, and acts. Solidarity says we are not alone, that we are profoundly interconnected, that we can identify with others in the same situation as ourselves and, most of all, that we can actually offer up our boredom and sufferings for others in the understanding that such connecting thoughtfulness will bring *them* comfort, solace, and a sense of being cared for and loved.

As the living Body of Christ, we can plead for one

another, pray for one another, comfort one another, and also offer up acts of courage, endurance, and suffering for one another. We can even die for others as, in fact, our brave soldiers have done for us and somehow, in the great mystery of life and love, it can benefit others. By the same token, others can help us. In other words, we are a part of a vast conjoined and spiritually interacting confraternity of fellow pilgrims. If we could only internalize that!

So, when life hurts us, then faith asks: Can I offer my asthma for those suffocating in dense slum tenements? Can I offer my sleepless nights for those whose nights are filled with acid fumes and gunfire? Can I offer my financial losses for those 65 million refugees today who carry their homes on their backs, whose children have no schooling and too often die from hunger?

Can we offer our migraines for the abused and exploited, our sadness for the depressed, and our unpopularity for those sidelined by racism, poverty, or prejudice? Do we believe that we can influence others just as they impact us? Do we believe in the powerful mystery of solidarity which says we can offer up much for others, that we can touch and comfort one another, and that other people's lives can touch and heal ours? For us, the answer to all these questions is a resounding "Yes! Yes! Yes!"

When I was a kid and had an ache or pain or disappointment, I was told, "Offer it up for the Souls in Purgatory." Today's teens or young adults would find this advice quaint if not outright laughable. But at least we knew, however vaguely, there *was* an "other" in play and that somehow we were connected and could influence one another. My pain wasn't just my own to squander in self-pity but a spiritual gift to others.

Who wants pain? Nobody. But it comes. Who wants to be unattractive, bored, unpopular, lonely? Nobody. But it happens. Who wants to say life is utterly useless and meaningless? Nobody, but we all have our down times. So, I ask: Who will seek out drugs, drink, or uncommitted sex to alter these moods? Who will feel bad for not making the team and pop a pill to feel - at least for a while, a pitiably short while—like they just won the Heisman Trophy only to wake up the next day caught in addiction?

Only those who do not know this great truth: we are never alone, and each of us belongs to a vast communion of Saints; we can choose to empathize with those who suffer like us and try to do something to make others' lives better; that, at the same time, others in the same situation are praying for us. These are the ones who feel a deep spiritual unity, who have a sense that, better than any drug, is doing good for others. As scripture says,

> Share your bread with the hungry
> Shelter the oppressed and the homeless;
> Clothe the naked when you see them
> And do not turn your back on your own.
> *Then* your light shall break forth like the dawn
> And your wound shall quickly be healed.

Drugs are an insidiously growing scourge: a powerful lift, a pleasant high, a brain pleasure center button-pusher whose price comes later, whose captive addiction takes over, whose last claim, death, is on the march.

I'm suggesting that a sense of solidarity may slow down the impulse to reach for a drug, that we can do something noble with our physical and emotional discomfort, and that, finally, the gospel truth "It is in giving that we receive" is the real high, and the better deal.

(PRECHED WITH SOME PASSION) 72

Seven Buses Worth

New Year's, 2018

It's a New Year and let's frame our homily with poet Robert Frost's question, "How many things have to happen to you before something occurs to you?"

How many things last year—like terrorist acts; the heavy, expensive security to protect the watchers at Times Square; the horrific, terrible drug epidemic that keeps on killing so many young adults and innocent children; the adolescent suicide rate topping and exceeding deaths by car accidents and illnesses; being held captive to our gadgets so that we check them twenty-four times a day, use eighty times a day or some 30,000 times a year; our endless and mindless ongoing consumerism; our deeply divided country suffering from a kind of soul sickness no one can seem to label but everyone feels it, knows that it's there.

How many broken values, broken relationships, broken dreams, and broken hearts before it occurs to us that something is wrong with the way we're living? Not quite the snappy holiday questions you expected, are they? But these are definitely questions for New Year's 2018.

At one time, I confess, I would look for answers to these questions among the wise and noble of country and church, yet somehow they seem to be in short supply. So,

I thought, as a sign of the times, I would look to the mean streets on the other side of the country, to a section of Los Angeles.

And there I found an "expert"—and what an expert! He's a Jesuit street priest named Father Greg Boyle, known as "G" in his neighborhood, a neighborhood that happens to harbor the murderous gang members of Los Angeles; in fact, it's a place recognized as the gang capital of the world.

To help these desperate, hopeless, heavily tattooed, gang members who live more of their lives in prison than out on the streets, Fr. Greg—or Father G—founded Homeboy Industries, which draws a lot of visitors and tourists curious about his hoodlum employees who are known as "Homies."

Every single day Father G deals with druggies, pushers, pimps, jailbirds, the poor, the fatherless, and the defeated. He gets them jobs, becomes their father figure, and also buries them when they become victims of turf wars and overdose. "Kids I love killing kids I love" is his lament. But every single day he relentlessly brings to them what we desperately need for the New Year: *hope*.

Anyway, I knew I found who I was looking for and so my New Year's message will be *his* message. I've raided his book, "Tattoos on the Heart," to share some of his searing stories. Listen in because they are our stories.

• • •

Father G:

Jose taps me on the shoulder.

"Jose," I exclaim, "When did you get out?"

Short little guy, his smile is bigger than he is.

Jose is fifteen and part of a gang. He's been discharged from a probation camp where he served six months for writing on walls and skipping school.

"Can I talk to you, G? In your office?"

I sit behind my desk and he takes a long envelope and slaps it in front me.

"My grades," he announces proudly, "from camp. . . Straight A's." I open the envelope and there it is: two C's, two B's, and one A—"Well," I think, "not quite accurate, not quite straight A's." I hand him back the transcript and say, "Wow, *firmé* [could not be one bit better]. Nice going,

Jose." Then I add, "If you were my son, I'd be the proudest man alive."

That does it! In a flash, this little fifteen year old who's been an adult all his life, with absent parents and a grandmother trying her best to raise him, whose best friend I just buried a month ago killed in our street for no reason at all, was unable to stop the flow of tears.

I let him cry it out and placed my hand on his shoulder. "You're gonna be okay," I tell him.

Jose sits up and wipes his tears. "I just want to have a life," he says. "I just want to have a life."

Do *you* have a life? A real life. Not the copy cat, Facebook, consumerist life that passes for living, but a deep life that gives, shares, and heals? Is one of your New Year's resolutions to go deeper this year than the surface of your life last year? Are you ready this New Year to embrace what you have been putting off: to become a saint?

Are you at a point when, weary of conformity and celebrity, you just want to have a life that counts?

• • •

Father G:

At a county detention facility, I was getting to know fourteen-year-old Rigo, who was about to make his first Holy Communion. The Catholic volunteers had found him a white shirt and black tie. We still have fifteen minutes to go, so I'm asking Rigo the basic stuff about his family and his life. I asked about his father.

"Oh," he says, "He's a heroin addict and never really been in my life. Used to always beat my ass. Fact, he's in prison right now."

Then suddenly, for some reason, a terrible memory jumps out of him. "I think I was in the fourth grade," he begins. "I came home, sent home in the middle of the day. Got into some trouble at school—can't remember what it was. When I got home, my father was there. He was hardly ever there. He said, 'Why did they send you home?' And 'cuz my dad always beat me, I said, 'If I tell you, promise you won't hit me?' He just said, 'I'm your father. 'Course I'm not gonna hit you.' So I told him."

Rigo begins to cry. When he is able to speak, he says only, "He beat me with a pipe . . . with a pipe!"

When Rigo composes himself, I ask, "And your mom?"

He points some distance to a tiny woman standing by the entrance. "That's her over there. There's no one like her. I've been locked up for more than a year and a half. She comes to see me *every Sunday*. You know how many buses she takes every Sunday to see my sorry ass?"

Then, quite unexpectedly, he cries again for a long time and then gasping through his tears, he says over and over, "*Every Sunday! Seven buses! She takes seven buses. Imagine!*"

New Year's question: Why do we have such a hard time grasping in our minds and hearts that we have a God who has taken "seven buses" just to arrive among us in a poor manger and share our lives and bring us peace? Why can't we grasp that we are loved by a longing God and that is our deepest identity? One week ago we celebrated the reality that

"*The Word was made flesh and took seven buses to dwell among us.*"

Believe *that* for 2018.

• • •

Father G:

After Mass at Central Juvenile Hall in Los Angeles, I spot a kid named Omar whom I had known for some years. I actually never knew him when he was out on the streets, only at a variety of detention halls or camps. He never seemed to be out very long before he'd find himself swept up, yet again, in gangbanging and life on the streets. He motions to me as he is being led back to his unit. "Come and see me," he mouths.

I locate Omar. He knows the drill. He quickly sweeps up two plastic chairs whose backs are covered with gang graffiti and carries them away from the others, landing near the windows, out of reach of earshot. He tells me he'll be leaving Thursday, but I can't help to think I'll be bumping into him again. After a half hour, I eye the clock on the wall and tell Omar, "Gottta go, dog." (Street slang for *loyal friend.*)

"Why so fast, G?"

I have an anniversary Mass at the cemetery for a homie I buried a year ago. So, gotta go."

Omar stays seated and is uncharacteristically pensive.

"Hey, G," he says, "Can I ask you a question?"

"Sure, *mijo*," [dear one] I say. "Anything."

"How many homies have you buried . . . you know, killed because of gangbanging?"

"A hundred and twenty-six, son."

"Damn, G, a hundred and twenty-six?" He shakes his head in disbelief, his voice a bare hush now. "I mean, damn . . . when's it gonna end?"

I reach down to Omar and go to shake his hand. We connect and I pull him to his feet, I hold his hand with both of mine and zero in on his eyes.

"*Mijo*, it will end," I say, "the minute . . . you decide."

The moistening of his eyes surprises me. He grabs my hand in his.

"Well," he says, "then I decide."

"Omar," I tell him, "it has always been as simple as that."

When's it going to end?

Do you think government, programs, institutions are going to answer this question? No, nothing will change until *you* decide—decide to respond to the One who every day says to you, "Come, follow me." It's always been as simple as that.

• • •

Finally, Cesar.

Cesar, a twenty-five-year-old whom I've known since he was a frightened kid in the earthquake of 1987, calls me. He's just got out of prison, his second home, and wants to know if he can come and see me. He has no place to stay and doesn't have any clothes. Can I help him? I say, "Sure," and promise to pick him up after work.

So there he is waiting for me, and when he sees me he jumps up and down, flies into my car and throws his arms around me. "When I saw you right now, G, I got all happy!" he says.

We go to JCPenney and I tell him he can buy two hundred dollars' worth of clothes. In no time, his arms are filled with the essentials . . . I drop Cesar off at his friend's apartment. He becomes quiet and vulnerable. He says,

"I just don't want to go back to prison. I'm scared."

"Look son," I say to him, "Who's got a better heart than

you? And God is the center of that great big ol' heart. Hang on to that, dog—'cuz you have what the world wants."

We say our goodbyes.

At three o'clock in the morning, the phone rings. It's Cesar.

He is sober and it's urgent that he talk to me.

"I gotta ask you a question. You know how I've always seen you as my father—ever since I was a little kid? Well, I hafta ask you a question."

Now Cesar pauses and the gravity of it all makes his voice waver and crumble. "Have I . . . been . . . your son?"

"Oh, hell, yeah," I say.

"Whew," Cesar exhales. "I thought so."

Now his voice becomes enmeshed in a cadence of gentle sobbing.

"Then . . . I will be your son. And you . . . will be my father. And nothing will separate us. Right?"

"That's right."

Now take in Father G's comment and internalize it:

"In this early morning call, Cesar did not discover that he has a father. *He discovered that he is a son worth having*."

And you? Remember that you are a son, a daughter, worth having. No matter what your history, what your experience, you are of inestimable value, ceaselessly loved, inerasably God's child—so your resolution for 2018 is *don't act less than who you are*. Bring into the New Year these words quoted by Nelson Mandela:

> Our worst fear is not that we are inadequate.
> Our deepest fear is that we are powerful beyond measure.
> It is our light, not our darkness, that most frightens us.
> We ask ourselves, "Who am I to be brilliant, gorgeous, talented, and fabulous?"
> Actually, who are you not to be?
> You are a child of God; your playing small doesn't serve the world.
>
> There is nothing enlightened about shrinking so that other people won't feel insecure around you.

> We were born to make manifest the glory of God within us.
> It is not just in some of us; it is in everyone.
> And as we let our own light shine, we subconsciously give other people permission to do the same.
> As we are liberated from our own fears, our presence automatically liberates others.

• • •

To this—with Jose, Rigo, Omar, Cesar and Father G—we add

Amen . . . Amen.

Notes and Credits

Notes and Credits

Chapter 2: Comfort My People
"With You Always" by Lisa Leshaw is reproduced with permission from *Guideposts*, Guideposts.org. Copyright 2014 by Guideposts. All rights reserved.

Chapter 4: Crossing Borders
The names listed here are contemporaneous minority figures who made the headlines of the day. They may need to be updated.

Chapter 7: For a New Year
Some thoughts here are taken from Ronald Rolheiser's book, *Sacred Fire*, Image, N.Y, 2014.

Chapter 8: The Passion of Elvis
I owe the facts of this homily to Jonathan Tulloch whose article, "I Want to Find God," appeared in *The Tablet*, 10, January, 2015, p. 14, website address, http://www.thetablet.co.uk. Used with permission.

Chapter 10: I've Got a Little List
The spiritual writer mentioned is Ronald Rohlheiser.

Chapter 17: Easter
One source for this homily is "An Afterlife for Our Times" by Greg Garrett, *The Tablet*, 7 March, 2015.

Chapter 18: The Wounds on Christ's Body
The litany is slightly modified from Father Thomas Berg's book, *Hurting in the Church*, Our Sunday Visitor Press, 2017, page 15. The quote is from Chris Lowney's excellent book, *Everyone Leads*, Rowman & Littlefield, 2017, page 42. This homily is only a teaser and begs for input. It's frustrating not to have the time to develop it as a longer piece, and counter-productive not to provide time either after Mass or another form to pursue it. Since the preacher cannot mention articles and books from the pulpit—people won't remem-

ber and they don't have paper and pen handy—a compatible bibliography of articles, books, and web sites should be in the parish bulletin, including what's being done.

Chapter 19: Alec, Fred, & Jesus
All the scriptures (the doubting Thomas gospel, for instance) were unusually well-lined up to encourage this homily.

The source for the Nicholas Kristoff citation is his column, "A Little Respect for Dr. Foster," *New York Times*, March 28, 2015. The archbishop referred to is the Anglican Archbishop, Justin Welby.

Chapter 20: Live the Questions
This and the following homily form an organic unit.

Chapter 21: Scandal
Homilies 21 and 22 both deal with the clergy sexual scandal. They present it from two different angles that give the homilist a choice of emphasis. I had previously treated the topic of clergy sex abuse in other books, but unfortunately, every once in while the subject surfaces and I must address it. In this case, the pastor of one of the parishes where I help out was accused and removed. In November of 2015, having pleaded guilty, he was sentenced to three years in prison, will be forever subject to parole supervision, and must register as a sex offender.

Chapter 22: Spotlight
This second homily was prompted by the November 2015 movie, "Spotlight," a well-made searing account of the revelations by the *Boston Globe* in 2002 of the clergy sexual abuse coverup in the Catholic Church. The U.S. Conference of Catholic Bishops was prepared for the movie's impact by offering ways and means of dealing with the movie with the emphasis on how much the Church has changed even while acknowledging its guilt. 'That was the (shameful) past, but this is the present' is the overall theme. "Spotlight" ends with a long list of dioceses, in both the U.S. and globally, where abuse and coverups have occurred—although critics are quick to point out that most dioceses have never posted an actual list of the names of the perpetrators.

The financial cost so far to the Church in the U.S. has been around four billion dollars. The moral cost is incalculable. The "scarlet letter" of clerical sexual abuse will be around a long time. It's time for the Catholic Church to downplay (not abandon) its motto of "One, Holy, Catholic, and Apostolic" and take on another well-known one, namely the "Church of Peter," and restart its evolution from Church leader, to shameful denier, to repentant sinner, to saint. As a reminder of this aim, "Spotlight" will be the rooster that always crows.

I've included this homily for its final image: arm in arm with flawed Peter, we move forward.

(The summary of U.S. Catholic Church impact comes from Dennis H. Holtschnedier's article, "Strategic Opportunities" in *America*, November 2, 2015.)

Chapter 23: Home
The David Brooks column cited is "The Devotion Leap," *New York Times*, January 22, 2015.

Chapter 25: Charleston, South Carolina
In this chapter as well as chapter 10, there are references to Atticus Finch and Jem from the famed *To Kill a Mockingbird*. In a new 2015 novel by Harper Lee, the iconic and revered Atticus has been deconstructed into a segregationist. Quite a turnabout. Preachers won't be able to use Atticus as a model secular saint anymore.

Chapter 27: Ascension
This story is modified from *Everyone Leads*, a must-read book on Church renewal by Chris Lowney. Rowman & Littlefield, 2017, p 113ff.

Chapter 28: Remember
This homily was inspired by a chapter in Martin B. Copenhaver's wonderful meditations in *Room to Grow* (William B. Eerdmans Publishing Co., 2015). This homily carries similar themes as other homilies in this book, and repeats some previous stories but puts them in a timely and challenging new context.

Chapter 31: The N Word
This homily was well-received. Especially affirming were a few Iraq veterans.

A good book to read is *Christian Persecution in the Middle East: A 21st Century Tragedy* by George J. Martin. Another ongoing aid to persecuted Christians is Solidarity with the Persecuted Church, 410 Constitution Avenue, NE, Washington, D.C. 20002.

A pastoral word: parish bulletins must be used more practically. It doesn't do, for example, to admonish the congregation to do more spiritual reading unless they have access to some suggestions in the bulletin. Likewise, there should be resources and references to topical issues mentioned in the homily.

Chapter 32: Emil Kapaun
This homily I lifted from my book, *An Anthology of Saints*, Twenty Third Publications.

Chapter 33: Violence
The local paper, the *Asbury Park Press*, is dated 2/2/14.

Chapter 37: The Church in Conversation with AA
A homily version of the excellent article, "Why Can't the Church Be More like AA?" by Kathleen Hirsch, October 1, 2015. Used with permission.

Chapter 38: Loving in Weakness
The story here is from *Portland Magazine*, Spring 2011 issue. Used with permission.

Chapter 39: Résumé Versus Eulogy
For this homily, I am raiding David Brooks' columns (May 29, 2015, "The Small, Happy Life;" and "Hearts Broken Open," June 19, 2015).

Chapter 42: E.T. Don't Call Home
If the homilist wishes, he or she can make the cellphone theme a parish Lenten project or goal, or a parish community effort. For example, I suggest the parish might issue car decals. Above the parish name, one decal would simply have the large initials "CIA." People will think the initials mean the Central Intelligence Agency or the Culinary Institute of America, but all will know it means "Cell in Auto." Perhaps another decal might carry the initials "CIH," meaning "Cell in Home." Maybe another would read "COF" for Cell on Fridays with a red diagonal line through the letters. If people ask about them, you have a chance to evangelize.

The Lenten rallying cry: Let's make this a communal effort to remind one another that we are subversive Christians fighting against those distractions which shrink human interaction, take lives and inoculate our souls against the power, beauty and living of the gospel. Let's help each other journey together in freedom.

Chapter 43: Annie and Friends
The story of Dr. Tom Caltena is found in a column by Nicolas Kristof, *New York Times*, June 27, 2015.

The story of Nicholas Winton is from various sources, especially *The Economist*, July 11, 2015.

The story of Rick Kearney can be found in *The National Catholic Reporter*, July 31-August 13, 2015.

Chapter 44: Sparking Joy
This homily, only the second personal one referenced in this collection, was inspired by Melanie McDonagh's article, "What Lies Beneath" in *The Tablet*, 9 July, 2016, p. 12.

Chapter 47: God's Time
This material is taken from *Guideposts.*

Chapter 48: The Atheists Among Us
Sources for this homily: "The Once-Born and the Twice-Born" by Gertrude Himmelfarb, *Wall Street Journal*, September 9-30, 2012; "Religion Without God by T.M. Luhrmann, *New York Times*, December 24, 2014; and a book review of *Atheists Awakening* by Richard Cimino and Christopher Smith, Oxford, 2015 in The *Wall Street Journal* by Naomi Schaefer. See also Riley's book, *Got Religion? How Churches, Mosques, and Synagogues Can Bring Young People Back.*

Chapter 49: "But Wait!"
I owe the germ of this homily to Martian Copenhaver. The reader will notice I'm back to a familiar theme that has already appeared in a half-dozen previous homilies: Christianity and what we might call the pressures of the modern anti-Christian era. It's an updated version of them and offers some more contemporary issues to reflect on. I tried to keep from hectoring, but I am not sure I succeeded. Anyway, the data may be helpful.

Chapter 50: The Cry of the Poor, Home-style
The restaurants mentioned are local upscale ones.

I added the postscript because this homily was delivered in the midst of the 2015 Synod on the Family, which gave great stress to domestic holiness.

Chapter 51: Cured on the Way
This is the only homily in this collection that is a repeat from a former collection. It has been revised because it resonated so fully with the congregation.

Chapter 52: The Mortara Affair
I wrote this homily before the film came out. By this time, you may know how it fared and what the reactions were. If, for some reason, the reality is far beyond my speculation, chalk it up to bad prognostication. Otherwise the homily may be of some help in giving it a wider context than the popular press might offer. My sources are Crux, John O'Malley, SJ, and the Catechism of the Catholic Church. The Vatican II quote is from *Lumen Gentium*, 8.

Chapter 53: Purgatory
I owe the development of this homily to my friend, Deacon Jim Knipper, and the thoughts on hell from Ross Douthat's "A Case for Hell," *New York Times*, April 24, 2011.

Chapter 54: Born Again?
The duet between Golda and Tevye is used with permission.

Chapter 58: Our Lady of Guadalupe
This homily is derived from Matthew Sewell's article that appeared in the *Mountain Catholic*. Used with permission. Matthew Sewell blogs at https://mtncatholic.com.

Chapter 60: A Premature Death: Why?
For the gospel, I eluded to passages from John 11 & 13 thus:

At that time [at the Upper Room] Jesus said to his disciples, "Do not let your hearts be troubled. Believe in God, believe in me." Then he added, "In a little while the world will not see me . . . I did not tell you this from the beginning . . . but now I am going away to him who sent me [and I know that] because I have said these things to you sorrow has filled your hearts . . . Yes, you will have pain now, but I will see you again and your hearts will rejoice and no one will take that joy from you."

This was well-received as it gave some direction to the "when bad things happen to good people." As I indicated, it's used best in conjunction with the preceding homily, although it can stand on its own.

Chapter 61. Helen Kazabo: Rest in Peace
This funeral homily is included for its story.

Chapter 62: Lillian Riley, Waiting for Death
This funeral homily is included as an example of bookending one good opening story that provides a serviceable three-point outline with another good ending story that leads to a memorable closing.

Chapter 63: Deaths of Despair
The inspiration and the data I have taken from Aaron Kheriarty's article in *First Things*, August/September, 2017, p. 21. *New York Times* reference is from July 13, 2017.

Chapter 64: Charlottesville, Virginia
In August of 2017, there was a violent confrontation among the white supremacists and neo-Nazis and opposing forces at Charlottesville, Virginia setting off a frenzy of commentary about free speech, polarization, racism, and national soul searching. I've recycled the movie allusions from homily 12, The Deep Well.

Chapter 65: Black Pioneer: Augustus Tolton
The homily about Fr. Augustus Tolton, the first black priest in the US, is or will be timely in the context of the healing of the races and America's racial history, not to mention his eventual canonization.

Chapter 66: One of Us
The homily on Mary (well-received and appreciated at several parishes) is a much-needed correction for a people looking to relate to Mary as a human being and not a glamorized icon beyond reach.

Chapter 67: The Barque is Sinking
The Barque of Peter (an old metaphor for the Church) proved to be a helpful comfort in times of Church decline.

Chapter 68: September 11, 2001—15 years later
This homily was very well-received and, of course, can be used on every new anniversary.